DISCREDITED

THE UNC SCANDAL AND COLLEGE ATHLETICS' AMATEUR IDEAL

Andy Thomason

DISCREDITED

University of Michigan Press
Ann Arbor

Copyright 2021 by Andy Thomason

For questions or permissions, please contact um.press.perms@umich.edu

Published in the United States of America by
the University of Michigan Press
Manufactured in the United States of America
Printed on acid-free paper

First published August 2021

A CIP catalog record for this book is available from the British Library.

ISBN 978-0-472-13281-2 (hardcover : alk. paper)
ISBN 978-0-472-12959-1 (ebook)

FOR SALLY HUNT, A FAN AND A FRIEND

CONTENTS

Digital materials related to this title can be found on the
Fulcrum platform via the following citable URL
https://doi.org/10.3998/mpub.10171336

Readers of a nonfiction book like this one expect the author to be an impartial observer. While I have striven to provide an evenhanded account of this book's events, I have some personal ties to the drama.

I was a student at the University of North Carolina at Chapel Hill between 2009 and 2013, where I was a reporter and ultimately editor-in-chief of the *Daily Tar Heel*, the campus newspaper. It was in this spirit that I interacted with some of the people I mention in this book well before the project was conceived. In the few cases where such interactions were not entirely journalistic in nature, I've made disclosures in the notes. But my connection to this story goes much further back than my college years.

I've loved sports for as long as I can remember. I grew up in Charlotte, North Carolina, in a neighborhood where you knew which college teams your neighbors rooted for. My dad went to N.C. State, so I grew up as a Wolfpack fan, rooting for Philip Rivers and Julius Hodge. Practically all my friends in middle school were rabid Chapel Hill loyalists; we'd argue around the cafeteria tables at lunch. I would always root for UNC to lose, especially in basketball. Mainly because they always seemed to win.

Then in 2009 I got into UNC and decided to go there. From the moment I stepped on campus, I was a Tar Heel convert, booing J. J. Redick, sneering at Coach K, and taking pleasure in the fact that N.C. State could never seem to beat UNC in basketball. Looking back I can hardly believe how quickly I turned. As I progressed through college, I watched fewer games as I got more involved at the newspaper. The scandal surrounding the football team and the infamous "paper classes" broke in my sophomore year, as I became an editor at the *Daily Tar Heel*. I helped steer coverage of the scandal for the rest of my college career.

In 2014, I got a full-time reporting job at the *Chronicle of Higher Education*. The UNC scandal was far from over, so I continued to report on it, making use of my campus expertise. In the past few years I've stopped watching football, but still tune into the occasional UNC basketball game. I was crushed when UNC lost to Villanova in the 2016 national championship, and delighted when they won it all the next year—an event that makes a prominent appearance in the book you now hold.

One other possible conflict of interest deserves special mention. In July of 2013, just after I graduated and before I became a professional journalist, I sent an email to the then-new chancellor of UNC, Carol Folt. (She appears several times in this book.) Among the things I told her was that I respected the university's commitment to athletic excellence, but that I feared that alumni emphasis on football and men's basketball was corruptive. I urged her to familiarize herself with the attempt of Frank Porter Graham, a famous UNC president, to deemphasize athletics in Chapel Hill—a story I've retold, in short, in the book that follows.

I make these disclosures at the outset and leave it to you, the reader, to judge my characterizations and conclusions as you see fit.

1

This wasn't how things were supposed to go for Holden Thorp.

He was the University of North Carolina at Chapel Hill's favorite son, the boy genius who'd fallen in love with the chemistry lab and followed that love all the way to the Ivy League, only to look homeward, still. He returned to Chapel Hill as a chemistry professor, but he was too talented to be kept off in a lab. So he was tapped to lead the university's planetarium, then its chemistry department, then its biggest college. When he was asked to interview for chancellor, the campus's top job, he didn't think he was a serious candidate.[1] The search committee, it turns out, was dead serious about Holden Thorp.

He seemed perfect for the role. Few had more impressive academic bona fides, featuring stints in the faculty and the administration. He'd also started a business and raised money for the college, critical skills in the world of university leadership. But perhaps most notably, the North Carolina native was awash with school spirit. His father had sung him the university's alma mater, "Hark the Sound," as he drifted off to sleep. He'd cheered on the university's legendary basketball team since he was a kid, starstruck by Dean Smith and his "Carolina Way" philosophy—an ethos of selflessness and excellence that must, admirers reasoned, be the source of the team's success.[2]

By the time Thorp took the podium for his inauguration—decked out in regalia of sky blue, the university's color—the Carolina Way no longer applied only to basketball.[3] It was a kind of thesis statement for

Chapel Hill, one that married its two prestigious halves: athletics and academics. Its teams won national championships and its students were Rhodes scholars. Its basketball players performed acrobatic slam dunks and nearly always got their degrees.

But one summer day two years into Thorp's tenure, the cracks in that gilded veneer yawned so wide that he decided he needed to tell the world about them.

He and his staff had spent the day playing detective, sifting through students' emails to try and find evidence of rule breaking. Now they prepared to go before the flashing cameras. Thorp hadn't known in the morning that he'd be holding a press conference, so he had to call his wife to bring him a suit.[4] A Carolina blue tie cinched around his neck, Thorp made a dark observation to those standing at his side.[5]

So this, he said, is the funeral for the Carolina Way.[6]

Thorp's remark was prescient. But what had begun to unfold before his eyes was much bigger than Chapel Hill, and much bigger than a campus myth.

UNC is among a few hundred colleges that participate in big-time sports, the football and basketball programs that provide one of the major sources of entertainment in American life.[7] Every one of these colleges signs on to a dubious assertion: that the young people who play on these teams are students first, athletes second.[8] Yet this ideal of amateurism is a myth that collapses under the mildest bit of scrutiny. The lives of most of the athletes who compete in the highest tier of college sports bear only a passing resemblance to those of their classmates. At universities like UNC, many of these students are admitted under different standards than nonathletes. When they get to campus, they have access to a separate team of academic advisers and tutors charged with ensuring their success, or at least preserving their eligibility. Meanwhile, a grueling schedule of practice and competition dominates their days, making coursework something close to an afterthought.[9]

This myth serves a clear purpose. By espousing amateurism, colleges prohibit their athletes from freely earning money for their labor.[10] Amateurism thus helps preserve big-time college athletics as it is today: a system that drives hundreds of millions of dollars to universities and television networks, but a piddly amount to the athletes themselves. It is through this system that universities can court donors, satisfy the public, and celebrate their histories. The amateur myth is a source of value for these schools, both financially and emotionally.

But it also carries costs, and not only for the athletes. The gulf between the players' lives and those of the students they are supposed to resemble creates seismic waves that travel far beyond the walls of the athletic department. It takes a village to make the amateur myth seem true. It is only accomplished, one UNC professor later wrote, "through the resourceful manipulation of smoke and mirrors and by a lot of winking and nodding."[11] Coaches wink, professors nod. Advisers wink, chancellors nod.

For many years in Chapel Hill, only amateurism's benefits were visible to the outside world. Once the cracks began to show, the costs of amateurism—hidden for all those years—finally became visible. The result was one of the most heinous sports scandals to visit a college in decades, succeeded only by the criminal trials involving Penn State and Michigan State.

This book, based on dozens of interviews and thousands of pages of documents, is a story of the myth of amateurism in three acts—how UNC embraced it, then watched in horror as the myth came unraveled, and finally embraced it again. At its core, this story is about a secretary who made it a personal mission to bridge the contradictions of amateurism, bringing scrutiny onto a university that had escaped it for half a century.

Amateurism was the clear cause of the scandal, yet the university never seriously entertained the notion that it should deemphasize its athletic enterprise or reexamine its allegiance to the amateur ideal. Indeed, the lengths to which it went and the conditions it endured to preserve its athletic dominance were extreme. Careers were ruined, a whole discipline shrouded in suspicion, lives soured. Even Thorp was driven out. But the lie and the cause it served lived on.

Much has been written about the substantial costs of amateurism to the athletes who must sign onto it; comparatively little has been written of late about the cost to the institutions of higher learning. As the public increasingly decries the exploitative effects of amateurism, the university presidents who endorse it may be forced to adapt. They would do well to look to Chapel Hill as a cautionary tale. The costs of American intercollegiate athletics may far exceed athletes' unpaid wages. At stake is nothing less than the moral standing of the most powerful intellectual institutions in the world.

On a cool January night in 1938, a man named Frank Porter Graham stood at the front of a classroom with a stack of paper in his hand.

It had been a hard few years for the president of the University of North Carolina system. A progressive icon in the state, he was known to pick good-natured fights for what he believed in. But this one had been the hardest yet, threatening both his career and his reputation. Alumni had come out of the woodwork to denounce him, students had chided him, and professors, some packed into the classroom before him, were skeptical. No one, it seemed, believed in his cause as passionately as he did.

To save your university from humiliation, he told the assembled faculty, help insulate it from the commercial forces encircling college athletics. Act now, he said, before it's too late.[1]

Amateurism wasn't always a paradoxical term. The patrician idea of the amateur sportsman who dabbled in multiple pursuits was eagerly embraced by American middle and upper classes who looked to Europe for inspiration on how to be elites. The young men who filtered through the nation's earliest colleges — think Harvard and Yale — embraced this amateur mindset when competing in sports like rowing, baseball, or football. "On college campuses before the Civil War," wrote scholars Allen L. Sack and Ellen J. Staurowsky, "the notion that college sport was recreation for participants rather than a form of commercial entertainment was pretty much taken for granted." College sports were thus for the benefit of the sportsman, rather than the audience.

After the Civil War, booming urban populations, the development of railroads, and the growing proliferation of newspapers fueled commercial interest in professional sports.[2] But people who lived outside metropolitan areas had few opportunities to witness the teams that were taking America by storm. The creation of land-grant universities designed to teach agricultural skills to the next generation also amplified rural Americans' access to sports.[3] New campuses cropped up across the country in places like Fargo, North Dakota; Reno, Nevada; and Auburn, Alabama. Those colleges became much-needed hubs of technical training, but they also gave local people something to do on the weekends: go to the local stadium and watch the boys play football.

The effect was especially pronounced in the South, where industrial development had lagged.[4] By the early twentieth century, football powerhouses such as Notre Dame and Yale were facing challengers, fueled by intense regional interest and support, from the South. The North Carolina Tar Heels played their first game in 1888,[5] and within thirty years, close to 10,000 people crowded the stands for the big games.[6] In 1926 a university alumnus, William Rand Kenan Jr., donated $275,000—$4 million in 2019 dollars—to construct a new football stadium that seated 24,000 people.[7] The student newspaper, *The Tar Heel*, praised the donation for addressing the greatest area of financial need on campus. "Twenty-four thousand seats may sound big now," the newspaper wrote, "but we venture to say that in five years' time, or less, every one of these seats will be taken at the big games."[8]

Just as emphasis on athletics grew, so did criticism of its influence. Evidence of such angst appears as early as 1893, when the *Tar Heel*, then an arm of the university's athletic association, lashed out at critics who "harp upon the evils of inter-collegiate contests and railroad traveling."[9] Such criticism found national currency in the ensuing years. Advocates of amateur competition watched in horror as colleges, eager for gridiron victory, enticed ringers to join their teams with jobs and financial aid—payment, essentially. This was a direct challenge to the supposedly amateur character of college sports.[10]

In 1929 a landmark study became a template for calls to return college sports to its amateur origins. The Carnegie Foundation for the Advancement of Teaching's report was among the first to call out the abuses that became so familiar to ensuing generations of fans and observers. Its author, Howard J. Savage, warned that college football, though played by nominal amateurs, was "a highly organized commercial enterprise."[11] He called on universities to rein in the twin practices that together made up "the deepest shadow that darkens American college and school athletics"—recruiting and subsidization. In recruiting, universities courted physically talented students to attend, then subsidized them through jobs, loans, or lump-sum payments once they got to campus. Both were examples, Savage said, of universities granting privileged status to a class of students based on factors outside of the institutions' intellectual missions. Such practices, Savage argued, were a first step toward institutional corruption.

But for colleges like UNC, where athletic passions were fiery, there was hope. "The man who is the most likely to succeed in uprooting the evils of recruiting and subsidizing," wrote Savage, "is the college president."[12]

Six years after Savage's report appeared in national newspapers, the Tar Heel football team traveled to Baltimore and trounced the University of Maryland by the score of 33-0 before a crowd of 15,000.[13] The blowout was all the more impressive because the coach, Carl Snavely, had benched a standout guard, John Sniscak. The sophomore was a promising force on the line, but shortly before the game someone alleged that Sniscak had previously played college football at Catholic University, which would have disqualified him from playing for UNC. The rules of the Southern Conference—the forerunner of the Atlantic Coast and Southeastern Conferences—prohibited transfers.

The allegation set off a firestorm in Chapel Hill. Coach Snavely initially offered the laughable claim that it was a case of mistaken identity: Sniscak had a relative of the same name, he said, who'd played football at Catholic. That defense rang hollow against Catholic's confirmation of Sniscak's identity.[14] The sophomore gave a statement to a newspaper accusing several Maryland players of also having illicit gridiron histories.[15] Meanwhile, UNC president Frank Porter Graham sought the truth. Within a week of the Maryland game, he expelled Sniscak, saying that the university "cannot take the position that a lie about athletic eligibility is less than a lie about scholastic work."[16]

The Sniscak case was on Graham's mind when, two months later, he unveiled an athletics reform plan that he hoped would be taken up nationally. The student life committee of the National Association of State Universities had been charged with preparing a report about college athletics, and Graham, who chaired the committee, took the opportunity to issue a provocative reform package. At the center of the plan was a controversial plank: the prohibition of athletic scholarships, either from inside the university or from outside of it. No student, Graham said, should be able to receive money primarily on the basis of athletic ability. Such a policy would return the college athlete to amateur status.

Graham didn't want his ideas to live in the abstract, so he convinced the Southern Conference to adopt the plan wholesale. The university's alumni went berserk in response, with chapter after chapter rising in protest. Less than a month after the conference adopted the plan, the state's newspapers reported that furious alumni had mounted a campaign to get rid of the president. This had been "the hardest and hottest fight" of Graham's life, he wrote.

Graham survived. His plan, however, collapsed amid messy accusations between the conference's universities about who was really complying with the rules. Less than a year after it had been approved, the plan was neutered.[17] One year later, it was killed.[18]

So Graham found himself before a full meeting of the faculty in Bingham Hall that January evening in 1938, hoping to salvage some of his plan's principles. He'd come ready to plead with his colleagues to ignore the Southern Conference and enshrine the Graham Plan at UNC.

He wanted to save college athletics from "self-destruction," he told the professors, and the colleges themselves from "self-degradation." When waged as an amateur enterprise, college sports had the potential to be among the purest expressions of a college's democratic spirit, he said. But without proper regulation of the money that was changing hands, athletics would inevitably become "a contest in subsidies."

Some of his plan's opponents favored athletic scholarships, administered in plain view by the college. Graham saw problems there. Where would the money come from? If it came from ticket revenue, then commercial forces in the stadium would become even more powerful. And what authority would the university have to prohibit alumni from handing off under-the-table payments, if it was doing the same in plain sight? Others had proposed that alumni raise the scholarship funds. That, Graham said, would lead to "unwholesome attempted control of the college" by outside forces.

Giving in to this pressure would put the university in shady moral territory. "Without attempts at regulation, the college is in danger of sanctioning the auction block, upon which boys in high school sell themselves to the highest bidder," he said. And blessing the distribution of money would also, Graham predicted, bring fallout. Administering scholarships on any other basis than "scholarship, character, and need" would create a campus of two classes—the athletes and the nonathletes—"and create campus problems undreamed of in our philosophy."[19]

It was a chilling forecast, but it did little to move the faculty. They declined to adopt the Graham Plan's key plank on subsidization, with all its teeth. Some questioned their president's vigor. After the plan was dealt its first blow by the conference, the *Tar Heel* declared that the "most regrettable feature of the incident lies in the fact that Dr. Graham, who is responsible for things far more important than athletics, has squandered much of his time and effort in behalf of an empty shibboleth."[20]

Graham lost the fight, but his ideas lived on.

In the late 1940s, the member universities of the National Collegiate Athletic Association, which until then had been a mostly passive lobbying organization, narrowly passed what would become known as the Sanity Code. The code prohibited scholarships tied solely to athletic ability, among other things, in the same spirit in which Savage and Graham had railed against them.[21] It seemed Graham had won the war; something resembling the central tenet of his plan was now the law of the land. And yet the same arguments that doomed the Graham plan to a death by a thousand cuts sprang up again, mainly that such a stringent code was impossible to enforce. The richest programs would skirt the rules while the more vulnerable programs would be punished for complying.[22] Thanks to notable objections by the University of Virginia—which had also played a leading role in sinking the Graham Plan—the code was killed three years later.[23] By 1957, athletic scholarships were explicitly allowed by NCAA rules.

If athletes were amateurs, why allow universities to pay them tuition, room, and board based primarily on athletic ability? As Graham had argued, the two simply didn't square. And they opened the door, as he had predicted, to "unwholesome attempted control of the college" by alumni. Walter Byers, the NCAA's longtime executive director, would later write that the sea change in the association's regulations would usher in a "nationwide money-laundering scheme."[24] Alumni of UNC and other campuses had long paid athletes under the table, and now they could do the same, specifically, via a scholarship fund that the university would then divvy up. The same system exists throughout higher education to this day.

The incorporation of athletic scholarships into the NCAA's rules, Sack and Staurowsky write, was the moment amateurism in big-time sports officially took on a different meaning. True amateurism, the idea that participation in sports is an avocation, had been replaced by a "counterfeit version" of the same idea.[25] The new notion of amateurism seemed to state that as long as the athlete was not paid by anyone other than the college and that they were a student, they remained an amateur. A rapid retreat from the amateur ideal was thus branded as a preservation of it. This is one reason that amateurism as espoused by the NCAA can be called a myth; it asserts that athletes are amateurs even as its own stipulations disprove the claim.

The paradoxical nature of the new amateurism, which allowed supposedly amateur athletes to be paid, was not lost on observers. Were they students or employees? In the years after the failure of the Sanity Code, the status quo of the athletic scholarship came under threat, Byers wrote, from "the dreaded notion that NCAA athletes could be identified as *employees* by state industrial commissions and the courts." So the association came up with a keen public-relations strategy to hide the truth, Byers wrote. "We crafted the term *student-athlete,* and soon it was embedded in all NCAA rules and interpretations as a mandated substitute for such words as players and athletes."[26] Using one word, "student," the association sought to imprint amateur status on a class of athletes who were quickly being professionalized. And it worked, proving a remarkably sturdy shield for colleges to fight off the legal action Byers had feared.[27]

As universities abandoned reform, athletics became more diversified. The pigskin was still the king of college sports, but college basketball was starting to gain on it, spreading outward from New York City in the years approaching World War II.[28] By the mid-1940s a heated basketball arms race had developed between UNC and nearby Duke and North Carolina State Universities. In 1946 N.C. State had hired Everett Case, a legendary high-school coach in Indiana, who in turn delivered conference championship after conference championship to the Wolfpack faithful.[29] UNC attempted to level the playing field by hiring a new coach, though the student newspaper—now *the Daily Tar Heel*—practically apologized for covering the news. "With a schedule of 10 football games staring us in the face . . . this is hardly a time to be thinking of basketball," the newspaper wrote. "But when you consider that one of the most fortunate happenings in the Carolina sports field during the past few years concerns basketball then we just have to put the pigskin away for a second and think about the round ball boys."[30]

The hiring of Frank McGuire was a more fortunate development than even the most bullish Chapel Hill boosters might have guessed. McGuire, previously the coach at St. John's University in Queens, New York, led UNC to a perfect season and a national championship in 1957, defeating a University of Kansas squad featuring Wilt Chamberlain. But a 1961 point-shaving scandal, in which players from both UNC and N.C. State took bribes from gamblers, tarred McGuire's tenure.

Graham's ideas resurfaced. The task of cleaning up after the scandal fell to Bill Friday, a protégé of Graham's who had taken over as president of the consolidated university system in 1956.[31] Friday and the chancellors of the system's three campuses considered implementing the Graham Plan, but instead opted for milder steps.[32] Friday canceled a popular regional basketball tournament called the Dixie Classic, banned athletic activity in the summer, and limited athletic scholarships. Friday, whose skepticism of athletics would echo through the decades, also declared that the jobs of the athletic coaches at the University of North Carolina did not depend "upon their obligation merely to win games or to achieve national standing for our teams."[33]

That message made its way to the new Chapel Hill basketball coach, who recalled the university's chancellor, William Aycock, telling him to "give the university a team it can be proud of" and not to "worry about the winning and losing."[34] That coach was a mild-mannered Kansan named Dean Smith, who would publicly reinforce Friday and Graham's spirit of reform for the rest of his decorated career.

Contrary to his chancellor's direction, Smith worried plenty about winning and losing. He did far more of the former over the next thirty-six years, racking up 879 wins to become the winningest coach in college basketball history by the time he retired in 1997.[35] Smith's dynastic record grew out of a steel-trap mind obsessed with the sport of basketball. He pioneered the use of the "four corners" offense, a method of ball control that allowed the Tar Heels to make offensive possessions last several minutes at a time, which gave trailing opponents limited chances to make up a deficit. The strategy was so effective—and made for such anticlimactic finishes—that the NCAA effectively banned it in the mid-1980s by introducing the shot clock.[36] He was also a fierce competitor, cramming for games, obsessing over losses, and haranguing referees he thought he could influence to his team's advantage.[37]

But his reputation was not just that of a winner. By the 1980s Smith had cultivated a buttoned-up ethos of moral rectitude that resounded both on and off the court. On Smith's teams, players who scored baskets were expected to point at the teammate who passed them the ball, a show of appreciation that continues today on basketball courts in rec leagues, high schools, and the NBA. In his private life, Smith was an avid churchgoer and a student of theology. Players spoke glowingly about his character, with Michael Jordan even calling him a second father.[38] Like any good father, Smith preached the value of academics. The college degree, he said, "is more of an equalizer than anything else I can think of," and a credential he made sure his players got.[39] Tar Heel basketball under Smith boasted a near-100 percent graduation rate for his players.[40]

Fused into Smith's ethos of success were also his progressive politics. Famously, Smith helped integrate a Chapel Hill restaurant by joining a black theology student there for breakfast. Less than a decade later he recruited UNC's first black scholarship athlete, Charlie Scott, onto the basketball team.[41] In the ensuing decades he became a fixture of the state's Democratic politics, protesting the Vietnam War and the death penalty.[42] He faced calls to challenge the hard-right Republican U.S. Senator Jesse Helms in the 1990 Congressional campaign, but resisted.[43]

All the while, Smith spoke of doing things "the right way" as a key to his program's success. "Long ago," he said in 1980, channeling Friday and Graham, "this University made a decision that we're going to do it the right way, even if we don't win."[44]

The prestige, the liberal politics, the emphasis on academics—all of it made Smith an irresistible figure for the scholars who shared his campus. Aycock recalled that Smith quickly won over professors skeptical of basketball's influence following the McGuire-era NCAA sanctions. "Our faculty quickly recognized that Dean was an excellent teacher," he wrote, "one of the best on the entire campus, and he taught his players much more than basketball." And when Smith's teams starting racking up winning seasons, "many of the faculty members were among his biggest supporters."[45]

Professors were not immune from the delights of fandom. Madeline Levine recalled starting as a professor at UNC in 1974 and being bewildered by the basketball-crazy culture. Levine, having grown up and gone to school in the North, had never seen anything like it. One day, she recalled, she was riding the city bus to campus with a few of her colleagues when, astonished, she watched them reenact plays from a recent UNC basketball game, jumping around, pretending to pass and shoot the ball as the bus made its way to campus. "I had never seen grown men do this," she said.[46]

By the early 1980s, as Smith's program prepared to reach its greatest heights, the faculty passed an unusual resolution in his honor, he wrote in his book, *The Carolina Way*. Smith was "far more" than just a coach, the resolution read, citing his players' high graduation rate, his service to his church, and his role in integration. But the faculty also applauded Smith for the fact that "he carries the Carolina colors to all corners, without hint or fear of blemish."[47] In 1982, after Smith's Tar Heels won their first national championship, North Carolina's governor called Smith "an institution, like a lighthouse," whose popularity in the state was paralleled only by that of Billy Graham.[48]

In Chapel Hill, basketball was religion. The sacred text was Smith's Carolina Way.

The Carolina Way might have been less spellbinding had it not cut so sharply against what the public was coming to expect from college sports.

In the 1970s and '80s, as Smith's Tar Heels reached their heights, the public became increasingly aware of college sports' seedy underbelly. Decades removed from the aborted Sanity Code, the NCAA in the '70s further backed away from enforcement of its amateur ideal. Allowing scholarships, essentially pay for play, wasn't enough. In 1972 the association ditched freshman ineligibility, meant to help athletes find their academic footing before stepping into the field of play.[49] The next year the NCAA got rid of a rule limiting scholarship eligibility to athletes projected to earn a 1.6 grade point average during their freshman year. With essentially no rules governing academic eligibility, a Wild West mentality took hold. Abuses were manifest.[50] Newspapers and magazines wrote exposé after exposé. A Creighton University basketball player competed all four years without knowing how to read or write.[51] A speech class at the University of Southern California gave dozens of athletes academic credit, even though they never showed up.[52]

By the end of the 1980s, the public had grown cynical about college sports. Two-thirds of participants in a national survey believed that "colleges overemphasize sports and neglect academic standards for athletes."[53] Perhaps this would have spurred reform, had big-time sports not also become more viable as a commercial product than ever before. The ubiquity of television, and the advent of cable television especially, took the giddy sports coverage previously reserved for the broadsheet and displayed it in living color, filling more and more hours of the day. Athletic conferences began making big deals with networks to show football games. The NCAA's March Madness basketball tournament became must-see TV, and member colleges cashed in on the advertising revenue.[54] Scandal-stricken institutions during this period didn't deemphasize sports, they just weathered the storm.[55]

Amateurism was becoming a mockery, and Smith spoke publicly about the need for reform. He urged the NCAA to restore freshman ineligibility.[56] He cheered a university president in California for taking control of a controversy-plagued basketball program by shutting it down.[57] He shunned commercial influence, writing in *The Carolina Way* that he turned down the endorsement opportunities that have become ubiquitous among coaches.[58] He pleaded with universities to take the lead in cleaning up college sports.[59]

In this way, Smith became something of a walking contradiction: speaking publicly about the flaws in the big-time sports amateur model while also emerging as proof that the system *could* work. Student-athlete may have been a fraught notion in the decades after the Sanity Code's unraveling, but Carolina basketball stood as enticing evidence that these student-athletes—the new amateurs—could be good students and still dominate on the court. A UNC chancellor in the 1980s summed it up when celebrating the Tar Heels' 1982 national title: "It shows that good guys can do it the right way and still win championships."[60]

Smith's Tar Heels were a balm for an unsavory era. When a national audience turned on the TV to watch UNC basketball, they saw teamwork, not scandal. When they read about the visionary coach in the paper, they read about the importance of academics, not craven athletics. They even saw the academic primacy of the Carolina Way when they went to the movies. In the first scene of the 1996 movie *Space Jam*, which earned $230 million at the box office, a young Michael Jordan tells his father that he wants to play basketball at UNC. His father responds by telling the future star that Chapel Hill is a "real fine school" where the young Jordan can get "a first-class education."[61]

The Carolina Way also permeated the insular ivory tower. A 1997 headline in the *Chronicle of Higher Education*, the academy's dominant trade publication, read, "U. Of North Carolina Is Proud of Its Balance of Big-Time Athletics and Quality Academics," and quoted then-chancellor Michael Hooker as saying he was "probably one of the few presidents who doesn't go to sleep at night and wake up worrying about the university's being embarrassed by its athletics program." Faculty, too, had keenly internalized the Carolina Way ethos. "There is a widespread feeling that on the one hand, we are part of big-time college athletics, but at the same time, we have the illusion—stoked perhaps by the long presence of Dean Smith—that we are better than the rest, that we are unsullied by scandal, that we have a high-class program," said Leon Fink, a history professor. "That may be an illusion, but that is the prevailing mood."[62]

It was a mood authored by Smith, carrying the heavy influence of President Friday. In 1994, the two giants shared a stage in Charlotte for a televised interview. Since retiring in the mid-'80s, Friday had helped start a nationwide group advocating reform in college athletics, the Knight Commission on Intercollegiate Athletics. In one exchange, they fleshed out the exceptionalism at the heart of the Carolina Way:

FRIDAY: In the work of the Knight Commission, we looked at all the programs all over the United States and I always took great pride in making the point that through all the years none of your teams has ever been cited for any kind of infraction, nor has any one of your athletes. Saying it more positively, you set the example in showing how you can play the level of basketball, intercollegiate basketball, and do it well and do it the way it should be done. . . . What's the system?

SMITH: I think it's the university for whom I work. They demand people who can do the work.[63]

Absent in Friday's rhetoric that day was the unflinching prophecy of his predecessor, Graham, who would have been surprised to behold the myth he'd helped set into motion. Seeing the commercial waves preparing to swamp campus sports, Graham had urged true amateurism—all students in one boat, admitted by and subject to the same rules as their classmates. Instead, the NCAA opted for creeping professionalism in amateur packaging. It was a recipe for scandal.

Graham's "campus problems undreamed of" hadn't been forestalled. They'd only been delayed, obscured by a Carolina-blue smoke screen. One of Tar Heel basketball's true believers would help demolish the house of cards.

As Smith and the Tar Heels grew into a dynasty, Deborah Crowder was one of the fans cheering from home. She grew up in the '50s and '60s in a one-story house near Charlotte, dreaming of attending the Chapel Hill flagship.[1] When she got there in 1971, she would say later, she liked it so much that she never left.[2]

Crowder, who declined to be interviewed for this book, arrived at a time of rapid change. For most of its history the university had served the state's white elite, barring African Americans and women. It had also been quite small. The campus Crowder entered in 1971 was stretched at the seams by people, many of whom did not fit the university's historical mold. The person Crowder became was born out of this changing campus—an increasingly bureaucratic apparatus with masses of struggling students and a rising athletic star. Crowder, who is white and goes by Debby, devoted herself to helping those students. In fashioning herself as their ally, Crowder found herself eagerly, and perhaps unintentionally, making the amateur myth and the Carolina Way it spawned seem true.

She paid a price for it, but not before she became a hero to many on campus.

In 1971, Chapel Hill was still feeling the aftershocks of the 1960s. As part of a nationwide wave of protest, in 1968 the university's Black Student Movement had presented the chancellor with a list of demands—one of which was the creation of an academic department focused on African and Afro-American studies.[3] The chancellor, J. Carlyle Sitterson, initially rebuffed the demand,[4] but soon a committee formed to discuss its possibility.[5] By 1969 African and Afro-American studies was enshrined in UNC's academic framework—not as a formal department but as a curriculum that could grant degrees.[6]

Activism 3,000 miles away at San Francisco State College, where a prolonged student strike had drawn the attention of the nation, paved the way for the concession in Chapel Hill. Activists there demanded that administrators give black-studies courses more prominence by housing them in a devoted department. This action provided a template for similar activism across the country. Within five years, more than 100 black-studies degree programs had been established throughout higher education.[7]

The creation of UNC's curriculum was a triumph of student activism, but also of desegregation. It had only been a few years prior that Charlie Scott joined UNC's basketball team, and a decade before that that the university had been ordered to admit its first black undergraduates. In 1969, only sixty black freshmen enrolled at UNC—making the Black Student Movement's achievements all the more impressive.[8]

But the successful struggle would have not meant quite as much if not for the runaway growth in higher education. Since the end of World War II, when veterans on the G.I. Bill flooded American campuses, enrollment in higher education had ballooned. By 1950, student enrollment stood at 2.7 million people, nearly double the pre-war total. A decade later that number had grown by roughly another million, and in 1970—the year before Crowder entered UNC—nationwide enrollment was a whopping 7.9 million.[9] Enrollment at UNC echoed these trends, increasing fivefold between 1945 and 1965.[10] As more Americans received a college education, the academy crept ever closer to achieving a spirit of mass access, and with it the understanding that the college degree was the quintessential American credential.[11] For black and other vulnerable students, the stakes were higher. As Dean Smith said, the college degree was the great equalizer, especially in the era of growing enrollment.

Mass access was also a double-edged sword. The influx of students strained a campus infrastructure that had never been so severely tested. The campus that Crowder entered in the fall of 1971 had overenrolled its freshman class by about 500 students. That made for less than ideal living conditions in the dorms, with some students tripled in rooms designed for two.[12] A similar dilemma struck at the beginning of Crowder's junior year, when just weeks before the beginning of the semester, the university notified hundreds of junior transfers that there was no housing for them on campus.[13] One housing official called it the worst overcrowding crisis the university had ever faced. Administrators looked to cram students in any space they could find, and had to borrow 100 mattresses from a local psychiatric hospital.[14]

Each fall's housing crisis was inevitably eased by the spring, leaving students to navigate what could be an equally impersonal apparatus: the curriculum itself. The university did little to simplify the path to a degree once students were on campus. The process of registering for a semester's courses was a good example. Each semester, students lined up outside Hanes Hall, forms in hand, to stake their claim to their preferred classes for the next semester. During Crowder's first on-campus preregistration, more than 4,100 students cycled through Hanes in a single day, and the line stretched for blocks down the street. Some students, desperately needing or wanting certain sought-after classes, even camped out the night before in sleeping bags.[15]

Because on-site preregistration offered no guarantees, students turned to the "drop/add" stage—a legendarily frenzied period featuring long lines of students mobbing Woollen Gym, hoping to claim what few open classes remained. Waiting for them inside were the university's undergraduate advisers. Though gripes about advisers were common among students, the professors who served in the role seemed just as frustrated with the system. In one *Daily Tar Heel* account of a drop/add period during the fall semester of Crowder's senior year, a dramatic arts professor describes the students' Sisyphean struggle: "people just keep coming back, asking if anything has reopened. It's just luck if they get something." Another art professor complained that "it's the constant usual hassle here"; the newspaper reported that at the time he was "holding an ice bag to his head."[16]

The registration system was frustrating and arbitrary. The university's director of records and registration, Raymond E. Strong, told the student newspaper in the fall of 1971 that not much had changed since he had started his job more than twenty years before. "The problems then were almost identical to those now," he said. "Now there are just more students."[17] That feeling of being one among many was not lost on freshmen. One new student, when asked about her impressions of her first week, remarked, "I have gotten used to getting around a large campus and am getting used to being a number."[18]

Other students never got used to it. Crowder was one of them. "Despite her love for the University," an investigatory report would later find, "she often told people that she had a difficult experience during her student years at Chapel Hill, feeling that she was left adrift by a faculty and staff that focused on 'the best and the brightest' and failed to pay attention to students like herself who needed direction and support."[19] That attitude, no doubt shared by many students, had consequences that reached far beyond hurt feelings. Toward the end of Crowder's first semester, Strong predicted that about 500 students were expected to drop out at the end of the term. The majority of these, he said, suffered from a "lack of motivation" that reflected "a disillusionment with higher education."[20]

But Crowder stayed afloat. She graduated with a degree in English in 1975, and within four years she was back on campus, having landed a job that only existed because a group of the most vulnerable students on campus had succeeded in making the administration feel their pain. She was the new student services manager in the Curriculum of African and Afro-American Studies.[21]

If Crowder was unschooled in the obscure mechanics of the academy, she got a quick education. Shortly after Crowder was hired, Sonja Stone, a popular black female professor who served as the curriculum's codirector, had her application for tenure rejected. Tenure is the highest professional status for a professor, guaranteeing virtually complete job security. When Stone was denied tenure, supportive students protested. At the root of their grievances was a sense that the university was not making good on its decade-old promise to value black scholars or students. The fact that the African and Afro-American studies program was still a curriculum, not a department, was the first piece of evidence. "We want an Afro-American Studies Dpt.," read one protester's sign at a demonstration sparked by the tenure denial.[22]

Curricula, like the one in African and Afro-American Studies, could grant degrees, but that's about where their power stopped. They were expected to draw faculty from other departments, instead of having professors on their own payroll. Those scholars' "priorities tend to leave the study of blacks and black Americans at the bottom of the totem pole," said the other codirector of the curriculum, Roberta Ann Dunbar, in 1978. This lack of status was a major frustration for supporters of the curriculum. Three years earlier, Stone and Dunbar had applied for departmental status but were denied by their dean, who later offered the rationale that "we were not in an expansionist period and did not have enough resources."[23]

What the curriculum lacked in status, it soon gained in popularity. In 1980 the university hired a new chair for the curriculum, a history professor named Colin Palmer who pledged to increase enrollment in the fledgling program.[24] He entered the university at a fortuitous time. Administrators were rolling out a new general-education curriculum that introduced new secondary requirements, called "perspectives," for all undergraduates. One of those perspectives involved taking a course in non-Western history.[25] Such courses were among the specialties of Palmer's program. By 1985, enrollment in the curriculum's courses had increased nearly eight-fold from just five years earlier.[26] Reginald Hildebrand started teaching in the curriculum in the '80s, and noticed over several years "a dramatic shift in both size and composition" of the black-studies classes he taught. His first such course, in the early '80s, enrolled just eighty students, 90 percent of whom were black. By the spring of 1985, 300 students were enrolled in the same course section, at least a third of whom were white. The curricular changes "alone would not have resulted in the increase," Hildebrand said, crediting Palmer's leadership, "but it cannot be ignored."[27]

But members of the curriculum bristled at still not being elevated to a department despite their enrollment numbers. In 1991, an editorial in the Raleigh *News and Observer*, known to locals as the *N&O*, applauded the university system for attempting to cut down on programs featuring "a perennial lack of interest from students." The featured example? Chapel Hill's African and Afro-American Studies curriculum, which, the newspaper pointed out, had only conferred ten degrees in the previous decade.[28] Trudier Harris, the permanent chair following Palmer, and another professor fired back with a letter to the editor pointing out that the curriculum had served more than 2,500 students that year, with just the equivalent of three-and-a-half faculty positions in its budget. "The major issue faced by the Curriculum," they wrote, "is not lack of student interest but the lack of personnel to offer sufficient courses to meet growing demand."[29]

Harris's dean had promised her three new faculty positions over the next few years.[30] One day in 1990 two professors in the curriculum approached the provost, a university's chief academic officer, about a promising young instructor who had an offer to teach elsewhere. They were "very anxious," a dean wrote, about that possibility, and wanted to keep him.[31]

That professor was soon hired full-time, and within two years, he became the new department chair. His name was Julius Nyang'oro.

Nyang'oro—who declined, through a former colleague, to be interviewed for this book—was by all accounts a rising star. Having grown up in Tanzania, he'd come to UNC in 1984 as a visiting professor, and soon wrote his first book as part of a postdoctoral fellowship.[32] After that he pursued a law degree at Duke, "more for the academic interest," he told the law school's alumni magazine, "since I wasn't interested in actually practicing law."[33] He returned to UNC in a visiting position in 1989, and it was soon after that that his colleagues scrambled to keep him in Chapel Hill. He was hired onto the tenure track in 1990, and two years later both earned tenure and became the department chair.[34]

Ascents as rapid as Nyang'oro's—from postdoc to tenured department chair in just five years—are almost unheard of in the academy. "He was a brilliant man, he had done exceptional work," Harris recalled later. "He was very much the kind of professor and scholar that one would want in any department."[35] And Nyang'oro also excelled as a teacher; in 1991 he won one of four undergraduate teaching awards bestowed by students.[36]

But Nyang'oro's identity as a promising junior scholar had drawbacks. "He's learning on the job," remembered Hildebrand, who'd taught in the curriculum when enrollment exploded in the 1980s. While Palmer, the then-chairman, had come in with a clear knowledge of how departments worked, Hildebrand said, Nyang'oro was green. "Administratively, in one sense, it meant it was Reaganesque in the sense that he wasn't micromanaging," Hildebrand said. "But it also meant he wasn't managing."[37]

It didn't help that Nyang'oro, as a scholar, had what an investigatory report would later call a "busy consulting and personal schedule."[38] He spent his first summer as chair out of the country in Africa.[39] The next year he did the same thing, each time informing his dean that Crowder would be able to contact him in the event of emergencies.[40] The amount of time Nyang'oro spent out of the office was "unique to him," Crowder later said.[41] The routine duties of the chairmanship eventually, if not immediately, fell to the longtime department manager. She later recalled that she and Nyang'oro would meet before his trips at Ye Olde Waffle Shop, a staple Chapel Hill breakfast joint across the street from the department's eventual home in Battle Hall, to go over "all varieties of things" before the chair began his months-long trips.[42]

There is some evidence to suggest the two had a good working relationship. Crowder was one of only ten people Nyang'oro mentioned by name in the acknowledgments of his first book, crediting her with "providing moral support."[43] He also on at least one occasion sided with her privately against what he characterized as the department's needy faculty. "I just don't like it when they all try to turn you into their hired help to do their little errands," he wrote in a 2007 email. "Remember: when you ask them to do a little adjustment to their schedules or help out a sinking kid they bitch as if there is no tomorrow."[44] But there is also evidence to suggest the relationship was not without strife. When a Swahili instructor named Alphonse Mutima later confronted Nyang'oro about evidence having emerged that his signature was forged on a class roll—perhaps Crowder's doing—Nyang'oro uttered, "That stupid woman!" according to a university letter that paraphrased Mutima.[45]

Whatever the nature of their relationship, Crowder emerged as what one instructor, Timothy McMillan, called "the de facto ruler" of the department.[46] She coordinated where faculty members taught and at what times. Michael Lambert, a longtime African studies professor in the department, remembered one instance in which she wielded this power in a way that made him sit up and take notice. Lambert typically taught on Mondays, Wednesdays, and Fridays in the fall, and on Tuesdays and Thursdays—preferred teaching slots—in the spring. Once he asked Crowder to schedule him to teach on Tuesdays and Thursdays in the fall, too. He proceeded to get a "horrendous schedule" of a morning class and an evening class with a big gap in the middle, and assumed Crowder was sending him a message. "I learned my lesson," he recalled, "and I'm like, 'I'm not trying that again.'"

Lambert found Crowder to be an off-putting presence in some ways. She had a "coterie" of work-study students often at her side, Lambert recalled, and he sensed that the socializing she did with them "was more important than the work that they were doing." In other words, Crowder's role at the university, from Lambert's perspective, seemed to her to mean something different than just a paycheck for services rendered. "She's not just there to do her job," Lambert remembers thinking. To him, that was dangerous. At some point, he says, he resolved to have as little to do with her as he could.[47]

Other professors recognized her as a formidable force in helping students. Hildebrand recalled, "If a student had a problem that I couldn't deal with, that if there was any wiggle room in the system, if there was any money to be applied for, if there was a way to get a credit, something, that she would know how to do that." Sometimes Crowder would ask Hildebrand to put together an independent-study course that would get the student enough credits to graduate. He found such requests a little annoying, he said, "when it seemed like everybody she had to save, she had to save through our department."[48]

Whatever its faults, the managerial setup delivered a coup that curriculum supporters had been waiting on for nearly three decades. Concerns still festered about the curriculum's low position in the university's academic ecosystem. Granting the curriculum departmental status would give the unit "freedom from the subordinate status of being a Curriculum," wrote Nyang'oro in his 1996 request to the dean, and assure other faculty, students, and people outside the college that it "has the same high academic standards as other units at the university." He closed: "In this regard, departmental status would signal that African and Afro-American Studies is not some lesser academic entity to be politicized whenever there is inside or outside focus on the African American population at the University. Thus, departmental status has the potential to place African and Afro-American Studies fully in the realm of the academic, where it belongs."[49]

In 1997 the curriculum finally became a department.[50]

By the late 1990s, with twenty years on the job, Crowder's reputation was beginning to travel far outside the bounds of her department. Her desire to help struggling students had earned her fans in academic advising. The advising department, housed in Steele Building, was one of the only places that could intervene when someone found themselves on the brink of failing out. Juniors and seniors with no one else to turn to would sometimes end up in the office of the university's graduation coordinator, Betsy Taylor.

Taylor's main job was to review graduating students' transcripts. That meant going over each sheet to make sure students had earned all the necessary credits and satisfied all the requirements of their degree. Among the boxes Taylor had to check, for instance, was the perspective requirement that had made African and Afro-American studies courses so popular. If a senior was missing a course or number of hours, the advising department would send them a notice in the mail, telling them to come to Steele Building. This is how many distressed students ended up sitting across from Taylor.

Sometimes a student's lapse was the result of some Kafkaesque provision of the curriculum. If students took the first level of the foreign language they took in high school, that class's hours couldn't be used toward the 120 hours required for graduation. Or if students repeated a course that they had previously passed, those hours could also not be used toward graduation. "Quirky little things" like that, Taylor said, could throw a student's academic plans into disarray. The panic that resulted was often compounded by personal problems—caring for children, working two jobs, or dealing with an illness. All of this resulted in a sharp sense of hopelessness.

Sometimes Taylor would have to tell disappointed students that they'd have to take summer classes and graduate later than they expected to. Other times she had more immediate solutions.[51] "She knew the system better than anybody," recalled Joseph Lowman, a former psychology professor who worked as an assistant dean in the advising office during the 1990s. "She was very good at knowing some of these roundabout fixes of doing things."[52]

This often meant getting a student into a brand new class, one that filled the missing requirement or supplied the needed hours. To accomplish that, Taylor tapped into what she and others called the "old girls network," the secretaries in academic departments across the university. These secretaries could get a student into a closed course in the department that they needed. Or they could help create an entirely new course—often an independent study, which was especially useful if a student only needed hours, rather than a certain class. These had to be approved and supervised by a willing professor, and no one had a better relationship with the professors than the secretaries who arranged their classroom space and printed their CVs.[53] And no secretary had more pull in her own department than Crowder, who was among the "old girls" Taylor called on.

When a student needed the ever-important, non-Western historical perspective—not just the raw credits an independent study could provide—Crowder's help was even more essential. Crowder herself remembered the first time she fielded a request from Taylor. A student had received incorrect information and needed a class that filled a perspective requirement in order to graduate. Could she ask Julius if he'd be willing to supervise one? "My question was, 'Can you do that?'" she recalled later, apparently having understood to that point that independent studies couldn't fulfill perspectives. "And she said, you know, 'Professors can do what they want to do.'"[54] So she asked Nyang'oro whether he was willing to supervise a course whose requirements would be the completion of a single paper. "He was happy to do it," Crowder remembered.[55]

Crowder recalled this as the moment the "paper classes," as they'd come to be known, were born. But they hadn't yet been institutionalized. To do that, she had to innovate. When she needed a paper class to fulfill a perspective requirement, she cloaked it in the course name and number of an existing class to which the relevant curricular requirement was attached. She called these "special arrangements." They were more sophisticated than independent study classes in that they filled specific curricular requirements, rather than just needed hours.[56]

Crowder wielded the independent study and paper classes liberally for at least a decade. An investigative report later claimed that Crowder designed this system, that she had sole control over enrollment, and that she graded papers herself—a clear overstep for a department secretary.[57] But she said the paper classes were inspired by Taylor, that Nyang'oro devised virtually all the paper topics himself,[58] and that she only graded papers when he was unavailable and the grades needed to be turned in.[59]

In less than two decades, more than 3,000 students enrolled in independent study and paper classes managed by Crowder.[60] Yet before these accommodations took on the stigma of scandal, they made

Crowder into a campus hero. Many times she got emails from advisers, students, former students, and professors grateful that she had helped a student out of a jam. "Thanks for being such a great advocate for students," wrote a student aid administrator.[61] One student, who had to take on a job and whom Crowder allowed to enroll in a class late, wrote that "I could not have managed it without your understanding."[62] An academic adviser wrote to her and Taylor: "You and Betsy have countless stars in your respective crowns in my book, and ANYthing that I can do to help I will do."[63]

But Taylor wasn't the only one in communication with Crowder. A separate team of advisers, working in an office attached to the football stadium, also sought her aid. One of them was named Jan Boxill.

Crowder would eventually become known for her efforts to keep students, including many athletes, in school. By doing so she helped cement the myth of the Carolina Way even deeper into the foundations of the campus she loved. If Crowder helped its spirit, Jan Boxill was among its greatest beneficiaries. That Boxill could ascend to such heights was improbable, given her origins. She grew up in circumstances more painful than many of her students and colleagues could ever imagine; the stories from her childhood are reminiscent of the grimmest scenes of *Little House on the Prairie*—infused with suffering and solidarity.

Boxill was born in 1939 on a dairy farm in the hills of upstate New York. Her parents were immigrant farmers who had moved from Illinois, where her father had been a coal miner, to the town of Worcester, N.Y. A Croatian immigrant, he had been a manager in the mines, aided by the fact that he spoke nearly a dozen Eastern European languages as well as English. Boxill's mother was Czechoslovakian and spoke no English.

The couple had no experience running a farm, Boxill remembered. They relied on the kids to shoulder their share of the unrelenting chores. The children milked the cows, fed the chickens, shoveled manure, weeded the garden, swept the floors, cut the hay, and planted and harvested the corn and potatoes. Work dominated the family's days. When Boxill was just a toddler, her mother died giving birth to her twelfth child.

Motherless, poor, and always busy, the children lived without comforts. They had no indoor plumbing, refrigeration, or everyday shoes to wear at home. They sewed their clothes from scraps of cloth. The winters were bitter, with only a potbelly stove and three-to-a-bed sleeping arrangements offering inadequate heat. The burden on Boxill and the younger children increased as her older siblings reached adulthood and began to move off the farm. She found herself helping her father, who could speak English but couldn't read it, with reading and writing letters.

Then one day when Boxill was twelve life got even more desperate. She was standing at the kitchen window washing the dishes and absentmindedly staring toward the barn her father was inside, raising clumps of hay. Suddenly, a mechanism on the tractor slipped and the big machine flipped over, pinning him to the ground. Boxill sprinted out the door and across the field to the barn, where she found her younger brother frantically pleading with the lifeless body. "Are you okay, Pa? Are you okay?" Her father's shoulders jutted out from under the overturned tractor. She ran up the country road to the next farm for help, but it was too late. Her father had been crushed to death. It was only when he was pulled out that Boxill saw his lifeless face, an image that would haunt her for the rest of her life.

Boxill and her siblings had nowhere to go. They had no other family to take them in. So they stayed on the farm, working as they'd worked before, just without parents. An older sister who by that time had two kids of her own became her younger siblings' legal guardian, but lived in town, visiting only occasionally. They would be forced to auction off the property, but the new owner agreed to allow the children to stay as long as they maintained the farm. Day after day of gritty chores and hard living birthed in Boxill a single goal: get away.

The solaces she found while waiting for her deliverance set the course of Boxill's life. In the summers she and her siblings would clear a hayfield for one of the only sources of entertainment they had: sports. They would fill a salt box with rocks and use it as a football. In the winter they would play hockey on the frozen pond—with a rock as a puck and their winter boots as skates. And they'd play basketball, which would later become Boxill's favorite, by mounting a bushel basket on a rafter in the barn where her father had been killed. Boxill was good at sports, and they made her feel good about herself.

School was another escape. Each day, after they'd each milked seven cows, Boxill and her siblings took the bus down from the hills to the public school, which was always warm and had a real toilet. But most appealing to the young Boxill was the fact that, following the death of her parents, school was where she found the only adults in her life: teachers. Boxill was particularly good at math, and in seventh grade, her math teacher would let her start each class by explaining the past night's homework assignment to the other students. That made her feel proud. Like sports, the classroom allowed the young orphan to feel good about herself.

School opened the door to another lifelong passion: music. The school loaned instruments to the children that they could take home and practice for band class. Boxill played saxophone. Even at a young age, she saw the similarities between sports and music. They were things you did for their own sakes, pure pursuits that made you feel good, distractions from the dire circumstances of rural life.

Boxill graduated high school when she was seventeen, and finally moved off the farm for good. She soon started on a path that several of her siblings had also taken: she joined the Air Force. Basic training, a harsh reality check for many new recruits, was for Boxill a delight. She had always gotten up at the crack of dawn, but now it was to eat a breakfast that had been cooked for her, not to milk cows. She had a bed all to herself and clean clothes to wear. It was always warm. She loved it.

Boxill's life away from the farm was defined by the three passions she learned while living there: sports, teaching, and music. She embraced music first. Boxill joined the newly formed women's Air Force concert and marching band, which took her all around the country. For a girl who'd felt stuck her whole childhood, the travel was exhilarating. She attended every state fair in the United States, and even watched the Kentucky Derby from the Churchill Downs infield. When she got out of the service in 1960 she was in San Bernardino, California, so she moved to Los Angeles, got a job, and—eager to get back into the classroom—enrolled in night classes at Long Beach City College. There she took a philosophy class with a good professor, and got interested. In 1965 she enrolled in the University of California at Los Angeles on a combination of the G.I. Bill and a work-study job as a student assistant in the philosophy department. This led to a stint at Los Angeles High School, an inner-city school whose student body was almost entirely black, to get some teaching experience.

A freshman biology teacher tasked Boxill with helping about a dozen of his worst-performing students. Boxill was in her twenties, less than a decade removed from when she counted her own teachers as her only role models. Now she stood at the front of a classroom full of students just as lost as she had felt at their age, if not more so. The Watts Riots, in which African American residents of the neighborhood rebelled against a police force they called racist and oppressive, happened around this time, underscoring the students' bleak circumstances. Not sure how to teach the unresponsive students biology, Boxill tried to level with them. She asked about their lives, and noticed a shift. When she asked honestly, the class of mostly female students answered honestly. Some of them, Boxill recalled, said they felt resigned to a life where they'd get pregnant early and go on welfare, just like their mothers had. Some had been abused by the men in their lives. "There was no hope," she recalled.

Boxill was surprised at how quickly they had opened up. "They just wanted somebody to listen," she said. And after she'd listened, she found the students were able to learn. She succeeded in teaching them some biology. The whole experience showed her the profound power of standing at the front of a classroom. "Here were kids that were going through—not the same things that I did—but I could understand how they'd felt no hope." She'd had no hope back on the farm—no money, no parents, and no idea of a future. She could relate, and then she could teach.

The one piece the white Boxill couldn't relate to was racism. That soon changed. The same year she started at Los Angeles High School a Saint Lucian graduate student named Bernard Boxill arrived at UCLA. A whirlwind romance ensued, and less than a month after they met, they knew they wanted to get married, which they did in 1966. The interracial marriage exposed tensions among some of the faculty whom the couple had thought were progressive. But nothing compared to what they encountered at their first apartment. When the elderly white landlord learned for sure that Bernard was black—he's light skinned—he sent them an eviction notice the next day. They couldn't move, so they kept living there in defiance of the notice. Every day the landlord waited for the Boxills to leave for campus, sprang out of his apartment, and spit on them. "There wasn't a day he didn't stand out there and spit on me," she recalled. "Every day."

Boxill developed an awareness of racial injustice that she channeled into activism. UCLA was a hotbed of the burgeoning civil rights movement, and Boxill attended speeches by Alex Haley, Stokely Carmichael, and Martin Luther King Jr. Once Boxill tried to get arrested as part of a demonstration, but a police officer declined to take her in. Her growing interest in activism translated to the classroom, especially the field of political philosophy, her husband Bernard's specialty.

As always, Boxill continued to feed the passions she'd developed back home. With several years of marching in the Air Force Band under her belt, Boxill asked the director of the UCLA marching band if she could join. "He looked at me like I had three heads," she recalled. Women, he told her, aren't strong enough to march and play an instrument at the same time. She'd probably marched more miles in the Air Force than his entire band put together, she told him, but he wouldn't budge. Spurned by one director, Boxill went to another. She and two other students asked the athletic director about starting a women's basketball team. He agreed. The director recruited the track coach to call the plays, and as John Wooden's legendary squad traveled on the university's dime to wallop opponents, Boxill and her team bought their own uniforms and drove themselves to the games.

When she graduated in 1969, Boxill stayed at UCLA and decided to earn her master's degree while her husband finished up his doctorate, a degree she also went on to earn. In 1979, Bernard accepted a professorship at the University of Kentucky, so they moved to Lexington. It was beautiful, and Boxill would get groups together to play pick-up basketball games in Rupp Arena during the lunch hour. But the Kentucky philosophy department, Boxill said, proved to be too harsh an environment for a black professor, so Bernard accepted an offer to teach at the University of South Florida. In 1980, the family packed up the car and moved to Tampa.

As she had at UCLA, Boxill quickly sought out any sports opportunities she could. In 1981 she became the Division II women's basketball coach at the University of Tampa; she was also an assistant professor there and had two young kids at home. But she loved it, and in 1984 was named conference coach of the year. In 1985, Bernard got a job offer for a fellowship at the National Humanities Center in North Carolina's Research Triangle Park. That led to a philosophy professorship at UNC, where Boxill landed as a visiting professor in the same department.

She was one of three scholars new to the department, and was told that only two would be awarded tenure-track positions. There are three components to every professor's job: the research they publish as scholars, the teaching they do in the classroom, and the service they perform to help the university. "You got tenure based on publication," Boxill said. "There was no question. Teaching was part of it, but very, very minimal." The same went for service, which was Boxill's strong suit. Practically as soon as she got on campus she did what she'd done at every other college. She gauged what she could do with sports. She had just stopped coaching full-time, creating a void she was eager to fill. So she met the then-women's basketball coach, who asked Boxill if she'd like to be the team's public-address announcer. Boxill said yes.

Her broad spectrum of interests proved detrimental to her tenure prospects. Just two years after she arrived, she was told that the department would be awarding the other two professors tenure. She apparently lacked focus. "You're not single-minded enough," she recalled being told. And while Boxill was disappointed, she realized it was true.

Spurned, Boxill accepted a tenure-track position at nearby Elon University, but only stayed for a year. She realized she didn't want to be on the tenure track. She liked teaching and she liked administration. She didn't want to focus on research. Since she was still doing public address at UNC, she decided to return as a lecturer.

When she got back, she pursued a wide array of responsibilities, just as before. As it happened, the university had just created a new office that was a perfect fit: the Student Athlete Development Center, a counseling office devoted solely to athletes. Boxill, who had long straddled the academic and athletic worlds, was hired.[1]

The center's work began in earnest on a summer day in 1984 when Brian Davis, a twenty-six-year-old from the Midwest, drove into Chapel Hill. Having just earned his master's degree from Iowa State University, Davis was accustomed to football stadiums that were visible from miles around, giant bowls that loom over the plains. He was surprised to find that during his first day in Chapel Hill, he couldn't find the stadium. Only after he got directions from a gas station employee did he finally find it, tucked into the woods in the center of campus.

Davis was the new academic coordinator for the UNC football team, hired before the university had even built a center to house employees like him. His title was more formal than his duties. "Basically," Davis recalled, "my job was to run study hall." The football coach had a rule that most players had to attend two hours of study hall five nights a week. In practice, that meant about seventy football players crammed into several rooms in the building that housed UNC's foreign languages department, a setting not adequate to the task. The players sat in old, worn-down wrap-around desk chairs. "And every once in a while," Davis said, "you'd just hear one snap and there'd be a 300-pound defensive tackle lying on the floor because his chair just broke from the sheer weight of sitting there for two hours."

While study hall took up much of his time, he also made sure players were enrolled in the right classes. To do this, he had to learn the same curriculum requirements that had bedeviled Crowder, Taylor, and so many students. So he put a curriculum worksheet side by side with the transcripts for 100 athletes, and began reverse-engineering the enrollment process. What classes had typically satisfied which requirements? What were the requirements for each major, and how could they be satisfied efficiently—keeping in mind the practice schedule that disqualified athletes for certain meeting times?[2]

This improvisation was characteristic of a profession in its infancy. Until the 1980s, across-the-board NCAA rules governing academic eligibility were virtually nonexistent. But sordid tales of illiteracy and dismal graduation rates prompted a group of college presidents to urge the NCAA to pass stricter rules. In 1981 members voted to implement a twelve-credit-hour minimum per semester for all athletes.[3] And in 1983, it passed the controversial Proposition 48, which raised entering eligibility standards for athletes.[4] Such rules would only grow more cumbersome in the ensuing years.

The new NCAA regulations coincided with the institutionalization of academic advising for athletes at the top programs in the nation, such as UNC and the University of Kentucky. Even as the NCAA stepped into the fray, professional advising was slow to develop. Davis recalled that at the first meeting of the National Association for Academic Advisors of Athletics he ever attended, the group was so small that each person stood up and gave their name and where they came from. The field's purpose, at least in the 1980s, was unmistakable. "Those jobs were really focused on keeping people in school," Davis said. For scholarship athletes, losing academic eligibility meant possibly losing their scholarship, which could mean being forced to drop out.[5]

Advisers felt intense pressure to keep that from happening. About a year after Davis started work, the university hired John Blanchard as director of athletic academic affairs. Blanchard, who had played free safety at Stanford University, recalled walking in the door to a hectic first session of summer school. There were "quite a large number" of football players whose grades in the previous academic year had been too low to make them eligible to return to school in the fall. So they loaded up on summer school classes, with a couple of athletes starting at 8 a.m. and working with Davis in study hall until 9 p.m. "It was completely crazy," Blanchard said. He didn't feel pressure from the outside to keep the players eligible, but he felt it internally. "I got to know these guys and they were about to be thrown out of school," he said.[6]

The university soon invested more money in the staff's mission. In 1986 it debuted the new Student Athlete Development Center, a $1.5 million addition to the stucco field house at the east end of Kenan Stadium.[7] Davis traded the worn classrooms of Dey Hall for the accoutrements of a brand-new facility—computer labs, offices for academic advisers, and separate tutoring rooms.[8] And the two-man staff soon got bigger. In 1988, Boxill arrived to advise women's basketball and a collection of other Olympic sports.

Boxill's new role was almost perfectly designed for her. Ever since she'd stood at the front of that Los Angeles High School classroom, she had loved working with students. As adviser to the women's basketball program, she was in a position to mentor students who reminded her of herself. Many were young women who'd grown up with few advantages, but found sports as a way to overcome their circumstances.

She threw herself into the responsibility.[9] Tanya Lamb enrolled as a freshman women's basketball player in 1988. Nearly 3,000 miles from home, Lamb found college disorienting. When it was time to register for courses, she picked her slate of classes more or less randomly.

Her schedule—including a biology lab and statistics—was too difficult, and she failed out of school in her first semester. Boxill started work as the team's adviser, Lamb remembered, while she was working toward readmission by taking correspondence courses. Boxill helped her decide which classes to take. As much as Lamb respected her coaches, they weren't there to help with the kinds of problems that she brought to Boxill. After Lamb rejoined the team, she began suffering from an eating disorder, which caused her to miss her target weight. After the coach, Sylvia Hatchell, kicked her off the team, Boxill and another adviser, Kathy Jarvis, worked to get her back on the roster the next year. Years later, on senior night, as other players invited their parents to accompany them to center court, Lamb asked Boxill. "She really was the mom I wish I had," Lamb said.[10]

But Boxill's enthusiasm for helping students one on one wasn't limited to her women's basketball players. Kit Wellman got to know Boxill as a philosophy student around the time Boxill started as an instructor. He ended up doing an independent study class with her on aesthetics and the philosophy of sport, a topic that was right in Boxill's sweet spot. The resulting paper, he recalled, was the piece he was proudest of writing at that point in his life. He went on to teach at nearby Guilford College, and when he got the chance he'd swing by Chapel Hill to visit with Boxill, whom he invited to his wedding. As a scholar himself, he was even more impressed with the initiative Boxill had taken in helping students like him. To advance as academics, professors have to carve out a space of ownership in their disciplines, and that means research. But Boxill didn't take that path. It's not that she wasn't single-minded enough, Wellman said, it's that she wasn't selfish enough.[11]

Boxill approached all her roles with characteristic appetite for work. The adviser for women's basketball, field hockey, lacrosse, and swimming, she also took charge of a program specifically for freshmen, to teach them how to get accustomed to college life. The normal duties of the role were legion: sending out academic progress reports to her players' professors, attending study hall every night from 7 to 9, traveling with the team on their away games, and setting up informal study halls. On the road, sometimes players would just come hang out and watch TV in her hotel room.

Boxill remembered on one trip, the night before a game, a few of the players came by her hotel room to hang out. One of them was complaining about her family. Over the ensuing years Boxill heard many stories about parents who beat their kids, who did drugs, who made their children stay up late and sleep on the couch, who put undue pressure on a player, now a star athlete, to save the family. There, in a hotel room full of black athletes, she saw it up close. "I thought, 'God, this is really sad,'" she recalled. And she remembered all the days she'd spent on the farm, knowing she would never see her parents again.

"I grew up without parents," she told the players. "At least you had parents."

There was a pause. And then one of them said, "You were lucky."

"I was lucky?" she shot back.

They talked about it until Boxill saw what they meant. Her childhood had been hard but she hadn't been beaten. They'd been poor, but there was no alcohol to abuse. Boxill had always considered herself fortunate for being able to make it off the farm, but she never truly understood the source of that luck. Part of it, she realized, was that she was white. Her white teachers had seen something in her and supported her, laying the groundwork for a career in the academy. By letting her teach the homework, her math teacher had given her the confidence and the self-esteem to feel comfortable in a classroom. As she looked at the black women in her hotel room, she realized they'd never had that. The most important people in many of their lives hadn't been parents, and it hadn't been teachers. It had been their coaches. Just as Boxill had loved going to school because it got her off the farm, some of her players loved playing basketball because it got them out of the house.

Those children she'd first taught in that high school classroom all those years ago had been hopeless. But the players Boxill mentored now had hope. That hope was basketball.[12]

For Boxill, this was a moment of confirmation. Ever since those days in the hayfield playing ball with her siblings, she'd believed in the power of sports. And her time at UCLA during the heat of the civil rights movement had shown her the gross inequities of American society, particularly along racial lines. Hearing her players' experiences triggered in Boxill a doubling down of sorts. She would approach the rest of her career with the dual belief that the mostly African American athletes who came into her office faced profound disadvantages, but that sports was their way to overcome them.

So when she sat down with her players to ask about their academic interests, she heard over and over again that they were interested in African American studies. Over the years she had attended some of the department's classes, and was impressed by the teaching styles of Nyang'oro and McMillan. Many of the classes they taught satisfied the students' perspective requirements, so Boxill would send them over to Battle Hall. Crowder, Boxill learned, was the point person with access to course enrollment, and a kindred spirit in that she, too, was the sort of helpful person who could get things done. "I made it my business to know where to send kids," Boxill said.[13]

Meanwhile, under Crowder's influence, independent study classes in the African and Afro-American Studies department had become especially accommodating to athletes. The exact conditions that resulted in this enthusiasm would later become a source of controversy. Crowder's own affinity for athletics and athletes no doubt played some role. Crowder remained an avid fan of UNC basketball.[14] She became close friends with the longtime academic adviser to the men's basketball team, a woman named Burgess McSwain. Crowder later told NCAA investigators that their relationship was like that of two sisters, adding that they were always careful to keep their personal relationship and professional duties separate.[15] They had met through Crowder's long-term partner, Warren Martin, a UNC basketball player she'd met when he was a student in the early '80s. "I am indeed part of the Carolina basketball family as a very distant relative," she told the investigators.[16]

She may have been a distant relative, but her passion for the game was undeniable. "She lived and breathed UNC basketball," recalled Lambert, the African studies professor.[17] A former graduate student who befriended Crowder in the '80s later recalled that Crowder became so upset after a big loss that she would sometimes not come to work the next day. She had the basketball team's promotional calendar in her office, and "glowed in anticipation of a big game," the student recalled.

Nyang'oro himself was also a fan of the basketball team, though more casually than Crowder. In a handwritten note to his dean in the '90s, Nyang'oro commented, "As you continue to be swamped by work, remember there is light at the end of the long dark tunnel: the basketball season."[18] A history professor named Jay Smith recalled attending a 1992 conference with Nyang'oro and watching the scholar tease two professors, Duke alumni, that the Tar Heels had landed a prized recruit named Jerry Stackhouse.[19]

Nyang'oro may have been a fan, but he also had a reputation as an unyielding instructor. A former student later recalled to the *Daily Tar Heel* that Nyang'oro was strict and demanding.[20] Perhaps he was too strict. An investigative report later found that Crowder told Nyang'oro that the advisers in the Kenan Field House thought he was "being an ass" for requiring too much of the athletes he supervised in his independent study classes.[21]

Lambert said he perceived Nyang'oro as someone who was motivated by a desire to be liked, and to keep people happy.[22] This quality may have motivated him to agree to teach Crowder's suggested paper classes. Timothy Shaw, an African studies scholar with whom Nyang'oro worked closely for a time, recalled that an essential pragmatism undergirded both the professor's scholarship and his personality. During a visit Shaw made to UNC in the '90s, Nyang'oro remarked to his friend that he found it interesting that black, male athletes seemed to be a key constituency of his department, Shaw remembered. "I can see that in the role he played at UNC, when the administration was trying to encourage a good basketball or football team, that he would see that that was something that his department could help with."[23]

Whether or not Nyang'oro intended it, his department became a popular destination for athletes. Between the spring of 1989 and the fall of 1999, the department chalked up 193 enrollments of athletes in independent study courses.[24] That averages to about 20 enrollments per year. Around 2000, however, things changed. It was ostensibly around this time that Crowder got the call from Taylor, and realized Nyang'oro could sign off not just on independent study classes but independent study classes masquerading as lecture courses, which could also supply key perspective requirements.[25]

The new type of class would prove remarkably helpful for athletes in the years to come.

During these years, Boxill became a prime exemplar of the Carolina Way. Just as that mystique assured the campus that its athletics and academics enterprises could excel simultaneously, so did Boxill thrive in her two passions, teaching and sports. Boxill relished the opportunities she found in Chapel Hill. As public address announcer for the women's basketball team, she was invited to announce basketball games at the 1996 Olympics in Atlanta, one of the most thrilling experiences of her life.[26] In 1998 she received an undergraduate teaching award alongside Holden Thorp, rapidly ascending the campus ranks, and alongside the author of the Carolina Way himself, Dean Smith.[27] Boxill got to know Smith personally; he occasionally spoke as a guest in her class on sports ethics. Ever the theoretician, the coach had a keen interest in the subject matter. In 2003 Boxill released her first major work of scholarship, an anthology on sports ethics. Smith authored the foreword. "Jan maintains that sports are the single most available means for self-development, self-respect, and self-esteem, when properly played, as cooperative activities," Smith wrote. "I think she is correct in this."[28]

But, as Boxill wrote on her syllabi each semester, to whom much is given, much is expected. She did far more than reap the rewards of a career that embraced the Carolina Way. She sat on committee after committee, board after board, continuing to throw herself into the life of the university. She helped agitate for the rights of adjunct faculty. She started an Ethics Bowl team in the philosophy department.[29] It was this nonstop service that endeared Boxill to her colleagues, eventually resulting in her election as chair of the faculty—an honor never before bestowed on a nontenured professor.[30] Boxill had come a long way from the farm.

By the mid-2000s, Boxill was working mostly from her philosophy department office, where she was the associate chair and director of undergraduate studies. She generally only visited the academic center for nightly study hall. A new learning specialist took over Boxill's old office, and the two became fast friends. Neither of them knew it at the time, but this newcomer would help expose the cracks in the Carolina Way that Boxill had come to embody.

One day not long after Mary Willingham started at Chapel Hill High School in 1999, a student walked into her office. He was an African American ninth grader, sent by his social studies teacher to talk about how he could satisfy the service-learning component of the curriculum. Sitting at her desk, Willingham, the service-learning coordinator, looked over the program's requirements and the student's textbook. But when Willingham asked him to read a few passages aloud, the student ran into trouble. He could pick out certain words by sight, but he couldn't read sentences. He was illiterate.

Willingham was shocked.[1] This was one of the most educated counties in America. Many of the students she passed in the hallway were the sons and daughters of professors, destined to follow in their parents' footsteps. The year Willingham was hired, an article in the *Wall Street Journal* had listed her new employer as one of the top ten high schools in the country based on "SAT, achievement-test and standardized-test scores."[2] How had this student slipped through the cracks?

Willingham sent the young man back to his class and walked over to the registrar's desk. They opened the file cabinets and found the student's transcript. He had advanced through every grade without passing his end-of-grade tests. Willingham was aghast. When she was a child her parents had impressed on her the injustice of societal inequities. Growing up on the South Side of Chicago, the Willinghams had mobilized with their church to welcome the first black family on the street. The Beverly suburb was predominantly Irish Catholic, but Willingham remembered learning to double-dutch with the new neighbors' children.

After eighth grade, Willingham's parents decided she wasn't reading at a high enough level. She rode her new Schwinn bicycle across town every day during the summer to spend the days reading and discussing Junior Great Books—anthologies of classic literary works packaged for children—at a reading-intensive program. The experience made her excited about reading, and she later knew she could do the same for others.

Since Chapel Hill High didn't have anyone who specialized in literacy, Willingham set out to become that person. She trained with a local nonprofit to learn how to teach teenagers to read, and changed jobs at the high school to work with struggling students. By teaching students to read, Willingham felt like she was making a real difference in their lives.

Then in 2003, her own children reached the age where they needed more attention. So she started looking for part-time work. Someone mentioned to her that the UNC athletics program hired tutors. Before she knew it, she had a part-time job there as a learning specialist.

Willingham and her then-husband, Chuck, had met at a biotechnology company in California and moved to Chapel Hill in 1999 looking for a career change. He started a chain of Irish pubs and she went into education. The newcomers realized that the university was at the center of Chapel Hill life. The fire trucks were painted Carolina blue, and road signs announced athletic championships. It seemed to Willingham that everyone in town wanted to work for UNC. Her neighbors told her how lucky she was to be part of the athletics program. Alums themselves, they told her how they probably wouldn't get in if subjected to the university's tough admissions standards today.

It was a dream job with a flexible schedule. Willingham could leave in the middle of the day to pick up her kids, then return at night for study hall. Robert Mercer, director of the academic-support program, was a great boss, she remembered, giving her latitude to do the kind of work she loved most: helping vulnerable students in the classroom. Her passion showed. Within a year, she was hired full-time as a learning specialist for the Olympic sports.

But Willingham was quickly struck by the similarities she saw with the high-school students she'd tutored before. One day she was working with a baseball player on a paper in the afternoon, and then helping her son at the kitchen table with a class assignment at night. The college student and the fourth-grader seemed to be reading at the same level. Willingham only had access to a relatively small pool of students, but if there were more athletes like this at Carolina, how were they passing their classes? And how did this square with the high admissions standards she'd heard so much about?[3]

She got a glimpse at the answer soon after she arrived. Jan Boxill would often stop by her old office at night, and the two women quickly hit it off. To Willingham, Boxill was full of energy, someone who seemed to do everything for everyone.[4] To Boxill, the new learning specialist brought passion and skill to the role, skill that Boxill quickly enlisted.[5] According to Willingham, soon after she started, Boxill sent her a women's basketball player for help with a paper. Willingham took one look at the paper and knew it couldn't have been the player's own writing. It read like it was taken from a book. Willingham asked the player what class the assignment was for.

A class in the African and Afro-American Studies department, the answer came back. All you have to do is turn one paper in at the end of the semester, the player told Willingham. She didn't even think anyone read them. Willingham went to the head of the Olympic-sports advisers and told her what the player had said. "Don't worry about it," she recalled being told. "It's been going on way before we got here."

Willingham had caught the first whiffs of the same problem that had left her so aghast at Chapel Hill High School: academically underprepared students were being passed along through classes without being given access to a full education. It was one thing to see this happen in a public high school, quite another at one of the most prestigious universities in the country.[6]

Athletic success depends on many factors, including coaching, teamwork, grit, and conditioning. But the tried-and-true way to win is to get the most talented players. In professional leagues like the NFL, teams select new players through a draft, and the most talented players are crowded in the first rounds. These players command lucrative contracts, and can command larger salaries by moving to new teams when their original contracts expire.

In college sports, things work differently. Because there is no draft, and because colleges restrict what they can pay players to roughly the value of a scholarship, coaches gain access to top talent via recruiting. In big-time NCAA sports, recruiting is the primary means through which programs compete. Elite programs are ostensibly on a level playing field here. This puts extra pressure on a coach and his or her staff, who must rely on charisma, relationships, personal assurances, the splendors of their campuses, prestige, or other intangible factors to land top recruits. For elite coaches, recruiting is the difference between national championships and being out of a job.

And yet, because NCAA rules also require that athletes be enrolled as students, institutions with high academic standards could face a disadvantage. The most talented high-school athletes in America tend to have lower academic profiles than their college-bound classmates. So if all scholarship athletes at big-time sports programs had to go through the normal admissions process, colleges with lower admission standards would have a decided competitive advantage. For example, every year UNC faces off against the University of Louisville, a fellow Atlantic Coast Conference member, in a variety of sports, including football and basketball. But their academic standards differ drastically: in 2018-19, nearly all of the students admitted to UNC had a high school GPA of 3.75 or higher,[7] while at Louisville that number stood at about half.[8]

To reconcile this, UNC long ago formalized a carve-out making it possible to accept athletes who are underqualified compared to their classmates. It works like this. Around the time Willingham was hired, UNC admitted about 170 athletes every year.[9] A small percentage of those met the same criteria as nonathletes. But the vast majority of the 170 benefit from a privilege known as "slots," where the athletic department recommends certain students for a specific number of seats. A slot generally guarantees an athlete's admission. But if an athlete's academic profile is very low, he or she has to be considered by a special subcommittee of professors who then vote to admit or deny the applicant. The number of athletes admitted through this process is small—a couple of dozen, at most, per year.[10]

In a literal sense, this process undermines the university's academic standards. But it has long been defended by university officials. College admissions is a cloudy and multifaceted process—holistic, in the favorite term of admissions professionals—so it is hardly uncharacteristic that factors other than academics come into play. The sons and daughters of donors and other alumni may have an advantage, and universities may also consider race when evaluating an applicant. Indeed, diversity is one factor university officials have used in defending the special admissions process. Students who bring special talents to the campus, the argument goes, bring a degree of vibrance and diversity. They make the whole campus better in that way.

But the carve-out creates conflict. Stanley Black, an economics professor who sat on the subcommittee in the 1990s, recalled that the group was charged with asking if these students could succeed in their classes. But the group wasn't doing any assessment or follow-up, he said, until he suggested it. "There was some reluctance," he recalled, but the report they produced the next year showed that the subcommittee had been "a little better than 50/50" in its forecasts. Those results, Black recalled, were "a little bit sobering." He couldn't recall whether the committee acted on the results in some way, and added that the group took its work seriously and did reject some athletes.[11]

The relationship between the coaches who recommended athletes and the professors asked to approve them was not without tension. Sometime in the 2000s, the chair of the subcommittee wrote to Blanchard, then the athletics department admissions liaison, with complaints about a particular student. That case left an "aftertaste" with the committee, wrote Peter Coclanis, a historian. (Coclanis didn't reply to messages seeking an interview for this book.) Some coaches, he wrote, "don't seem to be taking academic/character issues seriously enough, and they haven't been doing the due diligence necessary to inspire any faith amongst committee members."[12] In presumably the same case, the committee planned to reject a softball player for admission, but admitted her when it learned she had already signed her letter of intent, and thus wouldn't have been able to attend any college in the fall if she were rejected.[13] Yet Trudier Harris, the department chair who preceded Nyang'oro and a member of the subcommittee in the 2000s, wrote in an email that she said she didn't recall any "drama" in the group's work.[14]

Athletics officials were mindful of who sat on the all-important committee. In 2009, the executive assistant to the football coach asked an athletics official for a list of subcommittee members. The list included rundowns of each member's reputation with respect to the athletic department, including descriptors such as "Very helpful to Athletics and a big fan," "works hard to see that we are happy," "Will do anything she possibly can for us," and "Strong advocate."[15]

John Blanchard, who by the 2000s had been promoted from the academic support program to a senior position in the department, recalled his growing disenchantment with what he perceived as the subcommittee's too-soft hand. The admissions subcommittee was responsible for enforcing academic standards, but it consistently faltered in that role, rarely saying no to any player, Blanchard recalled. And yet focusing on the couple of dozen exceptions admitted each year may obscure the larger issue. Admit roughly 150 students through slots or exceptions each year, multiply that by four, and that becomes 600 students. A sizable percentage of that number, Blanchard said, were at a disadvantage when pushed into a classroom filled with more academically prepared students.[16]

That disadvantage can be expressed, if imperfectly, through numbers. According to internal university data, between 1998 and 2012 the average combined verbal and math SAT scores for admitted first-year athletes at UNC stayed steady, at a little below 1100 out of 1600. In that same period, though, the average score for all first-year, admitted students grew by nearly 100 points, to about 1350. The gap between the two types of student—184 points in 1998—was a whopping 262 points by 2012. The director of admissions, Stephen Farmer, acknowledged in a 2012 email to an athletics administrator that the gap between first-year athletes and all first-year students, as measured by SAT scores, was "much wider" in 2012 than it had been fifteen years before.[17]

Blanchard aired his concerns about this vulnerable population for years, using his annual reports as director of the program as an opportunity to sound a warning. For several years during the 1990s, he included some version of the following passage in his reports, under the heading "Principal Problems":

> Our students face a tremendous amount of pressure to compete in the classroom at a rigorous academic institution and to perform athletically at the highest collegiate level. The demand on their time and on their mental and physical energy is immense. College athletics is

too big an enterprise at the Division I level and is most taxing to students. The Department of Athletics at The University of North Carolina does an excellent job in supporting its student-athletes, perhaps better than any department of athletics in the country. However, the demand even on our students is great. . . . It is critical to note that in this context students who do not have a reasonable chance to graduate and are admitted to this academically rigorous university can have a difficult experience. The difficulties they encounter in the classroom are so severe that it impacts every area of their lives.[18]

It is easy to default into jock stereotyping when discussing athletes' academic preparedness. But consider the powerful forces that rule their lives. Big-time athletes are unlike nearly any other population in a university setting in that their academic ability is an afterthought in admitting them to the community. The athletic scholarship—a one-year contract that does not automatically renew—hinges on each athlete's ability to excel athletically despite a grueling schedule of practice and competition. They are athletes first, students second. It is only natural that this core truth manifests itself in the classroom. Willingham later came to think of it as if she'd suddenly enrolled in medical school. After a long absence from college coursework, "if you gave me a free scholarship it would be worthless because I couldn't do it," she said.

Social differences complicated matters. Many athletes were bewildered by college. Willingham remembered one athlete, enrolled in a drama class, who attended a play. He'd never been inside a theater, and when one of the actors turned to the audience and asked them, rhetorically, for help during the production, the player took the line as an actual invitation. So he walked on stage, causing the rest of the audience to gasp. Mortified when he realized what he'd done, he hurried out of the theater. Another student turned in a first-person paper about being a child and being told by his mom to kill his own dog with a baseball bat because the dog had bitten his sister. After he turned in the paper, his instructor reported him to academic administrators, considering him violent and a danger to the university. He was removed from the class.[19]

Another learning specialist who worked at UNC, Bradley Bethel, recalled much the same phenomenon. He'd come from Ohio State University, an elite athletic institution with lower academic standards than UNC. Bethel hadn't expected a significant cultural difference; he was skeptical of the Carolina prestige. But he noticed little things, comments athletes made to him about not fitting in, about not belonging. There was an elitism inherent in the UNC student experience, one that was especially hard for the mostly black students on the university's revenue teams to relate to.[20]

If campus is a foreign land, the sports themselves don't help with assimilation. In the 1980s, two sociologists conducted a years-long study of a Division I basketball program in the Southwest, embedding themselves in the day-to-day operations of the team. Through diligent interviews and observation, they observed a common trend among all the players they studied, that of role engulfment. Athletes entered the university with genuine interest in cultivating three components of their identity: athletic, academic, and social. But the athletic role crowded out the other two as players struggled with its demands and incentives. The academic role, the sociologists found, didn't stand a chance against the disorienting effect of the college classroom and the time demands and rewards of athletics. As one player put it:

> I've got two finals tomorrow and one the next day. I should be up in the room studying right now. But how can I get my mind on that when I know I've got to guard Michael Jordan tomorrow night?[21]

The two sociologists, Patricia A. Adler and Peter Adler, watched as the other two facets of the athletes' identities collapsed before them.

The supremacy of the athletic role was clear to many UNC athletes, as were its consequences. "You're not there to get an education, though they tell you that," said Rashad McCants, a member of the 2004-5 men's basketball team that won the NCAA championship. He added: "You're there to bring prestige to the university by winning games."[22] Chrystal Baptist, who played women's basketball in the early 2000s, learned early on that her scholarship was essentially an employment contract, and it hinged on her athletic skill. "There is nothing really, truly, that you can do without having approval besides going to class every day," she recalled. "You have to have approval to move off campus. You have to have approval to get a job. You literally, you work for the university."[23]

When the unstoppable force of athletic incentives meets the immovable object of academic requirements, there's conflict. That's why, Blanchard wrote, those charged with deciding whether to admit recruited athletes "must not waiver at the admissions table when these critical decisions are made. The consequences on the young people are too severe and the integrity of this great university is challenged when students who have limited chances of competing in the classroom at UNC are admitted."[24] Those young people were the students Blanchard had grown so attached to, and who Willingham was now tasked with helping.

With an exceptions system that was unable to enforce academic standards, the "campus problems undreamed of" that Graham had predicted were at hand. "In terms of higher education and athletics," Blanchard said, "higher education's original sin is admissions."[25]

Willingham started in the Academic Support Program for Student Athletes with the limited charge of making sure athletes with learning disabilities were getting appropriate accommodations. She and a psychologist hired by the university screened every athlete who attended the university's second session of summer school—mostly football and basketball players—for learning disabilities.

But with Mercer's encouragement, she expanded her role, working to help the most academically underprepared athletes succeed in their classes. She trained in supplemental instruction, designed to help students succeed in historically difficult classes. In 2005, she recalled, Wayne Walden, the men's basketball adviser, asked her to help with a few athletes who were struggling. Involvement with basketball, the crown jewel of the athletics department, lent her credibility among the rest of the athletes. Soon players from all sports were coming by her office.

As she saw more UNC athletes, she saw more discouraging signs. One athlete couldn't read or write. Another couldn't read long words; she had to teach him to sound out the word Wisconsin. Another asked her to help him get his reading to the level where he could read about himself in the newspaper. She asked one student who couldn't read well how he'd managed to score a 500 on the verbal portion of the SAT, and he replied that someone had taken it for him.

Just as she had at the high school, Willingham resolved to work within the system to correct these injustices. She drew on her literacy training. She oversaw study sessions for hard courses. When she noticed a female athlete squinting, Willingham reported it to others in the office, who bought the player her first-ever pair of glasses. Her reading abilities improved immediately. Willingham found working with athletes rewarding. They had so much positive energy and resilience. They wanted to work hard to show teachers who had doubted them that they were capable of making good grades. And they wanted to come through for their families. "I'm my family's lottery ticket," one athlete told her. "I have to succeed."

Willingham watched as the brunt of that pressure was transferred onto the office's advisers, people like Boxill.[26] Advisers had teams of their own, and were responsible for making sure team members were enrolled in the classes that fulfilled their requirements. These advisers reported directly to coaches on their players' progress. And even though the program itself had a reporting line to the College of Arts and Sciences, the athletic department funded it. Advisers later told investigators they were, in reality, reporting to coaches and athletics administrators.[27] Advisers in academic-support offices nationwide may consider themselves educators, Blanchard said, but their day-to-day lives are inflected by the culture of athletic departments:

> There's some weird transference of athletic mentality upon the academic-counseling world. If you're a wide receivers coach, and wide receivers aren't running good routes or not catching the football, that's your job. If you're a quarterbacks coach and the quarterback's not making the right checkoffs, the right reads, the right progressions, that's your fault. If you're an academic counselor and your football players aren't getting sufficient grades, that's your fault.[28]

Such responsibility sometimes manifested itself in stark terms. Carl Carey was an academic adviser in the program in the late '90s when a star prospect named Julius Peppers showed up on campus. Peppers played both football and basketball, excelling at both. Carey was in charge of keeping the star eligible. "All he knew," wrote *ESPN The Magazine* of Carey, "was that two coaching staffs were calling him at all hours, saying: Keep him eligible, keep him eligible." Once Carey banged on the office door of an instructor, according to the article, to demand a retest when Peppers risked flunking out.[29] He later became Peppers' agent when the player turned pro.[30]

But the advisers' role, still laden with pressure, had become more complex by the 2000s. Fresh off the abuses of the '80s and the passage of Proposition 48, the NCAA doubled down on academic regulations. In 1991 it passed a bylaw mandating that athletes have access to academic support services,[31] while at the same time college presidents—urged on by Friday's new Knight Commission—led a movement to raise academic standards for athletes.[32] A decade later the NCAA mandated that to stay eligible, athletes had to complete a higher percentage of courses required for a degree each year.[33] And it created the "Academic Progress Rate," or APR, which measured athletes' eligibility and translated it to a score that, if it fell below a certain threshold, triggered penalties.[34]

About the time Willingham arrived at UNC, the thicket of academic rules had never been more complex. For the advisers, monitoring athletes' academic performance was already a high-stress job. The process of selecting classes was not altogether different from the process Davis had used in the mid-'80s: what sorts of courses both satisfy degree requirements—critical to satisfy the APR's mandate—and aren't so hard or inconveniently scheduled that they threaten athletes' eligibility?

Jaimie Lee, who became an adviser in the program in 2007, recalled the set of questions she and her colleagues had to weigh when advising players. Many, though not all, of the football players she worked with were animated by their athletic ability, she said; they believed that if they worked hard enough at it, they'd be able to play in the pros. Academic success was not their first priority. "Should we pretend as though their sport is second? Why pretend? If it's first, it's first," she said.

That meant that convenience could take precedence. For the foreign language requirement, Lee often encouraged athletes to take Swahili or Portuguese, rather than Spanish or French. Fewer students came into those courses with prior knowledge of the material, meaning that the instructors had to start with the basics. Often, Lee said, the question of what course to recommend to an athlete came down to the professor. Was he or she known to be engaging and helpful? Did they reliably use the same syllabus year after year, a way for advisers to help plan players' academic calendars well into the future? Did they appreciate the challenges, scheduling and otherwise, of being an athlete? "If you know there are professors out there like that," Lee said, "and you give that recommendation—that that would be seen as a negative is backwards to me."

This is how clustering happens—by which athletes disproportionately end up in certain courses and majors. "If there's a class that's more of a go-to for folks who don't want to spend hours and hours to get that requirement done, of course you recommend that," Lee said. "Do they have to? Absolutely not."[35] Knowing these options is what advisers were hired to do. It was part of their job.

Few courses were more tailor-made for this brew of incentives than the African and Afro-American Studies paper classes. They could satisfy any number of perspective requirements, depending on the course number. And if the athlete was a major in that department, it could also satisfy major requirements. It also freed up time, a critical resource for busy athletes. Baptist, the women's basketball player, recalled having an ironclad schedule. Work out in the morning. Go to class. Practice in the evening. Study hall at night. Stretched for time and struggling with personal demands—she had a young child—Baptist looked for any means to wrest back some of her freedom. That's when she heard about the independent study classes in the Department of African and Afro-American Studies.

So nearly every semester Baptist walked to Battle Hall—sometimes on her way to Sutton's, a popular Chapel Hill diner—and stopped by Debby Crowder's desk. She recalled that Crowder kept a list of topics she could write on, and that the secretary was available to provide direction and support if she had questions. And Boxill, her academic adviser, was available to give her draft a look if she needed it. Baptist estimated she probably took more of these classes than any of her teammates. "As a student athlete who was extremely probably overwhelmed at times, you need some of your free time back. And independent study where I only had to write a paper worked for me."[36]

Willingham saw that some underprepared and time-starved athletes, buckling under the pressure of academic requirements, were using the paper classes as a release valve. But soon another ingredient was added to the cauldron, one that stretched the abilities of Willingham's office even further and convinced her that change inside the system was impossible.

On November 13, 2006, the university announced that Butch Davis would be its next football coach.[37] The hiring of Davis, former head coach of the University of Miami Hurricanes and the NFL's Cleveland Browns, was a statement. The Tar Heels, who had struggled since the late '90s, were rarely if ever a contender. Davis's appointment meant they were ready to join the upper echelon. But inside the academic support program, Willingham was nervous. A more vigorous recruiting apparatus, which Davis would almost certainly bring, meant even more underprepared athletes.

When the Davis era began, Willingham recalled, the number of athletes who found themselves in trouble academically ballooned.[38] That impression wasn't uniformly shared; Blanchard said he didn't recall a visible difference in the academic caliber of the students during the Davis years.[39] But the academic profile of entering football players was certainly low compared against all students. University records show that the average combined verbal and math SAT scores for entering football players in Davis's first recruiting class was 1013,[40] about 70 points behind the average for all entering athletes and 324 points behind the average for all entering students.[41] By 2010, the fourth year Davis's recruits landed on campus, that gap had widened. The average SAT score for entering football players was 953,[42] about 120 points below the athlete average and a whopping 391 points below the student average for that year.[43]

The students Willingham now viewed as in trouble were in desperate need of remediation, but UNC, the public Ivy, didn't offer those kinds of courses. Among the only such courses the university offered was English 100, a remedial composition class for students with low test scores. Willingham sat with players in the class and met with them every day. She knew many of the athletes needed further remediation, but at least this was something.[44]

Forced into a challenging academic setting, without the option of comprehensive remediation, athletes needed classes they could pass. So they relied on what Willingham would come to think of as a "shadow curriculum," the keystones of which were the paper classes in the African and Afro-American Studies department. With eligibility pressure more intense than ever, classes that didn't meet and that carried high grades were more important than ever. The advisers needed to enroll so many athletes in the courses that eventually Crowder began asking for them to send a list over; sometimes the advisers even included with each name the rough grade they needed to stay eligible. Crowder would wait until night to put them in the system, turning out her office light and entering names into the computer under the cover of darkness—so that no one would see her light on, she said, and bother her.[45]

She was also eager to facilitate in other ways. In some cases she acted like the counselor herself. In an email to Walden, the basketball counselor, she once second-guessed the decision to enroll a student in a class by a certain professor, calling her "too theoretical."[46] In another instance, noticing that a student was enrolled in one of the department's classes in the fall, Crowder cautioned Lee: "I would never, ever suggest that for any student athlete," she wrote. "It is just too risky under that instructor."[47] Once, when it appeared that Nyang'oro was making stricter demands on independent study courses he was supervising, Crowder suggested to Brent Blanton, another counselor, that she could run interference on a player's behalf: "They need to make sure they put [the papers] in my hands at the end of the semester and I'll straighten it out."[48]

In the summer of 2007, Marvin Austin, a top-flight recruit at defensive tackle, enrolled in English 100 during summer school. (Austin did not answer messages seeking an interview for this book.) But, Willingham recalled, he was showing up so infrequently at the remedial class that he was switched into African and Afro-American Studies (AFAM) 428 as a paper class that didn't require him to attend, in order to be able to be eligible to play. Willingham was disturbed.[49] If we can't keep athletes in even the modest remedial courses this university offers, and instead steer them into easy courses to keep them eligible, how could she and her colleagues call themselves educators?

Willingham became disenchanted. She was complicit, she saw, in passing underprepared students through the education system, just as she'd seen in that ninth-grader's transcript all those years ago. She had even dirtied her own hands. She recalled once accompanying an athlete who was struggling in a basic English course to the office of the student's instructor, and more or less pressuring the instructor to ensure the athlete passed the class.[50] Another time she strategized with the advisers about how to keep a student eligible for a crucial bowl game, when she lit on the clever hack of changing the student's major, allowing him to have enough relevant courses, before switching him back after the game.[51]

All along she had told herself that, even as she saw how underprepared her athletes were, she was helping them get something they wouldn't have had access to otherwise: a college degree. Chatting with Jan Boxill over coffee, she argued that the students they worked with day in and day out were being exploited for their athletic talent. Degrees in which paper classes made up a majority share were nearly worthless, and they weren't getting paid either. Boxill disagreed. Where would these players be without this opportunity? A college degree meant the chance to get ahead in life, and sports was the only avenue available. Given what sports had meant to Boxill, and her sterling campus reputation, Willingham had to respect her position, even if she didn't agree.[52]

And even as Willingham grew more cynical, the two remained friends. When it became clear that she'd need to get a master's degree to stay in her position, Willingham enrolled at UNC's Greensboro campus and wrote her thesis on the conflict between academics and athletics at universities with major sports programs. She wrote about paltry SAT requirements, special admits, and easy classes—all the things she'd personally witnessed.[53] Ever the doer and friend, Boxill was an adviser on the paper and challenged Willingham with counterarguments. Even as Willingham became disenchanted with an enterprise so close to Boxill's heart, the two remained friendly. One day when Willingham slipped on some black ice, Boxill drove her to the hospital.

In 2010 Willingham got a job offer from within the university, at its Learning Center. Soon she'd be out of the academic support office, no longer complicit in what she regarded as its unethical mission.

In the fall of 2009, Crowder retired after thirty years at the university. Practically the whole office left to attend her retirement party at Kenan Stadium, but, still wanting little to do with the paper classes—and never having met Crowder in person—Willingham stayed behind.[54] Soon she, too, would be gone, taking with her the sober experience of someone who'd seen the underbelly of the Carolina Way.

You can see for miles from the luxury box at the north end of Kenan Stadium. The yawning football field, stretching from side to side hundreds of feet below. The press box straight ahead. Beyond that, out in the distance, signs of the university's breakneck expansion. Its burgeoning hospital system, tall buildings clustered off to the right. Look left and you'll see a high tree line, beyond which stand the South Campus dorms that sprang up around the time Crowder got to UNC, fueled by the influx of students of which she herself was a part. Further out is the basketball arena, named for Dean Smith, the man who'd helped inspire her love for Carolina.

This was the view that greeted Crowder when she arrived at her retirement party. People from across the university came to celebrate her, many of whom would never be able to pay back the favors she had done them. It was this character trait that made her such an asset to the academic support program. The advisers there had sometimes been overwhelmed by the steep hill some of their athletes needed to climb. Crowder was always available to help them.

As her retirement date approached, Crowder was becoming more tired. An investigative report later claimed the source of this strain was the paper classes she arranged, and her fear that they would be found out.[55] But Crowder said she was just overworked.[56] "I admit that I am ready to get away from it," she wrote in an email to a football counselor, Cynthia Reynolds. "Somehow it used to be a challenge and at many levels rewarding. Now it is largely frustrating and draining."

Reynolds responded with reassurance. "You've put in your time," she wrote, ". . . counseled, helped and graduated more students than anyone can count." She added: "The students under my supervision could not have done it without you. Nor could I."[57]

Other advisers in athletics paid similar respects.

"The day that you retire will be a very sad day indeed," wrote Walden, the counselor for men's basketball, "because you have helped so many students who have been on this campus."[58]

Blanton also expressed his thanks: "Our students would not have survived without your assistance."[59]

The program sent her out in style, hosting her retirement celebration in the plush Pope Box overlooking the field.[60] Faculty from her department walked from Battle Hall across campus, passing Alumni Hall, where Crowder had worked for her first two decades, and Bingham Hall, where Graham had warned against overemphasis on athletics. Advisers walked the short distance up to the box, leaving Willingham behind. It was a beautiful autumn day.[61]

But the academic support office was already grappling with the implications of a post-Crowder world. She'd been a lifeline for struggling athletes, often able to find wiggle room in the unforgiving academic bureaucracy. Her paper classes had been critical to keeping some students eligible. Now they were poised to dry up.

This wasn't the first time the paper classes had been under threat. By the mid-2000s, Blanchard and Mercer, the director of the academic support office, knew about the independent study courses masquerading as lectures. Both later said they hadn't known the classes were so shoddily administered, but they knew enough to look for some clarity on what exactly these courses were.[62] They went to the Faculty Athletics Committee, the group of professors that met to advise the athletic department, who, according to the two men, told them that the way a professor teaches a class is his or her business. The subtext, Blanchard said, was clear: don't criticize the faculty.[63] The professors on that committee later denied that any such concern was ever raised.[64]

An investigative report later found that, around the same time, the senior associate dean who oversaw the university's academic advising program, Bobbi Owen, grew skeptical of the number of independent study classes being offered by the department. The report found that she chided Nyang'oro and instructed him to "get [Crowder] under control." Owen maintained that she only asked Nyang'oro to give her a copy of his signature, because one of her administrators had noticed variance in forms being turned into the advising office, and was suspicious. That, Owen said, is where her intervention stopped.[65] Whether or not she explicitly warned Nyang'oro, the effect was the same. Professors in the department and advisers for athletics recalled a subsequent deemphasis on the independent study classes. Yet the paper classes masquerading as lecture classes continued unabated.

In November 2009, two counselors for the football team gave a presentation to the coaching staff in which they made the academic stakes plain. There were twenty-four days left until final exams, and some "at risk" players were still struggling with tasks such as "attendance," "taking notes," "staying awake," "understanding the material," and "doing assignments," to name a few. "What was part of the solution in the past?" the advisers asked. They laid out the answer in what would become an infamous PowerPoint slide:

- We put them in classes that met degree requirements in which
  - They didn't go to class
  - They didn't take notes, have to stay awake
  - They didn't have to meet with professors
  - They didn't have to pay attention or necessarily engage with the material
- AFAM/AFRI SEMINAR COURSES
  - 20-25-page papers on course topic
  - **THESE NO LONGER EXIST!**

The team was on its way to sporting its worst GPA in a decade.[66] The post-paper classes era had begun.

Few people outside the circle of athletics advisers knew why Crowder was so important to UNC. To those who admired her, she was the consummate do-gooder, lending a human face to a cluttered, impersonal bureaucracy. She was also the lynchpin of the shadow curriculum that so disturbed Willingham but that had helped prop up the myth of the Carolina Way.

Lambert, the African Studies professor who had worked with Crowder since the mid-'90s, remembered stopping into her office shortly before her last day on the job. Huge stacks of paper towered over her desk. Lambert imagined the entire history of the department must have lived in those pages. He wondered how she would ever have time to sort through it before she left.

Shortly after she retired, he peeked into her office. The papers were gone, her desk wiped clean. It was almost as if she'd never been there.[67]

Crowder was gone. But what she'd been to Chapel Hill—revered saint, conniving sinner, or something else entirely—wouldn't stay secret for long. As she left the university, the Carolina Way was more fragile than ever, and about to collapse.

The day that Holden Thorp formally assumed the chancellorship dawned warm and beautiful.[1] He stood on a black platform flanked by the stately portico of South Building, resting his hands on a big wooden podium. He faced an admiring audience of university leaders and others. Behind them sat Wilson Library, which housed more than a hundred years of Southern history, stored in cardboard boxes. Behind that, in the woods, was Kenan Stadium.

Thorp devoted most of his speech to outlining his vision of the university's future, including the importance of research, town-gown relations, and service to the state. He worked himself into a sweat as he laid out these priorities, his twangy Fayetteville monotone echoing between the enormous oaks that towered over the sun-kissed grass.

But before he did that, Thorp gave special thanks to one man. "To President Friday:" he said, "Sir, without you, none of us would be here."[2]

Thorp and Friday cut similar profiles. Both had degrees from Chapel Hill, and both were relatively young when they stepped into the roles that would come to constitute their campus legacies. Friday was just thirty-six when he became system president, having served in a few minor administrative roles.[3] Thorp, forty-three, was a grizzled veteran of the academy by comparison. He had been a PhD student, a postdoc, a professor, a department chair, and a dean. Ascending to the chancellorship was just the cherry on top of a career in which, the alumni magazine observed, he was promoted "about as fast as he could move his books from office to office."[4]

Thorp was born in Fayetteville, N.C. His father was a lawyer and his mother ran a community theater. As a child he was a polymath, channeling the creative energy of his upbringing into jazz guitar and composing music. Once, while at a music summer camp, he read about a Rubik's Cube competition in a magazine, with a first prize of $500. Thorp had never solved a Rubik's Cube for speed before, but he practiced for a week, and won. "His brain scared me to death," recalled his childhood friend, Patti, who would later become his wife.

He was on the premed track as an undergraduate in Chapel Hill, but became infatuated with the lab after joining a chemistry professor's research team. That led him to Cal Tech to study inorganic chemistry, then to a professorship at nearby N.C. State University, and soon back to UNC.[5] The positions flowed from there: director of the campus planetarium, department chair, and dean of the College of Arts and Sciences, where in 2007 the search committee charged with choosing the next chancellor courted him for the role.

He went into his first interview thinking he'd just give the group advice on what they should be looking for.[6] But Thorp's credentials were eye-opening. First, he was a good fundraiser. He'd overseen $57 million in donations to the College of Arts and Sciences during his short time as dean. And he was clear-eyed about the importance of the task. "The dean's job, as I see it," he said while he held the position, "is to (a) raise money, (b) tell our story, and (c) oversee the largest school on campus." Perhaps more striking than anything, though, was his story: a North Carolina native whose brain had taken him all over the world, even into the biotechnology sector, where he'd help start two companies. But he just couldn't quit Chapel Hill. He seemed perfect for the top spot. "There will be no cultural learning curve for Holden Thorp," said Erskine Bowles, the system president who hired Thorp. "He knows the campus's strengths and weaknesses inside out."[7]

Thorp knew how to lead a college, not a university. A college or school, like the College of Arts and Sciences or the law school, is fairly self-contained. The modern research university contains multitudes.

American universities have long embraced the German model of the research university, which prioritizes faculty's pursuit of knowledge. Research is the coin of the realm at universities like UNC: it is how professors get tenure, and administrators value it as a mark of prestige and a major source of funding. Thorp was an eminently experienced researcher, having written more than 130 papers and holding 19 U.S. patents at the time he was named chancellor.[8]

UNC's vast medical system, UNC Healthcare, was also under the chancellor's watch. The year Thorp took office, revenue from patient services in the university's hospitals roughly equaled operating revenue from student tuition and fees.[9] Doctors were some of the highest-paid faculty and highest-profile researchers, bringing in federal grants that made up a large percentage of the university's research budget. Steeped in the world of science, Thorp was a quick study.

Finally, there was athletics. Thorp's predecessor, James Moeser, and the longtime athletic director, Dick Baddour, had revived Tar Heel athletics from its nadir at the turn of the century, when Dean Smith had just retired and Mack Brown, the successful football coach, had left for Texas. For years, both teams struggled. But by 2008 the programs were dominant again, with Roy Williams, a Smith disciple, leading the basketball program, and Butch Davis running football. In 2009, Thorp's first full year as chancellor, the basketball team won the national title. The team also had the highest APR of any team in the tournament that year.[10] The Carolina Way seemed as strong as ever.

But Thorp knew that casual fans like him know very little about the inner workings of the athletic department. So early on in his chancellorship, Thorp called Baddour and said, "Teach me." He soaked up the information like a sponge.

Thorp learned about the UNC's contract with Nike, first signed in 1993.[11] Nike paid UNC nearly $5 million for the rights to supply it with its equipment, ensuring that viewers saw its logo when the Tar Heels played on national TV.[12] The contract was renewed several times, including in 2008, for a grand total of about $37 million over the next decade.[13] Nike also paid the university royalties on the UNC merchandise it sold, and gave it $2 million for academics, which Thorp then divvied up.[14]

He learned about the proposed renovation of Kenan Stadium, expanding from its historic horseshoe shape to an all-the-way-around design, adding luxury boxes, and expanding the academic center from the fieldhouse into a more state-of-the-art facility.[15] Thorp knew this was important to fans and boosters and would cost millions of dollars. He told administrators, he recalled, to lower their ambitions on the scale of the renovation.

And Thorp learned that athletics had a way of setting the chancellor's schedule. When the slate of competition for each of UNC's more than two dozen varsity sports comes out—especially football and men's basketball—it lands right on the chancellor's calendar. The coaches expected the chancellor to be in attendance, as a sign of interest and support. And they'd notice if he wasn't there for a home game.[16]

Much of Thorp's public-facing work centered around athletics. In the fall of 2009 a student emailed him with concerns about the cost of a military jet flyover before a home football game. Thorp wrote a page-long reply.[17] Someone sent a $100 check to the chancellor's office with a note complaining about the football team's new dark blue uniforms. Thorp wrote back a handwritten note, and said he'd pass along the criticism.[18] The next year one Chapel Hill resident sent Thorp a clipping of a news article in which a UNC football player was quoted as saying, "We can't go out on no L," complaining about his grammar. Thorp replied with a handwritten note, assuring the woman that the player had "passed writing-intensive courses that require proper syntax & style."[19]

Much of the time, Thorp's role with athletics was just plain fun. He attended games, flew with the teams, and learned about the strategic intricacies of each sport from some of the finest coaching minds in the business.[20] Roger Perry, the chair of the Board of Trustees when Thorp was hired, recalled seeing the chancellor go from a man with a subdued interest in sports to someone who was extremely invested in UNC athletics. "It was just almost like it was an overnight transformation," he recalled. "It didn't take long." From Perry's perspective, Thorp seemed to be enamored of the new role. "I don't think there was anything wrong with it especially, or anything unusual about it," Perry said. "I just didn't expect it."[21]

Implicit in Thorp's early experience managing the athletics enterprise was the understanding that these systems would continue to run smoothly. He wasn't prepared for what to do if something went wrong.

Even in the best of times, the stakes were high.

Two decades earlier, Friday and his Knight Commission had issued their landmark report calling for reforms to college sports. At its center was the idea that the president, or the chancellor, should bear the ultimate responsibility for an institution's athletic program.[22] The NCAA adopted the principle in 1996, lifting the Knight Commission's proposal "chapter and verse," the *New York Times* said,[23] setting up a governance structure that put college presidents firmly in charge.

And yet by 2009, Thorp's first full year as chancellor, it was becoming more clear that the doctrine of presidential control couldn't be realized by presidential authority alone. The Knight Commission that year commissioned a survey of nearly 100 university presidents whose football teams played at the highest level of competition.[24] The portrait that emerged was one not of empowered vigilance, but of profound resignation.

"In terms of control over big-time college athletics, I don't believe we have control," one president bluntly told the surveyors. "Show me a president who won't meet the demands of a winning coach who has the chance to walk out the door for a higher salary somewhere else."[25] At the root of this powerlessness, some presidents said, was the fact that they were beholden to people who happened to love athletics, donors, for instance. As one president put it:

> Presidents do find the athletic program provides the opportunity to sell the institution to the larger community and they want to preserve that. Presidents are also expected to raise a lot of money from the private sector and they are trying not to alienate their major donors. Even if major athletic donors are not giving to the rest of the university they can make your life miserable.[26]

This is not to mention trustees who advise the president or the legislators who control the state's purse strings—two groups that appreciate a winning team. The surveyed presidents, too, were not shy about professing their own admiration for what sports can mean to a campus. They're the "intangible, social glue" that binds the campus together, one said.[27] "Brand identification," said another.[28] Visibility. An increase in student applications after a spectacular year.[29]

Yet several of the presidents were clear-eyed about the risks that overemphasis on athletics posed to their campuses. "Our biggest battle is not about revenue," one president told the commission, "it's about the balance between academics and athletics." While faculty fight for pay raises, coaches drive around in new cars.[30] The time demands on the athletes themselves made one president doubt whether they were getting a fair deal.[31] To another, athletics was a foundational issue of perception. "There's too much identification of a university with non-academic aspects," the president said, "distracting from values of higher education and from desirable values in society."[32]

Several presidents said it was clear that athletics, for them, was an existential issue. "The real power doesn't lie with the presidents;" one said, "presidents have lost their jobs over athletics."[33] Another employed more vivid imagery: "The presidents who have had their heads handed to them? A high percentage of them had that happen because it was something to do with athletics."[34]

The overall impression that emerged was one in which college leaders were riding the tiger. Thorp would soon learn what would happen if he fell off. In the summer of 2010 Baddour called him with news that didn't square with the ideals of the Carolina Way.

NCAA investigators were coming to Chapel Hill.[35]

On May 29, 2010, Austin, the defensive lineman whose early switch out of a remedial English class had so unsettled Willingham, tweeted a quote from the Rick Ross song, "Sweet Life."

I live In club LIV so I get the tenant rate . . . bottles comin like its a giveaway.[36]

Austin later said he was actually at the Miami airport when he sent that tweet, not the famous LIV nightclub in South Beach.[37] No matter: The tweet caught the NCAA enforcement staff's attention.

For players with professional prospects, the temptation to take under-the-table payments or gifts is ever-present, as professional agents are always scouting for great talent well before a player is eligible to go pro. The NCAA enforcement staff's bread and butter is policing violations. Enforcing amateurism's prohibition on outside pay has resulted in a complex web of rules that is often derided. "NCAA has created the largest rule-bound bureaucracy on the face of the earth," one president told the Knight Commission. "There are big problems in athletics and it isn't whether the coach buys a player a cup of coffee."[38]

But the apparent violations by Chapel Hill players far outstripped a cup of coffee. It turned out Austin had been in Miami on a trip he hadn't paid for.[39] At the same time Austin was in Miami, so was his teammate Robert Quinn, whose lodging had also been paid for by someone else.[40] The very same weekend, another Tar Heel football player, Kendric Burney, had been in Las Vegas, his plane ticket booked by a former UNC football player, who covered his hotel room, too.[41] And this was only the beginning.

Thorp, Baddour, and other senior administrators adopted an approach of frenzied disclosure. Find out as much as possible and show it to the NCAA. An internal investigation ensued: who got paid, and by whom? Thorp was constantly on the phone with Baddour that summer, busy charting the university's response to the investigation. Investigators interviewed players, and with the football season rapidly approaching, the key question was whether the football team would be playing at full strength in its much-hyped September 4 opener against high-ranked LSU at the Georgia Dome in Atlanta.

It was against this backdrop that Thorp ended up in Baddour's office in late August, where the two reviewed a troubling new piece of evidence. A tutor named Jennifer Wiley had written portions of football players' papers for them, a clear example of improper assistance— and one that was a lot more pernicious than a free piece of jewelry or a plane ticket. As they talked, Thorp and Baddour saw an ominous piece of news cross the ESPN screen crawl. The tutor whose academic misconduct they were about to reveal had also worked privately for Butch Davis's family as a tutor for his son. This thing has just shot into the stratosphere, Thorp thought. There was no way they could not hold players out of the team's opening game.[42]

Under-the-table payments are one thing; in the highly commercial world of college sports, the NCAA's rules are, to some degree, made to be broken. Real-life academic fraud—especially at a university like UNC, which prided itself on high academic standards—was quite another. The Carolina Way was as much about high academic standards as it was about athletic success. What administrators had discovered about Wiley posed a direct challenge to this mythology. The university's reputation—celebrated from academic trade publications to major motion pictures—rested on the fault line that was the Carolina Way. Now Thorp and his team were feeling tremors.

Thorp resolved to come clean. He, Baddour, and Davis held a press conference, where backstage Thorp lamented the death of the Carolina Way. "To everyone who loves this university," Thorp told the assembled crowd of reporters, "I'm sorry about what I have to tell you." He announced the news about the tutor, and updated the press on the ongoing nature of the investigation.[43] The message was clear: the investigation now had a second prong.

Rapidly, more shoes dropped. Austin was suspended indefinitely,[44] and twelve other players sat out of the LSU game,[45] which Thorp spent lying on the floor of a private box, overwhelmed by both the suspense of the game and the weight of the burgeoning scandal.[46] The day after the game, which the Tar Heels lost only narrowly,[47] an associate head coach named John Blake resigned. Later in the month it was revealed that Blake had been linked to one of the agents who had apparently bankrolled travel for the UNC football players.[48] News of a corrupt go-between inside the UNC program was yet another terrible development.

It also raised questions about whether this would be Davis's last season. News of his relationship with Wiley and his trust in Blake brought the scandal even closer to his office. Meanwhile, his team was able to string together a respectable season, defeating the No. 24-ranked Florida State as well as archrival Duke, then earning a bowl bid against Tennessee,[49] which it won in a thrilling double overtime.[50] Thorp and Baddour publicly supported Davis. "Competitive, big-time football is a hazardous undertaking," Thorp said in September, "but the plan right now is for him to be the coach next year. He's done everything we've asked him to do to get to the bottom of this, and we're pleased with him." In November, he told the Chapel Hill Board of Trustees that neither Baddour nor Davis were going anywhere. "They're going to be here next year, and we're excited about Carolina football," he said.[51]

Though he sang one tune publicly, Thorp had done the opposite in private, he recalled. He wanted to fire Davis. The revelations had been too damaging, the threat to the university's integrity too grave. Before that November meeting, he recalled, he met with six trustees at the chancellor's mansion to take their temperature on a possible coaching change. (He chose six, he recalled, because that was the largest number of members who could congregate without triggering the state's open-meetings law.) But he didn't have the support.

There was a wing of the board, Thorp recalled, that he and his South Building brain trust called "the sports trustees." These were the people who loved Carolina athletics and even sat on the board of the Rams Club, the foundation that funds UNC's athletic scholarships—a clear conflict of interest, given the ability of athletics to hurt a university's academic reputation. These trustees loved Carolina sports, Thorp said, and were invested in its success. They opposed firing Davis.[52]

Bob Winston, the board's chair at the time, said he didn't recall a specific meeting in which Thorp floated the idea of firing Davis, but said during those months there was a constant back-and-forth between Thorp and board members over what to do with the embattled coach. "Holden was pushing more towards moving on Butch, as far as letting him go, and I was on the other side of that," Winston said. He added that he opposed firing Davis because he wanted to make sure the university didn't punish the coach unfairly for things people under him did. It wasn't, Winston said, because there were some trustees concerned primarily with UNC's athletic dominance. The reservations, whatever their source, undoubtedly influenced Thorp. "I do think Holden felt the influence from me and some others to not make a move in the early stages," Winston said.[53]

With Davis safe in his post, for now, the university awaited the dreaded Notice of Allegations from the NCAA, essentially the association's version of an indictment. When that document landed, in June 2011, it relieved Thorp and the university of any misplaced optimism they might have felt. Although the university wasn't hit with a "lack of institutional control" charge, which typically is associated with the harshest penalties, the allegations were wide-ranging and extreme. Seven football players had pocketed more than $27,000 in benefits.[54] Jennifer Wiley had crossed several bright lines both financially and academically.[55] Perhaps most disturbingly, John Blake had been on the payroll of an agency firm, and he expected to use his position to direct athletes toward that agency.[56]

If this had been it, the university could have moved on, sobered by a serious but isolated fissure in the university's "right way" rhetoric. But the very next month, Thorp received news that the scandal might stretch far beyond the NCAA's investigatory timeline—news that came from the unlikeliest of sources.

Americans love to watch college sports. The average TV viewership for a men's basketball NCAA Tournament game in 2019 was 10.5

million.[57] That year's college football national championship game attracted a whopping 25.3 million viewers.[58] A cable subscriber in an urban TV market can expect more than two dozen college football games within reach of the remote control on any given Saturday in fall.[59]

But people do more than just *watch* sports. Many of them have a fanatic interest in a single college or team. These fans hang team flags on their doorsteps, wear jerseys to bars, gloat on Facebook, and paint their faces, yell, and scream when they go to games. Charles Clotfelter, a Duke University economist, conducted an analysis for his book *Big-Time Sports in American Universities* in which he looked at the breakdown of specialty license plates issued by the state of Florida in 2016. The runaway most popular plate, beating "Helping Sea Turtles Survive," "US Army," and "In God We Trust," was the University of Florida's "Gator Nation" plate. The second most popular plate was Florida State University's "National Champions" plate, celebrating the Seminoles' 2016 football championship.[60] People are not just interested in sports as a pastime. It is a source of identity.

Identification stems from one's own college attendance and loyalty as an alum. It also comes through family ties or the nostalgia of childhood memories. A survey of Tar Heel basketball fans found that 46 percent said their fandom had been influenced by their parents. Seventy-four percent said they were already fans when they were just twelve years old.[61] Such identification breeds a sense of investment in the team's brand and performance. Some scholars have used the word "equity" to describe the emotional investment fans make in their favorite teams. Many fans no doubt feel they have a personal stake in their team's success.

With equity in a team's brand comes a responsibility to defend that brand when it's under attack. Scholars at the University of Alabama examined two athletic scandals—the Jerry Sandusky sex-abuse scandal at Penn State and a booster scandal at the University of Miami—and found that loyal fans behaved on Twitter essentially as crisis communicators, employing four strategies familiar to those in the business: ingratiation, encouraging solidarity among other fans; reminder, pointing to the program's previous successes; scapegoating; and casting blame on someone outside the program, such as media outlets.[62]

Loyal fans may air their best defenses on social media, but they also have friendlier havens online where they can lay down their armor and enjoy the company of others like them. These are the message boards, team-specific sites where paying members can grouse, gossip, and give their own takes on the latest program news, such as signing a prized recruit, intrigue inside the athletic department, or even rumors of a chancellor's resignation.[63] If the fans are a university's online standing army, these sites are the soldiers' barracks. And they're primed not just to defend, but to launch an attack.

In July 2011, Michael McAdoo, a former UNC football player, sued the university and the NCAA for reinstatement. The NCAA had declared the defensive lineman permanently ineligible, saying he had accepted improper help from Wiley, the tutor. In his suit, the former player argued that Wiley had merely reformatted a works-cited page in one of his papers. The university and the NCAA had acted improperly, the lawsuit argued, in declaring him ineligible on that basis.[64]

Tucked away in an appendix to the lawsuit was the paper itself.[65] It didn't take long for a user on the site PackPride.com, the watering hole for N.C. State fans, to dig in. The user, going by the screen name Wuf-Wuf1, got suspicious when he read the word "Mohammedanism," an obscure and rarely used synonym for Islam, in the paper. So he pasted sections of it into Google and found a clear example of plagiarism. "LOLOLOL," he wrote on a PackPride message board. "I can't wait till the media gets this and breaks this down. Let's help." The users put together a marked-up and color-coded version of the paper that catalogued each instance of apparent plagiarism. A few blogs picked it up,[66] followed by the *Daily Tar Heel*[67] and the *N&O*.[68]

The rival fans' motivations may not have been pure, but the questions they raised were entirely legitimate. The university's student-run honor court hadn't seemed to detect the plagiarism, nor had—disturbingly—the professor for the summer class, none other than Nyang'oro himself. The revelation seemed to raise questions that transcended the focus of the NCAA investigation. "The worst academic/athletic scandal in 50 years continues to linger at the University of North Carolina at Chapel Hill, and the clouds are darkening as more information is revealed," wrote the *N&O*'s editorial board, adding that "neither Athletics Director Dick Baddour nor Chancellor Holden Thorp has demonstrated a grasp of just how serious this crisis is."[69]

An overzealous tutor was one thing; a football player's plagiarized paper promised more attention, more questions, more scrutiny.

The editorial may have influenced the chancellor's thinking. Perry, the board chair when Thorp was hired, recalled sending it to the chancellor, who was on vacation. And although Perry didn't tell Thorp to take any specific action, "I had recommended to him that now that he was under attack publicly by the newspaper that he needed to do what he needed to do to defend and protect himself."[70]

Thorp was beginning to appreciate the scandal's severity. It wasn't going to just go away when the NCAA issued its sanctions, especially with the intense interest from the journalists and editors at the N&O. So Thorp did an about-face. He called a meeting of what one attendee called "friends of the university"—current and former board members and administrators. There he announced his decision, which he presented as a fait accompli: Davis would be fired. Then he called Baddour, who lodged objections. The football season was just days away, and firing a coach would leave the team very seriously in the lurch.[71] But Thorp had made up his mind.

On the evening of July 26, Thorp sat down with Baddour and Davis in his office and gave the coach his notice.[72] Davis recalled being shocked by the decision.[73] When the news broke after the next day's Board of Trustees meeting, the college sports world was equally shocked.[74] Thorp seemed to acknowledge the importance of symbolism. "I have lost confidence in our ability to come through this without harming the way people think of this institution," he said in a statement announcing the firing. "Our academic integrity is paramount, and we must work diligently to protect it. The only way to move forward and put this behind us is to make a change."[75]

Some fans were furious, and Thorp got emails threatening him with violence the next time he stepped into Kenan Stadium. The university beefed up security at the chancellor's mansion, and assigned security to Thorp during football games. He and Patti used to walk the back trails from the chancellor's mansion to the stadium; now they rode with public-safety employees.[76] But others applauded Thorp for trying to wrest back control. The N&O's editorial board, which had just that month ripped the chancellor for not appreciating the scale of the crisis, now credited him: "Thorp, an alumnus of the university and a man whose devotion to it cannot be doubted, does not deserve these most extreme reactions to what he did. And what he did happens to have been the right thing to do."[77]

Perhaps most important was the opinion of one very important retiree. Friday had fifty years earlier taken decisive and symbolic action in canceling the popular Dixie Classic basketball tournament when gambling allegations had surfaced. History remembered that moment kindly. Now Friday himself gave Thorp his stamp of approval in an interview with the N&O. "This sad story has now come to an end," Friday said. "The university is a resilient institution and can turn this around. The university has suffered from it; there's no doubt about that. But there will come a time when everybody will look back on this and say, 'It's time to lock arms and move ahead.'"[78]

Willingham was getting frustrated. In the fall of 2010, she'd sent her thesis, spelling out what Blanchard had called the "original sin" of college athletics, to several influential people, including the admissions director, the faculty athletics representative, and Thorp. Only two responded. One was Bill Friday himself, and they arranged a meeting to talk through her experience.

She walked over to his campus office with a new blouse on and chocolates in hand. The legendary Friday, whom Willingham had only seen on TV, was warm and friendly, and had a copy of her thesis in his hand. He asked her about her findings and her experiences working with athletes. He said he'd arrange for introductions to some of the university's prominent figures to talk through her concerns about the value of the education athletes were getting in Chapel Hill. She walked away feeling grateful.

The second person who replied was Dan Kane, an N&O investigative reporter who had recently taken over coverage of the scandal. Friday had mentioned to Willingham that he believed in the value of investigative journalism, so she agreed to talk with Kane off the record. He'd call her up with a piece of information and she'd confirm it, or add context, or be a sounding board. If people at the university—aside from a good-natured and influential retiree—didn't want to hear her story, she'd tell it to a reporter.[79]

Meanwhile, Kane had unearthed more troubling information. In August 2011, just a month after reporting on McAdoo's paper, he reported that Austin's transcript revealed the 400-level class in the

African and Afro-American studies department that he had taken instead of remedial composition. Most striking was that Austin's professor in that class was the chair of the department and the same person who had graded McAdoo's clearly plagiarized paper: Julius Nyang'oro.[80]

Thorp decided he needed to act again. He called the general counsel's office and asked them to get copies of the student rosters from Austin's 400-level class and a handful of others. When the university's public records officer had the rolls in hand, she got on the phone with Thorp. He asked her to read the names on the roster. As she ticked them off, his stomach sank. They were a who's-who of Carolina athletics. He hung up the phone. Then he called his boss, the president of the sixteen-campus UNC system, Tom Ross.

He told Ross he needed to see him about something. When Ross responded that he was at dinner, Thorp said he would be on Ross's porch when he got home. That night Thorp walked up to the president's residence, a hundred-year-old house with a wraparound porch and two-story Corinthian columns framing the front door. He sat in a rocking chair, the class rolls in hand. When Ross's car pulled in, Thorp showed him the documents. They needed to investigate.

The first step was talking to Nyang'oro, the common link between the two most damning revelations—McAdoo's plagiarized paper and the 400-level class filled with athletes. Around the time he met with Ross, Thorp called the department chair's boss, a senior associate dean named Jonathan Hartlyn. When Hartlyn questioned Nyang'oro, he confirmed that these were not normal college courses, and there had been more than just a few of them. As Hartlyn told him about the meeting, Thorp heard a name he didn't know: Debby Crowder.

Around this time Thorp turned forty-seven, and one night his son asked him what he wanted for his birthday.

"I want to be forty-eight," answered the weary chancellor.[81]

The rough contours of the story became clear to Thorp rather quickly, he recalled. Crowder had managed academically suspect classes with some degree of participation from Nyang'oro, and the courses probably stretched back as long as each had been there, to the early 1990s. With evidence that athletes had seized the opportunity to take these improvised courses, the university alerted the NCAA, which was in the final stages of its investigation. Meanwhile, the university started its own internal probe. Thorp based the investigation's charge on a records request the university had recently received from Kane: to look at the period between 2007 and 2011. Two deans started digging up old course records and interviewing members of the department.[82] At the administration's urging, Nyang'oro agreed to resign as chair.[83]

The university alerted the NCAA to what it knew just days after the *N&O* published the story about Austin's transcript.[84] Thorp fully expected the association to add a charge to the list of allegations against the university, which would be heard by the Committee on Infractions—essentially, the jury in cases like this—in October. A combination of the association's investigators and university officials set about conducting interviews about the dodgy classes. Boxill, who had that summer become faculty chair, giving up her advising responsibilities in the academic-support office, was among the people they interviewed.

Minutes before she went into the room, Thorp talked with Boxill by phone. He was worried about her. If there had been heavy enrollment, broadly, among UNC athletes, then Boxill, as women's basketball adviser, might have been at the heart of it. If she needed to tell them something she didn't want to admit, Thorp wanted to know about it. So he asked her point blank:

Jan, did you think faculty were grading the papers for these classes?

Yes, the answer came back. I thought Julius was grading the papers.[85] Boxill herself recalled being surprised at the question. What other possibility was there?[86]

Thorp accepted that answer. Then, a little over a week after the university notified the NCAA of what it had discovered, he got a call from his general counsel, Leslie Strohm. It was the Friday before the first football game of the year, and Strohm had unexpectedly good news. No players would need to be held out of the game. And the NCAA hadn't found anything wrong with the classes; they were going to let it lie. Thorp was floored. "I said, 'You gotta be kidding me,'" he recalled. "I mean, how could that have possibly been true?" Amid the good news came one caveat. The NCAA had instructed the university to keep the decision quiet.[87] It would be a year before the university revealed that the NCAA had given the classes a look and decided not to pursue them.[88]

Even as the fast-unfolding investigation of the paper classes did not play a part in the NCAA investigation, the university still braced for penalties. In September, UNC announced it was vacating football wins from several prior seasons and imposing scholarship bans and a $50,000 fine on itself.[89] The action was viewed by observers as an effort to keep the NCAA from being too harsh in its penalties. No such luck. In March of the next year, 2012, the NCAA handed down a scholarship penalty and a postseason ban, declaring that the university had failed to monitor the program. "The university did a great job of investigating it," said the chairman of the infractions committee. "They tried to get to the truth, and that's not always the case, but in this case it was clear that they did. . . . Nevertheless, it was a serious case and we had aggravating factors."[90] The penalties were more severe than Thorp had anticipated. He would not have the luxury of an untainted football season ahead.[91]

But the new investigation threatened much worse. In May, the deans released their report. Nine courses from 2007 to 2009 were declared "aberrant," meaning there was no evidence that the professor listed actually supervised the class. An additional forty-three courses, all taught by Nyang'oro, seemed to have been taught not as the lecture classes that they were supposed to be, but as independent study courses. Signatures on grade rolls for the nine classes appeared to have been forged. The report laid blame at the feet of Crowder and Nyang'oro,[92] who officially retired shortly after the report's release.[93]

The new report was a shock. Revelations of forged signatures and fraudulent courses would have been unthinkable two years before. Crowder and Nyang'oro had engineered academically deficient courses. Two major unknowns remained. The first was scope: what if this scheme went further back than 2007? The second, and most important, was why. Every crime needs a motive, and the report had no answers. The two perpetrators were also off campus and not answering questions.

In the days after the report's release, Kane revealed that a whopping 39 percent of the enrolled students in the classes covered in the report were football and basketball players, although such players represented a minuscule percentage of all students on campus.[94] Maybe these classes existed to boost the GPAs of athletes.

But UNC and the NCAA weren't the only bodies with the authority to conduct an investigation. After the university's internal review, the State Bureau of Investigation launched a probe into the classes under the suspicion that Nyang'oro had been paid for classes that had not actually been held.[95]

On the horizon was the third fall semester in a row that Thorp would spend under an athletic controversy. The scandal, which Thorp had sought to end by firing Davis, was only beginning.

Five thousand miles away, a UNC physics professor named Paul Frampton was sitting in a decrepit Argentine jail.

He'd been caught at the Buenos Aires airport with two kilograms of cocaine in his suitcase. He claimed innocence, saying he'd been tricked. The *New York Times Magazine* later reported that it appeared someone posing online as a Czech bikini model had suckered Frampton, who may or may not have had some knowledge of the scheme, into smuggling the drugs. (The magazine characterized his friends as saying the professor was "a kind of idiot savant."[96] A former student of Frampton's told the *Daily Tar Heel* that the professor "was so oblivious, it wouldn't surprise me if someone had duped him.")

The bizarre story made waves back in Chapel Hill, even as the athletic scandal raged. The administration took him off the payroll as he awaited trial; as a senior scholar, he had been making six figures.[97] "It makes the faculty worried," one scholar told the student newspaper. "What if I was in that situation? Would I be treated the same way?" Two scholars set up a website to raise money for Frampton, and dozens of academics—from UNC and elsewhere—wrote a public letter objecting to the suspension.[98]

Reginald Hildebrand watched the Frampton saga with disappointment.[99] As the athletics scandal continued churning, skeptical observers had—in the absence of a motive or more detail about the suspect classes—turned their gaze on him and his colleagues in the African and Afro-American Studies department. He had been interviewed by state agents and asked whether he, a respected scholar with decades of experience, had ever accepted money in exchange for a grade.[100] Letters were flowing into the local newspapers casting aspersions on the department's integrity. "'Black studies' are nothing more than a politically correct sop by our institutions of higher learning to a preferred minority group," one resident wrote in a letter to the *N&O*.[101]

One student suggested to the *Daily Tar Heel* that the entire department should be eliminated. "The actions of a single department have brought shame and embarrassment onto the entire UNC community," he wrote.[102] A member of the Board of Governors, which oversees the university system, also floated the idea of shutting down the department—a grave and extreme prospect.[103]

No evidence suggested that anyone other than Nyang'oro and Crowder had been involved in the wrongdoing. But that didn't stop the generalizations and accusations. Where, Hildebrand wondered, was the faculty support? Why did professors across the university seem more willing to support a white physics professor ensnared in an apparent narcotics scheme than their colleagues in African and Afro-American Studies?[104] The trial had echoes of history. Nyang'oro himself had implied, in his request to bring the department into being, that its subservient status as a curriculum made it seem like "some lesser academic entity to be politicized whenever there is inside or outside focus on the African American population at the University."[105]

The problem wasn't the department, Hildebrand wrote to the *N&O*. It was that the university was attempting to run a minor-league sports franchise while asking the players to double as full-time students. "We are forced to confront the fact," Hildebrand said, "that this charade can only be kept going through the resourceful manipulation of smoke and mirrors and by a lot of winking and nodding. The system will find, or create, enough academic wiggle room and gimmicks to keep things moving along."[106] Crowder had supplied that wiggle room, Hildebrand suggested, but just because the locus of the latest revelations centered on the department where she worked didn't mean that the department was rotten.[107]

Faculty silence carried a cost. "Such silence reads loudly as consent," wrote one professor to his colleagues, "in the face of the ongoing firestorm whose flames would consume us."[108] Hildebrand and his colleagues wrote letters defending their department's integrity. At a meeting in the fall, the UNC faculty endorsed a resolution that "affirms the integrity and validity of the intellectual disciplines represented in the Department of African and Afro-American Studies and expresses our solidarity with those members of the faculty of that department whose professional lives and work have been in no way connected with academic irregularities."[109] A scholar in the department, Kia Caldwell, read a statement on behalf of her colleagues,[110] which was greeted with applause. "That meant a lot," Hildebrand wrote, "and it helped heal some wounds."[111]

But years later, the faculty's show of support came to rankle Hildebrand. Expressing solidarity with only the faculty who were "in no way connected with academic irregularities" implied that the suspicion that clouded the department was legitimate—that scheming professors lurked in the offices of Battle Hall. "They aren't saying, 'Until you prove he's done something, he's a member of this community and needs to be respected as such,'" Hildebrand said. "That statement never came."[112] And the first part of the statement, the validation of the department's integrity, implied that the department's foundations needed validating. The well-intentioned statement of solidarity both honored and demeaned Hildebrand and his colleagues.

It reminded Hildebrand of a monument the university had erected less than a decade earlier.[113] It was meant to memorialize the enslaved people who built much of the university's grounds, but the form it took—a low, black table propped up by a mass of muscular statuettes inches off the ground—struck some as far from an honor. When it rained, the "unsung founders" got splattered with mud, Hildebrand remembered. They were used as footrests. It was hard to even see them. "Suppose we were trying to honor the chancellors of this university," Hildebrand said, "and got little images of all of them, and put them as table legs, and had us put our feet up on them. It would be so outrageous and unacceptable. . . . Nobody would even consider it."[114] Like the faculty's statement in support of his department, the statue was both gratifying and insulting.

Hildebrand came to view the entire academic-fraud scandal through this lens. The racists who conspired to defame the enslaved builders or to drag the black-studies department through the muck don't exist. But the conditions that prevailed in both cases amount to something "that still looks and feels and tastes like racism."[115]

Taylor Branch, the civil-rights historian and UNC alumnus, argued in his 2011 cover story for the *Atlantic*, "The Shame of College Sports," that big-time sports has begun to carry "an unmistakable whiff of the plantation."[116] The saga that played out on Branch's own campus carried more than one such whiff. The African and Afro-American Studies department stood in the shadow of a statue of a Confederate soldier, erected at the height of the South's white-supremacist terror campaign, and that statue towered over the Unsung Founders Memorial. (Protesters tore down the statue, known as "Silent Sam," in 2018.) The mostly black athletes who took classes in that building to stay eligible lacked the right to earn money of their own, and were—as Willingham would come to argue—also being deprived of an education on par with their classmates. Even when the football players took the field, they did so under the auspices of a white-supremacist history. Until 2018,[117] Kenan Stadium was named for William Rand Kenan Sr., the donor's father, who in 1898 captained a squad of machine-gunners that carried out a violent coup d'etat against Wilmington's biracial government. Historians estimate that at least dozens and possibly hundreds of people were killed in the rebellion, many of them black.[118]

The mostly black players competing in a stadium built to honor a white supremacist killer were thus deprived of the right to be compensated at a market rate, and the right to a full university education. Black professors who worked in the shadow of a Confederate statue were shrouded in unfair suspicion. "This would not have taken the bounce it did if, somehow, in the background, we weren't talking about what people perceive to be a black department, a black subject, and black athletes," Hildebrand said. He went on:

> The assumption that gives people license to make the assumptions about me, and what I'm doing and not doing about my ethics and integrity, flow from my being black and what they perceive to be in a black department with making life easy for black athletes, who are somehow getting by with doing something and defaming the reputation of this university.[119]

In the wake of the scandal, Hildebrand was approached after class by one of his students who asked whether he thought she should mention in her graduate-school application that she was a major in his department. "I felt like somebody kicked me in my stomach," he recalled. "She felt, just by saying that, it would be a signal that she wasn't a serious student. That she'd learned nothing in my class." This was the worst shame of all, the professor said—what the scandal did to the department's students.[120]

But he also paid a personal toll. As the scandal raged, Hildebrand attended an event in honor of the Emancipation Proclamation, then on display at the North Carolina History Museum in Raleigh.[121] The event no doubt had personal significance for the professor; his family had long traded stories about how their last name came from a distant relative who, on emancipation, refused to take the name of the man who enslaved him, instead choosing Hildebrand.[122] At the event, while Hildebrand was making small talk with a former state politician, she asked him what he did for a living.

When he told her he taught Afro-American Studies at UNC, she laughed in his face.[123]

Chancellor Thorp would visit the besieged department and expressed solidarity with its scholars.[124] But he wouldn't be able to deliver the closure that they longed for.

The revelations continued throughout the summer of 2012. A public-facing "test transcript" hosted on UNC's website turned out to belong to star player Julius Peppers. A PackPride user discovered it, and noted that Peppers had taken twelve courses in the African and Afro-American Studies department, including three independent-study classes.[125] The university's silence on the scope of the irregularities was deafening.

Meanwhile, Thorp was getting more pressure from the outside. After the internal review was released, the N&O's editorial board wrote that the saga "does not reflect well on his leadership."[126] Someone started a Change.org petition calling on Thorp to resign. He received several emails from people still embittered by his decision to fire Davis. "The real academic fraud at UNC has turned out not to be in the football program," one wrote, "but rather in the African-American Studies department overseen by yours truly. Mr. Thorp, it is time for you to resign."[127] Wrote another: "As you forced out Coach Davis without cause, as leader of the University you SHOULD RESIGN over this scandal."[128] One email with the subject line, "What more do you need?" simply said: "You can't blame Coach Davis for this fiasco."[129]

Emails from the public were one thing. But pressure was building from the board that hired Thorp, the UNC system's Board of Governors. Burley Mitchell, then a member of the board with well-known ties to N.C. State University, wrote in an email to Thorp and another member of the board that "a real investigation by an independent source is needed, but if only those of us from NCSU say so I'm afraid it will be painted as us just picking on Chapel Hill."

"You are exactly correct," the board member responded, forwarding the chain to Tom Ross, the system's president. He forwarded it to Thorp with a piece of advice: "You may want to consider taking the time to call each of our Board members within the next few days and discuss this matter with them."[130] If Thorp wasn't in the hot seat yet, he would be soon. He was caught between three forces: athletically minded supporters of Chapel Hill who viewed further digging as pointless and masochistic; reform-minded observers and journalists who craved answers; and fans of rival teams who wanted to see Carolina suffer.[131]

When August came, Thorp announced another investigation. This one would go back further than 2007, and it would be led by a figure whose loyalties couldn't be questioned: Jim Martin, a former Republican governor. He also announced that he would bring in a panel, led by the prominent academic leader Hunter Rawlings, that would help "analyze the proper future relationship between academics and athletics."[132] He won praise for both. "Your creation of the Martin Commission is an excellent move," wrote the critical board member, Mitchell, to Thorp after the announcement. He continued: "As a Davidson and Princeton man he will not be suspected of bias or being part of a whitewash."[133] Jay Smith,[134] the French history professor who had emerged as the most public faculty advocate of further investigation, also applauded the creation of the Rawlings panel.[135]

It seemed that Thorp may have righted the ship again. But in September, a new scandal cropped up in an area that had been key to Thorp's ascent: fundraising. The university's chief fundraiser, the N&O reported, had tried to hire his girlfriend, who was also the mother of a former UNC basketball star, for a fundraising position in his office. Thorp had prevented the hiring, citing the university's nepotism policy, but records showed that he flew on private university planes with the couple after the girlfriend had been hired for another fundraising position that did not report to the chief fundraiser.[136]

Just as with the Davis firing, Thorp realized he had not done enough to stem the controversy, which he now saw he would never be able to escape as long as he was chancellor. So on September 17 he announced he would resign at the end of the academic year. "I will always do what is best for this university," Thorp said in his release.[137] And what was best, he had realized, was for him to step down.

Years later, Thorp would be able to spot his mistakes. He thought that by carefully vetting every decision with the constituencies who lent him his authority, he was ensuring that he would be able to keep his hands on the reins. Ever the dramatists' son, Thorp realized that he'd missed his cue. When he wanted to fire Davis after the 2010 football season, he should have followed through, even though it may have meant daring the powers that be to send him packing. When the NCAA walked away from investigating the paper classes, Thorp should have publicly disclosed that decision and what the university knew about the classes. The university should have been more transparent, he said, revealing what it knew more often.[138] "What happens is that there comes a time when you have to stop trying to figure out how to bring everybody together and put your shoulders up and say, 'I'm the chancellor of the University, and this is what we're going to do,' and then deal with the consequences," Thorp told the *Daily Tar Heel* years later.[139]

But as Thorp prepared to relinquish the chancellorship, he hadn't realized all that. "When you're in the blender," he said, "you don't know what's going on."[140]

After his announcement, Thorp was buoyed by a wave of support. Faculty members asked him to reconsider. Supportive students and employees held a rally outside his office, encouraging him to change his mind and stay on.[141] But his mind was made up.

Now a lame duck, Thorp didn't shy away from public commentary. The same month he announced his resignation, he went before the N&O's editorial board with what he predicted would be, when formalized in a few months, "national news." The university's admissions office was working on a new formula to better predict athletes' academic success; that formula, Thorp said, would allow the university to raise the bar for athletes who would be admitted to UNC. "Academics are going to have to come first," Thorp said. "And it's clear that they haven't to the extent that they should."[142]

The resulting article, with the headline "Thorp: UNC's Standards for Athletes Will Rise," caused a stir among Chapel Hill faithful. A former trustee emailed Thorp and the board chair, Wade Hargrove, with praise. "Couldn't agree with you more," Hargrove responded. "But already, emails to the contrary are coming in."[143] An alumnus emailed the trustees expressing his displeasure: "UNC will soon be mediocre on the playing field in sports like men's basketball and football, if Thorp is allowed to implement his crazy plan."[144] One of those trustees confided to another over email that "HT stepped in it."[145] A few weeks later, Roy Williams, the high-powered basketball coach, seemed to drive the final nail in the coffin. "I'm not trying to criticize my chancellor here," Williams said of the N&O story, "because I love him to death, but there are some things that can't be done."[146]

It was abundantly clear that some university constituencies had no interest in plans that might make them less competitive athletically. Thorp thus decided the best thing he could do in his final months as chancellor was to be honest about the choice Chapel Hill was making. He'd been taken in by the Carolina Way, he admitted, but now saw it was just a hallucination.[147] UNC had decided it needed to continue being in the big-time sports business, so it needed to be realistic about the price, he told a panel, sitting beside Boxill. For two-and-a-half years he had tried to play for a tie between Chapel Hill's sports fans and those who believed it should live up to the ideals of Friday and the Knight Commission. A tie was impossible. The fans would win. "What you're seeing is sort of the five stages of grief," Thorp said on the panel, "as different people on the campus go through accepting that we're gonna be competitive in sports, we're gonna do it by the rules, but occasionally—probably more frequently than once every fifty years— we're gonna have some problems."[148]

In other words, as Thorp told a local columnist, "We thought we were different from Auburn, but now we know that we're not."[149]

In October 2012 a fittingly morbid piece of news came just on the heels of Thorp's resignation. Bill Friday, who had helped author the idea of presidential control, who preached against the influence of athletics, and who influenced the Carolina Way mythology, had died at ninety-two.[150] State and university leaders gathered for a memorial service on campus.

Thorp sat in the front row, taking in the Shakespearean irony of it all.[151] He'd followed Friday's lead, trying to protect UNC's reputation while also trying to mollify the constituencies that kept him in charge. In doing so, he'd been dashed against the rocks.

Hodding Carter III, once president of the Knight Foundation, stood at the podium and hailed Friday and his partners in the reform group. "If, as cynics often remark, theirs was a quixotic mission, their targets were not windmills," Carter said. "They were and are real destructive dragons and as recently as only yesterday they have done sickening damage to institutions as diverse as Ohio State, Penn State, USC, Harvard, and Chapel Hill." Carter again invoked the scandal by name, quoting Friday from an interview he'd given in the *Washington Post* shortly before he died:

> There are thousands of alumni who look upon what happened with serious concern and I don't think they're going to tolerate it. People don't want their lifetimes to be measured by how much their football team won or lost. There is something valuable they want measured on that intellectual tombstone when the time comes, and it will come.[152]

Just like Graham, his predecessor, Friday had a prophecy to deliver on athletics: reasonable alumni would strike back.

But Thorp, who always revered Friday, nonetheless ended up jaded by his experience with the genie Friday longed to put back in the bottle. People *did* want their lifetimes to be measured, in part, by the success of their teams. They didn't want reform. The work of the Knight Commission, Thorp came to conclude, was nothing more than a waste of time. Retired presidents with nothing to lose would push reform. The presidents and chancellors with skin in the game who joined the cause would just get spit out of Division I leadership, as Thorp himself had been. Months later, Thorp got an offer to become the provost of Washington University in St. Louis, an elite private institution that competed in Division III athletics. Rather than rejoin the Chapel Hill faculty, he left.

Those who worked with Thorp lamented the circumstances that sent him packing. "We probably did Holden a great disservice by hiring him to be chancellor at that moment in time in his career," said Perry, the board chair when Thorp ascended to the role.[153] Winston, who'd urged Thorp to act cautiously in firing Davis, said he felt similarly about Thorp's downfall. "He got a raw deal because he was a great leader who walked into a real tough situation that went from bad to worse," Winston said.[154]

John Drescher, the *N&O* editor who had overseen Kane's investigative coverage of UNC, offered a kind of eulogy for Thorp's chancellorship. It's not that Thorp was any lesser than the Grahams and the Fridays, the stubborn reformers. In fact, Thorp was of the very same ilk, Drescher argued—smart, trusting, and approachable. It's that college athletics had finally become unmanageable, uncontainable, and invincible as a commercial force.

"The athletic-industrial complex yields to no one," Drescher wrote. "Not even Frank Graham could have tamed it."[155]

7

Mary Willingham, however, wasn't ready to give up. She had seen the shadow curriculum with her own eyes. She knew all about the paper classes. She had the information people were clamoring for. But she had kept quiet, wanting to have nothing to do with the scandal.

But when she heard that Friday was dead, she remembered their one-on-one meeting where he had encouraged her to tell the truth, no matter what. She was one of the first people in line for his memorial service, and she sat and listened to the remembrances. As Thorp sat in the front, worn by the scandal and jaded by the power of athletics, Willingham was coming to a different conclusion. Friday had shared her disillusionment with the influence of commercial athletics on the university's educational mission. Carter's fiery eulogy resonated with Willingham. Who would carry that torch now that Friday was gone?

She resolved to break her silence. She thought about giving Kane a call for an on-the-record interview, but her husband made another proposal. It's your story, Mary, he said. Put it in your own words. So she started a blog, Athletics vs. Academics, and wrote a post alleging that she had witnessed academic fraud during her time in the academic support office. Soon after she got a call from Kane. So you must be willing to go on the record now, he told her.[1]

The resulting article, headlined "UNC tolerated cheating, says insider Mary Willingham," was the first time someone from inside the university described how they used the paper classes to keep athletes eligible. More importantly for Willingham, she described how under-prepared athletes were being admitted to the university and kept eligible through a shadow curriculum of easy classes. "There are serious literacy deficits and they cannot do the course work here," Willingham told Kane. "And if you cannot do the course work here, how do you stay eligible? You stay eligible by some department, some professor, somebody who gives you a break. That's everywhere across the country. Here it happened with paper classes. There's no question."[2]

The article made waves. The university president, Tom Ross, sent an email to board members with a one-word question raised by the article: "Mole?"[3] The N&O editorial board urged action: "A great university has been embarrassed by wretched excesses and academic fraud connected to its athletics program. The reins must be pulled, and hard."[4]

Willingham did as much as she could think of to force such action. She spoke to Martin, the former governor Thorp had hired to investigate the suspect classes, and recorded the conversation. She told him she sensed professors were afraid to fail athletes. She told him she didn't have a problem with athletics; she had a problem with fraud. And she told him the university was steering athletes into the same classes over and over, including the paper classes. In one seconds-long exchange, she described the essence of the classes:

> What used to happen is they would just pick up the phone, like Cynthia Reynolds would just pick up the phone, and she would call Debby Crowder and she would say, "I have a student who needs a paper, an independent studies/paper class." Then Debby Crowder would say, "Well what does he still need credit for?" And then I would hear, "History," or something, whatever, "History before 1700," or whatever. Then they would figure out what class they were going to put him in.[5]

Meanwhile, an informal committee of the faculty that called itself the Athletic Reform Group got in touch with Willingham. Jay Smith, the French history professor and the most vocal leader of the group, invited her to meetings. She was a straight arrow, he said, speaking directly from the heart. The group of critics recognized they'd found a kindred spirit.[6]

It was Smith's group that was among the most alarmed when, in December 2012, Martin released his investigative report, claiming,

"This was not an athletic scandal. It was an academic scandal, which is worse; but an isolated one."[7] The report found that the suspect classes stretched back to 1997, and numbered them at 216—far more than the 54 previously identified.[8] University officials, including Boxill, said they were distressed by the breadth of the scandal, but that they were taking action to fix the problems. Smith was horrified. "It's a stunner," he told the *N&O*. "I mean, I just can't believe that they had such a blind spot for athletics."[9] Willingham wrote on her blog that the report was a missed opportunity to point out how advisers had been steering athletes to paper classes as a way of maintaining eligibility. Why, Smith asked, had Martin left Willingham's allegations unaddressed?[10]

More troubling questions would emerge about Martin's report. In defense of the academic support staff, Martin noted how Blanchard and the then-director of the academic-support office said they tried to bring the classes to the attention of the faculty committee that advises the athletic department.[11] But Martin only interviewed one member of the committee, and all its members denied ever learning about these classes. Martin was forced to clarify the report after a faculty outcry. Even he later admitted that the report came to be viewed as a whitewash.[12]

The scope of the irregularities had grown, but there was still no known motive. Martin hadn't been able to interview Crowder and Nyang'oro, and he said he didn't have time to do a thorough review of emails between them and academic-support staff, which were on university servers.[13] The truth was out there, but it seemed Martin hadn't found it. Thorp's hope, that Martin's report would bring an end to the long-running scandal, was not realized. Willingham thus was the only witness who was willing to speak publicly, and her words carried extra weight. She talked to anyone who would listen, including Thorp, who admitted being naive about the university's athletic enterprise.[14]

Among those inclined to deemphasize athletics, Willingham became a nationally known voice. In the spring of 2013, she learned that she had received an athletic reform group's annual award, the Robert Maynard Hutchins Award, named for the University of Chicago president who eliminated the university's football program. She would receive the award from the Drake Group during the annual College Sport Research Institute conference, held in the UNC center named after Friday himself.[15]

Her father was in the audience as she stepped up to the podium.[16] Willingham had become a Tar Heel in the fall of 2003, she told the audience, and felt she was lucky to get the job. She loved what eager learners the athletes she worked with were, and how proud their families were of them. But as she spent more time in the job she'd seen how unprepared about a quarter of the athletes were for college-level work, how much they struggled in the classroom. She'd worked with about three dozen struggling athletes every year, she told the crowd.

Taking these athletes and throwing them into a full-time job with intense travel and physical demands wasn't a good idea. It would be like giving her a jersey and asking her to play in a college football game. She would pretend to know what's going on as the action swirled around her, much the same way the athletes she'd worked with were forced to act in the classroom. As an educator, she felt responsible to advocate for these students, many of whom played for the two sports—men's basketball and football—that subsidized the rest of the varsity sports. Think about the racial dynamics of that, she told the crowd. The mostly black teams subsidizing the white ones.

But every year the system asks those involved to hold their tongues, Willingham said, to greet injustice with silence. She had been guilty of this, too. She had even lied, signing her name each year to the statement that she had not witnessed any cheating. But she had. She rationalized that choice. She was helping these athletes have a chance to get a college degree. "But I really know," she said, "that they leave here without the one thing they need most in life: a real education."

An athletic scholarship, she said, was just a golden ticket to the athletics factory. During the tour you might get injured, in which case there'd be no workers' compensation. You'd get room and board, but no salary. "The NCAA cartel owns us," Willingham said. "They need us. Do we really need them?"

The university had a duty to provide intense remediation for the most unprepared students, Willingham said. And this idea actually had a precursor in the university's history, she'd discovered through research. In its very early years, the university offered a program to prepare admitted students for the college classroom before they actually started. Willingham proposed reopening this program, which she called the Academy. "Let's be honest and do the right thing, meet our talented athletes where our K-12 system failed them."

Invoking the spirits of Frank Porter Graham and Friday, Willingham made a striking pitch: Thorp was wrong. The Carolina Way was not dead, it just needed to be reclaimed. The mythology had unraveled; that didn't mean it couldn't be stitched up "The Carolina Way could be the right way again and we could lead the way," she said. "I am a Tar Heel."[17] The crowd gave a standing ovation.[18]

But elsewhere at the conference, Willingham wasn't getting such a good reception.

In their screenings since the mid-2000s, Willingham and the psychologist she'd worked with had found that 40 percent of the screened athletes showed signs of learning disabilities such as ADHD. They presented a poster summarizing those results at the CSRI conference. A group of academic support employees, said Bradley Bethel, then a learning specialist, saw the brief and grew concerned that Willingham, despite no longer being in the office, was still accessing data about athletes, which posed confidentiality problems.[19] That word apparently traveled up the ladder, and soon Willingham's partner, Lyn Johnson, found her contract with UNC canceled.[20] In an email to Boxill, the psychologist wrote that she and Willingham were "quite taken aback by the reaction" of some academic counselors to the poster session. "I think it is a disservice to the athletes," she wrote, "and it is unfortunate for me, that some of the staff over there appear to be taking their anger against Mary out on me in such an unprofessional and unethical manner."[21]

An internal document explaining the change in disability screening cast doubt on the reliability of one of the administered tests, suggesting that Willingham's methods may have led to overdiagnosis.[22] Bethel said in an interview that he had previously expressed a desire to contract with a psychologist with more experience in distinguishing between learning disabilities and factors related to language or lack of preparedness. Concerns about confidentiality prompted by the poster brief were the final straw in the psychologist's contract being canceled, Bethel recalled.[23]

For Willingham, the whole affair carried the stink of retaliation. It was the first of many times she felt under attack. In late June, she met with her boss, Harold Woodard, for her annual performance review. Up to this point, they had all been positive, with the exception that Woodard had noted that Willingham had declined to take on supervisory roles within the office.[24] Willingham explained that she had been wary of being responsible for some long-tenured and low-performing employees, and having to take the blame for their continued low performance.

But that day, when Woodard handed his review across the desk to Willingham, she was shocked.[25] She had been demoted. Referencing her "unsuccessful attempt" to supervise some of the center's staff, Woodard determined that she would no longer be an assistant director, just a learning specialist. Her office would be moved from the second floor, with its natural light, to the basement. She would also become a graduation adviser, checking boxes for students on the verge of receiving degrees,[26] "because you love graduation so much," Woodard said. (Woodard did not answer messages seeking an interview for this book.)

Willingham was stunned. She had been in human resources, and knew this was not how things were done. Effective demotions like this needed to be foregrounded with performance plans and warnings. But Woodard hadn't discussed Willingham's performance with her at all over the past year, she said.

You don't want to do this, she told him in that room.

No, we do, he said back to her.

She filed a grievance and resolved to stick it out in her new role until she was vindicated. She would walk from her new, basement office north, past the Kenan Field House, to Steele Building. There she did the same work once done by Betsy Taylor, whose initiative had unwittingly kicked off the whole scandal: checking off students' requirements for graduation. Willingham and Smith had by this point begun work on a book about the UNC scandal, a large portion of which was to be about Willingham's discovery of the shadow curriculum. So she pulled athletes' transcripts off the system she now had access to.[27] She saw familiar patterns. Dozens of African and African-American Studies classes carried higher grades, outweighing the Ds and Fs. Other course names popped up often: Elements of Stagecraft. Naval Weapons Systems. Boxill's classes, too, seemed to pop up often.

Willingham's awareness of the effects of the shadow curriculum thus came full circle. She had seen athletes steered into African and African-American studies classes, Portuguese, and hand-picked drama, education, and communication courses. But she hadn't seen the other side. The students who came to see her as they prepared to graduate had taken rich arrays of classes. Journalism. Chemistry. History. Linguistics. Religion. Subjects she rarely saw on the transcript of a revenue-sport athlete. This was what a UNC education was supposed to be.

Meanwhile she told everyone she could think of about the problem, and about about her idea to reopen the Academy. When the dean of the business school, Jim Dean, became provost, Willingham emailed him with the findings from her and Johnson's study. Large percentages of football and men's basketball players, she wrote, were reading at levels one could expect from fourth- through eighth-graders. They lived under constant threat of losing their eligibility because they just weren't prepared for the college classroom. "Keep in mind," she wrote, "that the bogus system of eligibility—UNC's paper class system—was assisting these players to stay on the court/field. That system no longer exists." Dean replied that he would be in touch.[28]

As 2013 drew to a close, she met with the university's faculty athletics committee and told them about the Academy. She told them about her research. She told them about how the university was failing to adequately educate these athletes. And, bolstered by her time poking through transcripts in Steele, she listed the component parts of the shadow curriculum. Education 441. Exercise and Sport Science 260. Drama 116. Recreation 430.[29]

Then, the next month, Willingham spoke with a reporter at CNN about athletes' literacy. The resulting story, "CNN analysis: Some college athletes play like adults, read like 5th-graders," was explosive. Its centerpiece was Willingham's research, which it used as a jumping-off point to examine the academic credentials of athletes admitted at twenty-one public colleges nationally. It included statements from Willingham about the paper-class system, and quoted an administrator at Iowa State who said that people who shuffle athletes from class to class to keep them eligible "should be arrested. We should make it against the law." Another expert concluded, "College presidents have put in jeopardy the academic credibility of their universities just so we can have this entertainment industry."

The story established a threshold for "college literacy"—the ability to read well enough, broadly, to be prepared for the college classroom—a score of 400 or above (out of 800) on the SAT's reading or writing section, or 16 or above on the ACT.[30] Willingham said she found 22 percent of the athletes she studied had scored below 400 on the SAT. And she cited a variety of other indicators that she and Johnson had used to measure preparedness.[31] In a videotaped segment with CNN, Willingham didn't hold back: "I mean we may as well just go over to Glenwood Elementary right off the street and just let all the fourth graders in here, third graders in here."[32] Stephen Colbert mentioned the story on his show.[33]

Willingham, now used to playing the scapegoat, received death threats over the story.[34] Some came through the university's switchboard. Willingham was not scared for herself, she recalled, but what would happen if someone followed through with a threat when she was around students? What if she was with someone else's kids and someone attacked? What would she tell their parents?[35]

The article created a furor in Chapel Hill. Administrators quickly responded, saying their own data contradicted Willingham's claims. In fact, 97 percent of the athletes admitted by exception between 2004 and 2012, the university said, met CNN's threshold for literacy. And every single athlete admitted by exception in the fall of 2013, the university said, met CNN's threshold.[36]

Dean, the provost Willingham had emailed with her top-line findings months before, met with Willingham and asked her to turn over her data so the university could examine it. (Dean declined to be interviewed for this book.) Smith, who was at the meeting and who recorded the conversation, told Dean that Willingham was afraid she would be scapegoated if she turned over the data in full.[37] But, at his request, she handed it over.

The data, it turned out, hadn't been collected properly. In every communication Willingham and the psychologist had made with the university's institutional review board, they had said that the data would be deidentified. In other words, that they would not be able to identify the athletes who'd been tested by looking at the data. But that wasn't the case; Willingham had worked with these students, so she knew who they were. "How would I do research if I didn't have the names?" she told the *Daily Tar Heel*.[38] The board had determined that approval for the study wasn't necessary, because Willingham had said the study was blind. In a letter dated January 16, the day the university released its response to the CNN report, the board effectively revoked that determination, making Willingham apply for institutional review board approval if she wanted to continue the study.[39]

The next day, the new chancellor, Carol Folt, and Dean, the provost, gathered before a meeting of the faculty to discuss Willingham's allegations. Dean, in particular, was vehement in his condemnation. Willingham had been sloppy with her metrics, using a test that measures vocabulary comprehension ability to make conclusions about reading ability. That made those conclusions "virtually meaningless," he said. "Using this data set to say that our students can't read is a travesty and unworthy of this university." The assembled professors rose to their feet and applauded. Smith, Willingham's friend who had been added as a co-investigator on the now-canceled study, was stunned. A scholar of French history, Smith knew a mob when he saw one. "In 25 years of faculty meetings, I've never seen anything like it," Smith told a reporter. "It was a public conviction and an intellectual execution."[40]

But Willingham didn't stop. On April 6, she sent a tweet that struck to the heart of Tar Heel fans' greatest fear: that a national championship would be jeopardized by the fallout from the paper-class scandal. Five starting players of the 2005 men's basketball national championship team, as well as one other player, had taken 69 paper classes that season, Willingham wrote in the tweet.[41] Widespread use of the paper classes by members of a championship roster presented a clear and present danger to the celebratory banner that hung in the Dean E. Smith Center. Carolina fans were outraged. "There is no legitimate educational purpose served in releasing this information to the media," wrote a pro-UNC blogger, of Willingham, "except to advance her own cause and possibly chase a banner, which has been her partner Jay Smith's stated goal."[42] She'd gotten that information by pulling transcripts from her computer in Steele Building, which prompted UNC officials to probe whether she'd violated the Family Educational Rights and Privacy Act. A faculty committee later in April released a statement urging that Willingham be investigated for possible FERPA violations.[43]

Five days after Willingham's tweet, the university released the reports of three independent experts contracted to study whether Willingham's screening data could be used to make conclusions about literacy level. The answer, the three concluded, was no. They pointed out flaws with the vocabulary subtest that Dean had referenced.[44] But those experts hadn't been studying all the variables Willingham said she used to determine reading level, she said. She had told Dean in their meeting that she'd used a combination of SAT and ACT scores, as well as the vocabulary subtest. But the university had directed the experts to focus on the vocabulary test, even though her determination, she said, had been holistic.

And why, she wondered, was the university being so defensive? She'd seen the use of the paper classes with her own eyes, and the university still would not acknowledge their true purpose. "Sadly, it seems that throughout this entire exercise, the University has been incredibly defensive and reactive in trying to discredit certain people rather than being proactive and accepting responsibility," she wrote in a response.[45]

That the university had recruited and admitted some athletes who couldn't read at anywhere close to a college level was a fact. Willingham had seen it with her own eyes.[46] Blanchard had, too. In an interview for this book, the longtime UNC athletics administrator confirmed that the academic support office had worked with some athletes who read only at an elementary-school level. Not very many, he said. "But we had a lot who didn't have enough," he added, referencing their academic preparedness. "And that was the frustration."[47]

The same month the university released its evaluation of Willingham's data, she met with Folt, the chancellor. A biologist with a composed demeanor, Folt confronted Willingham about what she'd said to the CNN cameras about some athletes being no more qualified than elementary school students. "Some of the things that you've said publicly are so dismissive of them as people. 'Go down and bring kids from fourth grade.' How can you say that?" Willingham blamed the media for distortion. Folt touted the reforms the university had put in place and decried polarization. Willingham said she wished athletes had true access to all the university's majors. Folt suggested it was time to stop living in the past and focus on the present and future. Willingham said what bothered her most was how many people had remained silent about the paper classes.[48]

Soon after this meeting Willingham decided she was finished with

UNC. She'd gotten into helping people with literacy because it made her feel like she was making a difference. But now she was toxic, getting annoyed by how she was being treated while also clearly annoying others who would rather let things lie. "I couldn't fix anything," she recalled. "I couldn't help anyone." She thought telling the truth could help make the university a leader in reforming athletics, just like Friday had wanted. But the university they both loved, instead of acknowledging her experience, made her into a scapegoat.[49] She resigned, and soon after she sued the university for retaliation.[50] The university eventually agreed to pay Willingham $335,000 in a settlement.[51] A review conducted by a panel of the university's Board of Trustees found that Willingham's job change had not been retaliatory; it was, the board found, motivated by "legitimate business needs" and part of a larger restructuring within her unit.[52]

Leaving the university didn't relieve Willingham of continued scapegoating. That summer, someone posted Willingham's thesis on InsideCarolina, UNC's answer to the Pack Pride site that had combed McAdoo's paper for plagiarism three years earlier. Just as N.C. State fans had used forums to attack UNC, now UNC fans were using the same methods to attack Willingham. They asserted plagiarism, which Willingham said was inadvertent. A UNC-Greensboro committee found enough evidence to conduct an investigation, citing ten instances of apparent plagiarism in the thirty-two-page paper. Willingham cried on the phone with Kane as she said, "Whatever I did, I did and, you know, whatever."[53] She was exhausted. All she wanted to do was teach kids to read, and still she was caught up in this mess.

Willingham tried to move on. She got a job at Durham Technical Community College as an adjunct. When a more senior job came open at the college, she interviewed for it. Willingham recalled that she made it all the way to a sit-down with a vice president at the college, who told her, from across her desk, that no one in North Carolina would ever hire her. She cried.[54] Reached by email, that vice president, Christine Kelly-Kleese, denied that she told Willingham that no one in the state would ever hire her. "I would never say such a hurtful thing to anyone, in the context of an interview or otherwise, and I certainly did not say that to Mary Willingham," she wrote.[55] Willingham soon left North Carolina for teaching opportunities elsewhere.[56]

There was, however, a sliver of hope on the horizon. The summer after Willingham departed from UNC, the NCAA announced it would reopen its investigation into the paper classes.[57] A new probe meant more questions and possibly more answers.

And that wasn't the only new investigation. In the spring, Folt announced a new independent review to be conducted by a former federal prosecutor, Kenneth Wainstein, one that would finally get to the bottom of the claims Willingham had made about the paper classes. "I am hopeful," Willingham wrote, "that Mr. Wainstein and his team will once and for all expose the extent to which a fraudulent system of eligibility was put in place for athletes at Carolina."[58]

In announcing the new probe, Folt said Wainstein "will have the freedom to ask the tough questions, follow the facts wherever they lead, and get the job done."[59] Investigators would have access to both Nyang'oro and Crowder this time, allowing them to finally understand the classes' intent. Were they meant to keep athletes eligible? Had they been used that way?

Jim Woodall, the Orange County district attorney who had charged Nyang'oro with accepting $12,000 for a class he didn't teach, had already gotten a preview of what investigators would discover. In reviewing email evidence for the case, Woodall had caught whiffs of what had eluded investigators: motive. He had seen corroboration for the claims Willingham had made, that advisers in the academic support office had seized on the paper classes to keep athletes eligible. So when Nyang'oro's attorneys came to Woodall with an offer—that Nyang'oro would participate in a new, UNC-commissioned investigation in exchange for dropping the felony charge—the district attorney made it happen. Crowder, who had talked to state agents as part of the criminal case, also agreed to participate.

In an interview with Kane years later, Woodall said that one person's emails, in particular, had suggested there was more to this story than she herself was letting on. It was Boxill, the faculty leader who found herself managing the scandal, even as her own emails suggested she had been an active participant in it.[60]

Boxill had faced questions the previous summer.

In 2012, she was charged with supervising a faculty report that would raise unanswered questions about the scandal by reviewing relevant reports to that date, and then make recommendations to prevent problems in the future. A year after the report was released, the *N&O* published email records that appeared to show that Boxill, in her capacity as faculty chair, had kept out of the report a reference to Crowder as "an athletics supporter who was extremely close to personnel in Athletics." Crowder's name was also cut out of that section of the report. "The worry is that this could further raise NCAA issues and that is not the intention," Boxill wrote in an email quoted by the newspaper. The article, written by Kane, concluded that Boxill wanted to "lessen the chances the NCAA would come back to campus." The article cast a suspicious gaze on Boxill's athletic ties, noting that she herself was a longtime member of the academic support program.[1]

The truth, according to Boxill, was more complicated. The report was written by a three-person subcommittee of the Faculty Executive Committee, but Boxill said she thought it was appropriate to give the larger body an opportunity to weigh in. She circulated a draft among the members, and they all came back with suggestions. One of those members, who had a son in a Division I athletic program, told Boxill that use of the term "booster" as applied to Crowder wasn't appropriate, as it meant a very specific thing in the context of the NCAA. The edited language—"an athletics supporter who was extremely close to personnel in Athletics"—seemed to some members of the committee like an unintentional jockstrap allusion, Boxill said, so they suggested it be cut. Boxill, the dutiful coordinator, passed along the suggestion to the co-authors.[2]

They weren't pleased initially, according to emails cited by the *N&O*. "It seems to me that we might need to tell Jan that there is a line we hope she does not cross," wrote one of the co-authors. "Why is it a good thing to remove Deborah Crowder's name from the report?" wrote another co-author. "The fact is, she was close to people in athletics." But all three members of the subcommittee wrote in emails to Kane that they didn't have problems with the final changes to the report.[3] And after the article was published, they spoke publicly in support of Boxill, saying the emails didn't tell the full story.[4] "Emails are not the best way to communicate," Boxill told a local radio station, "because you read them as you want to read them not as perhaps they were intended."[5]

Some on UNC's campus saw the article as a misfire for Kane, who had been the driving force behind the revelations that forced the university to continue investigating. Perhaps, by targeting a beloved senior faculty member, he had bitten off more than he could chew. The article would soon be viewed in a much different light.

As faculty chair, Boxill often spoke about the university's management of the scandal at Faculty Senate meetings, to newspapers, and on panels. She did not share the fact that she had worked with Crowder quite closely, as she had with several department managers. In this capacity she sent players to Crowder to sign up for what she says she believed were independent study classes with Nyang'oro. She would tell Crowder a player needed a "cushion" class—a shorthand term, Boxill said, for enrolling in one more class than what was minimally required so that they could drop a class if they were overwhelmed. And she passed along players' papers directly to Crowder by email, commenting on their quality.[6]

In other words, she had worked directly with Crowder, experience that was directly relevant to the many questions surrounding the paper classes—including whether she tried to scrub Crowder's name from the report. Blanchard, the longtime athletics administrator, recalled attending a Faculty Council meeting and being flabbergasted by Box-ill's role in addressing topics related to the scandal. "I was thinking, 'What are you people doing? I mean, she knows Debby Crowder and works more closely with her than anybody on campus.'"[7] Boxill didn't bring it up, she says, because Crowder was just another student ser-vices manager located buildings away. She didn't think to bring it up, she says, because she knew as little about the paper classes as every-one else.

Boxill's experience with Crowder would not stay secret for long. In 2014 Wainstein called her to be interviewed for his investigation. Boxill wondered if she should bring a third party with her, but a col-league advised against it. That would change the whole dynamic, he said. It was a piece of advice Boxill later regretted taking. She sat in a conference room overlooking UNC's iconic Old Well, as Wainstein, who cut a trim, polished figure, told her, she recalled, that her deco-rated reputation preceded her. He and another attorney then interro-gated her, often referencing emails that they had stacked in binders in front of them. They were years old in some cases, and she had trouble recalling specifics. Some of them showed her discussing grades with Crowder. Boxill was bewildered.

She left the room after several hours alarmed at what Wainstein's report might say. She worried that blame for the scandal would land at her feet.[8] She called Thorp, he remembered, soon after the interview. "She was barely making sense," the former chancellor recalled. She told him about all the emails Wainstein had shown her, and the hours they'd spent in what she perceived as a merciless interrogation.[9]

Boxill received another ominous sign in the fall when she went to see Dean, the provost, to ask him if the Parr Center for Ethics, which she led, could host a panel about the proposed renaming of Saunders Hall, a building on campus that at the time was named after a former Ku Klux Klan leader.

"I suggest you don't do it," he said, she recalled.

"Why?" she asked.

"There are a few emails I've heard about," he said, referring to the Wainstein investigation.

"There are no emails in there I can't defend," Boxill said, to which Dean replied that he hadn't seen the emails in question.

Boxill left with a queasy feeling. She met with Dean again on October 22, the day the Wainstein report was to be released.[10] She walked in with a statement in hand. It said she had never known that Crowder graded papers for Nyang'oro. She sent players there because she knew from experience that they responded well to the material. Every class she ever sent a player to was listed in the course catalog. And so many of her players had been successful.[11]

She handed the statement to Dean. She was handed a letter right back. She started reading it, but when she saw what it said, she couldn't bear to finish it.

Boxill had been fired.[12]

After years of questions and speculation, the Wainstein report finally painted a clear and damning picture, delivering the final nail in the coffin of the Carolina Way.

In authoritative prose, the report described how Crowder, a lifelong Chapel Hill loyalist with a soft spot for struggling students, had come to run the system of fake classes with Nyang'oro's tacit approval. She graded the papers, the report found, and typically awarded A's and B's for often shoddy work. The academic support program had seized on the courses as a tool to keep athletes' GPAs up, just as Willingham had been saying for years. More people had known about the system of classes than had originally been thought, though fewer seemed to know that Crowder was actually awarding the grades. More than 3,000 students had used the classes, the report found, a whopping 47 percent of whom were athletes. Red flags flew up along the way, but no one had acted on them.[13]

Administrators revealed the results of the investigation at a press conference. A Carolina blue curtain draped behind her, Folt, wearing a matching scarf and a pin with UNC insignia, said that the Wainstein investigation was "the most thorough and complete investigation possible," and that she was "deeply disappointed" with the revelations.[14] But, the chancellor stressed, just as she had in private with Willingham, that there was a big difference between "then" and "now." The wrongdoing had stopped years before. The cloud that had hung over the university since the summer of 2010 might now, more than four years later, begin to lift. She turned over the podium to Wainstein, who outlined his findings in all their excruciating detail. Folt took questions from reporters.

"Does this suggest," one local reporter asked, channeling the CNN report that had been published that year, "that there are students who have gotten into North Carolina who probably shouldn't have gotten in here to start with? Is that at the crux of this? And does this justify Mary Willingham's research and the findings that she had years ago?"

It was a good question. The report found that Crowder had offered her classes to all students, but the real problem was the Academic Support Program for Student Athletes. The scandal itself was not that Crowder had supplied the wiggle room, it was how the wiggle room had been systematically exploited. The pressure advisers felt to keep athletes eligible was motivated by the contradictions of amateurism, which relies on athletes' identities as students to keep them classified as amateurs rather than employees. On campuses like UNC this means forcing revenue athletes—with their harsh schedules and comparative lack of academic preparation—to compete with students who do not have those demands, free to choose whatever course of study they like. Curricular loopholes could be used to bridge that gap.

Willingham had been right, and the university—backed by the disturbing Wainstein report—now had a chance to be honest about the toll wrought by the amateur myth. But instead Folt demurred. The "main failure," she said, was that a handful of people had made unfair assumptions about what athletes were capable of, and "we didn't provide the proper services." Amateurism wasn't at the root of the scandal, she seemed to say. Instead, a handful of people simply hadn't trusted enough in the students' abilities, and took matters into their own hands. The problem wasn't the system, Folt seemed to say. It was the people who hadn't believed in it.[15]

She faced a similar question later in the day. At a town hall meeting a student in a Nike-branded hoodie raised his hand at the back of the room. The conversation around the report, he said, seemed to focus on the work of a few individuals. But wasn't this whole scandal just a symptom of overemphasis on athletics in a university setting?

Folt answered the question directly. It was wrong to talk broadly about athletes as a class, she said. Every student at the university comes from different levels of readiness and brings different strengths to the campus. "What I think failed here," she said, "was that we had individuals who believed that they knew better." They didn't go through the proper channels to get athletes help or good advice, and those channels had since been shorn up. Just this year, she said, several hundred athletes had been on the conference's academic honor roll, and their GPAs were improving.

But the student persisted. He wasn't demeaning the intelligence of Carolina athletes. He was asking, big picture, what the university's priorities were. If the university didn't give out athletic scholarships—as Graham had urged—the scandal never would have happened, he told the chancellor. The people who acted outside the system were doing it because athletes were struggling, full stop. Take away that gap, the one that had so disturbed Blanchard and Willingham, and you get rid of the problem. You couldn't just ignore that truth. The student, his voice wavering, was bringing Graham's prophecy into the lecture hall and placing it before Chancellor Folt. What did she have to say to that?

I believe academics and athletics can coexist, Folt told the student. The chance to get a college degree was a chance many of these athletes would have never had otherwise, she said, channeling Boxill. The athletics enterprise was about encouraging diversity at the university. Every student admitted brings a range of talents and weaknesses to the table, she said. It's the university's duty to encourage that kind of difference. "At its best," she closed, "that's what the university of the people tries to do." The audience applauded.[16]

About a week later, Folt faced similar questions in a meeting of the Faculty Senate. Smith, Willingham's friend, said he was concerned by the focus on a few bad actors. What happened wasn't the result of "a cabal of evil people, but good people who thought they were acting ethically because they were working within an unethical system." Hodding Carter, who had eulogized Friday and helped drive Willingham to act, chimed in in agreement. The administration owed Willingham an apology for the way it treated her, he said. Other professors made similar points. One said Carolina should reform special admissions. One wondered how the reforms would be monitored. One encouraged their faculty colleagues to take a firmer hand in governance, and stand up to the administration.[17]

If the funeral for the Carolina Way had been held four years earlier, the Wainstein report was its interment, wake, and death certificate. It had been constructed amid a convenient faith in the amateur myth and runaway passion for college sports. It had been deconstructed by university investigations, Kane's reporting, Willingham, and—finally—unmistakable proof of its failings.

In the epic story of the UNC scandal, these were the first two acts—a rise and a fall. In the third, the university would decide that, despite all evidence to the contrary, the amateur myth was worth recommitting to. Before it did so, the university would need to perform one final bit of penance by punishing the people who allowed such a shameful scandal to materialize in the first place.

In the days after the report's release, its gory details made waves in the national media. The "shadow curriculum" appeared as a teaser on the front page of the following day's *New York Times*.[18] People on social media passed around some of the most interesting and outrageous snippets of evidence. There was the alarm from a Steele Building adviser that word of Crowder's classes had gotten into "the frat circuit."[19] There was the adviser who told a colleague to lower the standards expected of an athlete's paper to "middle-school" level.[20] And there was the finding that many of the papers submitted to Crowder were rife with plagiarism.[21]

But the most attention by far was affixed to Boxill, the sports ethicist whose "own ethics were malleable," observed the *Chronicle of Higher Education*.[22] Above every other piece of evidence implicating Boxill was one email. In 2008, she had sent a player's paper to Crowder, who replied, "Did you say a D will do" for the player? "I'm only asking because 1. no sources, 2, it has absolutely nothing to do with the assignments for that class and 3. it seems to me to be a recycled paper. She took [another class] in spring of 2007 and that was likely for that class."

In a now-infamous reply, Boxill wrote, "Yes, a D will be fine; that's all she needs. I didn't look at the paper but figured it was a recycled one as well, but I couldn't figure out from where."[23] In just one exchange, Boxill had seemed to prove that she knew Crowder was awarding grades, that she was directing her which grades to award, and that she was willing to tolerate "recycled" papers. In one email, she was implicated fully in the paper class scheme. That email was cited in articles by the *New York Times*,[24] the *New York Daily News*,[25] and the *Chronicle*.[26]

The report noted that Crowder and Boxill had "admitted their collusion," but added that the case had nothing to do with eligibility; that student was no longer playing basketball and was on the verge of getting her diploma. But that wasn't the only instance cited in the report. In 2010 Boxill emailed Crowder's successor, Travis Gore, with a player's paper and the comment, "I would give it an A- or at least a B+." The player was given an A- in the course, which was led by Nyang'oro. The former department chair told Wainstein that he didn't remember that course, but that he did recall giving women's basketball players specific grades if Boxill asked him to. "He recalled one particular situation," the report stated, "when he gave a women's basketball player a B+ even though he felt her paper was 'terrible' and was a 'clear F.' He assigned that grade because Boxill had suggested that he do so."[27] But it didn't stop there. The report also found that there were instances of Boxill adding snippets to her players' papers, possibly crossing the line into effectively writing portions of their papers for them.[28]

Boxill, whose reputation had long preceded her on the campus, was now a focus of intense suspicion. In an article with the headline, "The Ethicist Who Crossed the Line," the *Chronicle* reported that "the person everyone's talking about" after the report was Boxill.[29] She was now a laughingstock nationwide, and a pariah at the university she'd served for decades. The overwhelming impression that emerged, based on the report, was of an ethicist who had been complicit in fraud.

Boxill says this is a false portrayal. She didn't know anything about the paper classes. Yes, she sent students to those classes, but she thought they were aboveboard; they were in the course catalog, after all. She didn't know that Crowder was actually grading papers, a clear abuse. She never suspected anything was wrong; why would she? She had no idea what happened in the African and Afro-American Studies department. If the vast majority of the professors in the department were blind to more than a decade of abuses, how could she be expected to have known about them?[30]

Crowder later told investigators that she never told anyone that she graded papers.[31] And multiple people interviewed for this book emphasized that the affairs of a professor are often a mystery even to their close colleagues. Having an office down the hall from Nyang'oro didn't tell one that he ran or tolerated a collection of classes whose papers were at least sometimes graded by Crowder.

Professors, at least culturally speaking, are not akin to employees in a corporation, with direct lines of authority above and below them.

As a former president of the University of Michigan put it, bolstered by academic freedom, "faculty members do what they want to do."[32] They are sovereign over their own teaching and research. "In academia, the fences are pretty high," said Lambert, the African Studies professor whose office was right next to Nyang'oro's. It's not that professors don't communicate, he said, it's that people assume the best of their colleagues, and "it takes something pretty egregious to justify violating that sovereignty."[33] Boxill's statement that she didn't know about the worst aspects of the paper classes is more believable in this context.

But what about the seemingly overwhelming evidence to the contrary? Start with the "a D will be fine" email. This wasn't even a paper class; it was an online course, Boxill says, where the professor was out of the country and only reachable by Crowder. The student, a women's basketball player, sent the paper to Boxill, her adviser, who then sent it to Crowder, the conduit to the professor. It was the player's final semester, and she didn't need a certain grade to graduate, she just needed to turn something in. So when Crowder asked Boxill, "Did you say a D will do?" Boxill knew the grade didn't matter. The player was in good standing and just needed to complete the class. So she responded that a D would be fine. Crowder had called the player's paper "recycled," but Boxill says that didn't mean it was plagiarized or fake. The student had submitted it in another of the department's classes, a practice that was not ideal but not akin to plagiarizing someone else.

In other words, the email seemed to show one thing—Boxill's complicity in the paper-class scheme—but showed something quite different when the full context was considered. In the case where she suggested a grade to Gore, Boxill said Nyang'oro had asked her to work with the student in the class. The suggestion, then, was that she perform the dutiful work of an instructor giving input to another, through Gore, the de facto department manager, not that she was a meddling adviser forcing a grade on an underling. To Nyang'oro's apparent claim, mentioned by Wainstein, that Boxill asked the department chair to award a higher grade to a women's basketball player, Boxill said it's false. "Never in my life would I have asked him to do that," she said.[34]

It's possible the claim was the result of a miscommunication. As an adviser, Boxill advocated for her athletes, and that meant being concerned with their grades. Jean DeSaix, a biology professor and Boxill's longtime friend, recalled that in one case Boxill reached out to DeSaix to ask what a student enrolled in a biology class needed to do to pass. "I knew, and she knew, she wasn't asking me to do anything to make it possible for the student to pass," DeSaix said. "Because she would never ask me to do that." In a university, professors who advocate for students will do what they can to give them a chance to succeed, including sending emails to colleagues asking what a student needs to do to get a certain grade. "If you care about students," DeSaix said, "you go down that path."[35] It's possible Nyang'oro read a grade request into such a communication from Boxill.

For every supposedly damning piece of evidence laid out in the Wainstein report, Boxill has a persuasive explanation. In general, she declined to reveal the names of the students involved out of a desire to protect their privacy.

Perhaps the most compelling piece of evidence against her is that Willingham, once a good friend, says Boxill did know that Crowder graded papers. She knew, Willingham says, because everyone in the office knew.[36] Smith, the faculty critic and Willingham's co-author, recalled the former learning specialist telling him, "Everything I tell you, Jan also knows."[37] But Boxill says she wasn't like every other academic-support employee. She was rarely actually in the advising office.[38] (Wainstein called her "unofficially, if not officially, a member of ASPSA.")[39] Things in the infamous PowerPoint presentation came as a shock to her, too.[40] Boxill and Willingham, once good friends, stopped talking in around 2014.[41] Boxill finds it hard to talk about their friendship today, while Willingham expresses puzzlement at Boxill's claims of ignorance.

For Boxill and her former friend Willingham, experience in the academic-support office made UNC's athletics program into a kind of Rorschach blot. In athletics, Boxill saw a ticket to a better life. Willingham saw an exploitative system that wrung value from athletes' labor, only to compensate them with a cheap simulacrum of a college education. Perhaps each person's approach to their work was determined by their past experience. Willingham, having once acted to help correct a systemic inequity, did so again by speaking out. Boxill, who viewed sports and education as buoys for disadvantaged students, continued to work within the system, person to person, to lift them up.

With the Wainstein report, the public tides turned in favor of Willingham's view. She was vindicated, while Boxill was humiliated. And yet they still had one thing in common. Both women viewed themselves as cast aside by a university acting swiftly to sew up an embarrassing scandal.

They weren't the only ones who had been sent packing. The university, as Folt had presaged, did not react to the Wainstein report by reexamining its commitment to the amateur ideal. It instead performed an exorcism: punishing the people who had been caught doing the work to make the myth seem real—with Boxill at the front of the line.

Folt, who in early 2021 was president of the University of Southern California, declined to be interviewed for this book. But she wrote in an email that the Wainstein report was "was not the kind of document that could be relied on to make employment decisions."[42] When presented with the fact that Boxill and at least one other employee were notified on the day of the report's release that they would be fired, and that Boxill's dismissal letter stated plainly that the Wainstein investigation was the source of the evidence against her, among other things, Folt replied that the report's findings were not accepted "without our own critical review and assessment." She went on: "A team of people, led by the UNC Provost and the VP for Human Affairs, worked very hard to review all the available information and to make the right decisions."[43] University officials received the Wainstein report less than a week before releasing it.[44]

Among the fired were Jaimie Lee and Beth Bridger, the academic counselors for football players who had presented the infamous PowerPoint presentation to the coaching staff.[45] Both were fired the day of the report's release, even though Bridger had switched jobs, and was working at UNC-Wilmington. Brent Blanton, a counselor for women's soccer, who according to the report had directed some players toward Crowder's classes, was fired about a year after the report was released following a disciplinary review. Timothy McMillan, a popular lecturer in African and Afro-American Studies, was close to Crowder and had passed along a few possible topics to her for paper classes. He resigned shortly after the release of the report.[46] Bobbi Owen, a longtime administrator and tenured drama professor, had, according to the report, chided Nyang'oro for his department's gratuitous use of independent study.[47] Her decision not to investigate further, the report

found, was "inexplicable."[48] Owen was barred from holding administrative duties at the university after a review, but retained her tenured
professorship.[49]

None of the fired employees had supervisory oversight over
Nyang'oro, a job that fell to a senior associate dean. Organizational holes
had prevented any meaningful oversight of the department. Because it
didn't have a graduate program, the African and Afro-American Studies department was exempted from receiving regular external reviews
every five years. Nyang'oro himself was never subject to post-tenure
review because university policy declared that department chairs were
exempt. Nyang'oro's three reappointments as chair, the Wainstein
report found, failed to raise any concerns about the paper classes.[50]

In the absence of any clear managerial failing, attention focused on
those lower down. A big part of the academic advisers' job was to keep
their athletes eligible to play. Boxill, Lee, Bridger, and Blanton were
fired for doing their jobs. McMillan, the adjunct lecturer, was beholden
to Crowder, the de facto head of the department, who had the power
to determine whether and how much he taught each semester. And
Owen, as senior associate dean for undergraduate education, had limited oversight. Nyang'oro's department was not in her purview, and she
claimed in the report that all she had done was ask him to turn over a
signature to the head of advising after noticing a few suspicious signatures on grade rolls. Each was punished not for starting or steering
the system, but for not speaking up. And yet the most senior of these—
Owen, who had the clout, if not the knowledge, to blow the whistle on
irregularities—was punished the least. She escaped with her job.

And then there was Travis Gore. The report had painted Gore largely
as an underling of Crowder and Nyang'oro, who had taken orders from
each. In one case after Crowder's retirement he had supplied Nyang'oro
with athletes' GPAs so the professor could base the grades he handed
out on what they meant for the athletes' eligibility.[51] A year after the
report's release, the university fired Gore. In his dismissal letter, the
university listed a strange body of evidence in support: first, Gore had
loaned out videos from the department that were supposed to only be
used by faculty; second, he had "falsified" an email from two students
to get Crowder to enroll them in an independent study class; third, he
had "helped a student receive a final grade" in a summer class that was
not his place to determine; and finally, he inappropriately disclosed
student information to a friend in another unit on campus.[52]

In sum, the findings had little or nothing to do with knowing about the paper classes. Instead, it seemed, the university had assembled a constellation of misconduct, and then cited it while firing a junior staffer who made $32,703 a year.[53] His firing seemed ridiculous to some of his former colleagues. Gore was a happy-go-lucky guy who was on the absolute lowest rung in the department, remembered Lambert, the professor of African Studies. Did the administration feel so insecure about the punishment they were handing down, Lambert wondered, that they had to beef it up with supporting evidence unrelated to the investigation? "I was embarrassed to be a part of the university when they let him go," he said.[54]

So was Hildebrand, the professor who had been so incensed at the effect of the scandal on his department. Gore, he recalled, was just a receptionist. He'd get coffee for professors, retrieve their mail, answer the phones, and set up chairs before department events. Hildebrand chided him about his not moving on: this job is fine for a couple of years, he told Gore, but eventually you need to be doing something else. Gore was nowhere near culpable for any part of the scandal, Hildebrand said. He couldn't be; he didn't have enough power. When Gore was put under review, the professor wrote to the provost on his behalf. "If you try to solve this problem by firing our receptionist, the gofer, you're going to make yourselves look ridiculous," he recalled writing. But that's not what happened. "I was wrong," Hildebrand said. "They fired him, and they make themselves look like heroes."

It struck Hildebrand that Gore's role was similar to that of the state agent who had asked him in his office whether he had accepted a bribe. The question had been insulting, but the professor recognized the officer was just following orders. Gore, too, had been following orders, doing what he'd been told to do because he had no other option. And yet the university had fired him, apparently untroubled by what they were doing to his life, career, and reputation. When Hildebrand saw news of the firing in his local newspaper, he realized something about the people he'd worked for all these years. That they could do something so ugly to a young man who'd had so little to do with the scandal left him deeply disturbed. It was a new low. He wasn't working for noble intellectuals, ethical stewards. Instead, he saw, "I'm working for a bunch of thugs."

The longtime professor had one more year before he planned to retire, but he gave it up. Both of his departments asked him whether he wanted emeritus status, and he said no to both. He wanted nothing to do with UNC anymore. He felt smaller every time he walked on the campus.[55]

The hits came quickly for Boxill. She lost her position as the director of the Parr Center for Ethics. Her ties with the athletics department were severed. She'd been voted the next distinguished scholar of the International Association for the Philosophy of Sport, but was asked to withdraw her name. She had been under contract to edit an anthology about ethics in sports, but that was canceled too.[56]

Her dismissal letter presented her with a single option to clear her name. She could request a hearing before the faculty hearings committee, which would consider her case. Meanwhile, she hired a local attorney to help her navigate the process. But such procedures were rough going. Because they knew Boxill through faculty governance, she said, nearly the entire committee membership had to recuse itself.[57] And at a prehearing of the committee, the presiding officer, a faculty member, ruled that the administration could introduce the Wainstein report as evidence, but wouldn't allow Boxill to take written statements from any faculty members in support, according to Boxill's attorney.[58] In an environment where faculty members were getting fired, Boxill sensed fear among the people who might have come to her defense. She found friendly colleagues hesitant to get on the phone, or to be seen with her in public. She definitely couldn't get them before a committee.[59]

To boot, the university initially wouldn't give her the email evidence that Wainstein had used as the basis for many of his conclusions.[60] When it finally did, it handed her a CD of hundreds of thousands of emails. She read the first 100 and decided it was pointless.[61] Meanwhile, her siblings—reminders of the hardscrabble world Boxill had escaped—were in ailing health. Two had passed away in the few months before the Wainstein report hit, and two passed away—one suddenly—in the months after.

Scarred by the already unfavorable headlines and reminded of her own mortality, Boxill faced the likely possibility that she would go before a committee and be dismissed: the ethics professor who got fired for ethical misconduct. She decided to retire. At seventy-six, she was well past the eligible age, and this way would be entitled to retirement benefits, which she would lose if dismissed. She was confident in her innocence, but it seemed that her institution was determined to usher her out. So she told them of her intent to retire.[62]

In what Boxill perceived to be adding a final insult to injury, the university then announced that Boxill had "resigned," and made public the dismissal letter Dean had handed her in October.[63] Listed in that document were the charges, in all their embarrassing detail and for the world to see, seemingly legitimized by Boxill's decision to leave. Included among them was the allegation that Boxill herself had created independent study courses with "minimal academic expectations" in the philosophy department.[64] (The *Daily Tar Heel* reported after the release of the Wainstein report that Boxill had offered 160 independent study classes between 2004 and 2012, and cited email traffic from the Wainstein investigation showing that the classes were used by athletes.[65] Boxill says that, as director of undergraduate studies in the department for part of that period, her name was signed to every one of the department's independent study offerings, even those taught by other professors, inflating that number in university records.)[66]

Any notion of a dignified retirement was buried. In the second-to-last sentence of its statement releasing the dismissal letter, the university wrote that Boxill "indicated her intent to seek retirement benefits."[67]

Boxill was publicly disgraced, her reputation in tatters. Even Smith, the history professor who had been suspicious and critical of Boxill, saw her dismissal as unfair. "I just think it's unfortunate that Jan, an untenured faculty member with divided loyalties from the day she first stepped foot on campus, and who had the respect of most faculty and who did a lot good things at the university over a 25-year period, that she and a bunch of other untenured, unprotected staff members are the people who bear the brunt of the backlash of the scandal. It's not fair. It's not right."[68]

Even after she was gone, the question hung in the air: had Boxill actually done what the Wainstein report alleged?

The harshest effect of what Boxill saw as scapegoating was that she was suddenly cut off from everything that had made up her life for decades. No more teaching. No more research. No more UNC basketball. The loss of the bevy of ever-multiplying tasks Boxill so eagerly shouldered now created an immense void at the center of her life.[69]

The university may have been eager to cut ties with Boxill, but her former players weren't. Tanya Lamb, the women's basketball player who Boxill had fought to get back on the team, was shocked when she came across the allegations. She logged onto the UNC women's basketball Facebook page. Nobody had heard from Jan.

Lamb thought back to what Boxill had meant to her, fighting to get Lamb back on the team when no one else would. Boxill was the mother figure she so badly needed, so far away from home. It's my turn, Lamb thought. She gave Boxill a call. I don't care about what they're saying about you, she told Boxill. I just want to know that you're okay. On the other end of the line, Boxill was embarrassed. She was humiliated. And she was worried that she was a risk to the women's basketball program she had served for so many years. Lamb offered reassurance. You need to know, she told Boxill, that there are a lot of alumni who care about you, who are there for you.[70]

Boxill received many such calls and supportive notes. But in the arena of public opinion, she seemed to be alone in the wilderness. Her daughters urged her to make a public statement declaring her innocence. But after everything that she'd seen written about herself, she couldn't bear to see her words twisted again. "No matter what I said, it wouldn't be what I said," she recalled thinking. Not to mention the fact that she could barely talk about what happened without breaking down. So she stayed silent, a decision she would later realize helped reinforce the Wainstein findings against her.[71]

A few months after she resigned, she got the chance to talk. The NCAA released its notice of allegations against the university—one of three that it would send in this latest iteration.[72] Boxill was heavily featured in each. The notices made allegations similar to those of the Wainstein report—basically, that she had provided impermissible academic assistance to players through heavy-handed editing and by enrolling them in paper classes and other independent study classes across the university. Each notice listed several examples, based exclusively on unearthed emails, showing how Boxill provided such assistance. By the final notice, the claims against Boxill focused nearly exclusively on alleged help—overzealous editing, basically—that Boxill had given to athletes. Gone were any intimations of Boxill's knowledge of a paper-class scheme; the case focused virtually entirely on

Boxill providing impermissible assistance to her athletes the way an overeager tutor might.

The enumerated claims gave Boxill and her lawyer specific claims to respond to. After the NCAA widened its case against her in its second notice, her lawyer issued a scathing response. "It did not happen," Boxill's attorney wrote. "Not one of the Allegations against Jan Boxill is true." The association had emails appearing to show Boxill adding content to students' papers, or creating sections out of the whole cloth. But the emails didn't show that at all, the lawyer wrote. In one instance, the NCAA alleged that the fact that Boxill had attached an introduction to an email clearly showed her intent that the student pass off that introduction as their own. But it was just a sample introduction, he wrote, not at all related in topic to the student's assignment. An example of what an introduction should look like, not something the student could rip verbatim. The NCAA had even interviewed this student, but hadn't asked about the allegation (though the student denied Boxill provided improper assistance).

In another instance, the NCAA cited an email that seemed to show that Boxill had sent a completed quiz to a player to pass off as their own work. But this was for Boxill's own class; why would she give the player a quiz to turn in to her own class? If she had wanted to help them cheat, she could have just given them an A in the course. Instead, the attorney wrote, Boxill was just replying to an email from the player seeking help, returning as an attachment something the player had already sent her.

Boxill's attorney refuted each item of evidence in similar fashion. Each seemed to boil down to the same thing. Just as had happened with the Faculty Executive Committee report, someone had looked at emails and jumped to conclusions without seeing the full picture. And in cases where Boxill had appeared to suggest text for papers, this was something that was well within a professor's purview.[73] Boxill has defended it as modeling, a simple tactic to try to improve a player's writing. It wouldn't have necessarily been appropriate for another counselor, but Boxill wasn't just any other counselor. She was a professor with credible and well-earned bona fides. If being a counselor and a professor posed a conflict-of-interest problem, it was one the university had fully endorsed for all the years it asked her to do both jobs.

The process continued to play out. The NCAA released an amended notice; the university responded. While the news kept filtering up, Lamb texted Boxill an emoji of an ocean wave. Here comes another wave of news; brace yourself.[74] On her living room wall Boxill has a famous photograph of a lighthouse, consumed by a tumultuous sea as a man stands at its rear, barely protected from the crashing wave. This is what it feels like, Boxill thought.[75]

Then in 2017, the big day came. It was the final stage in the NCAA investigation—the trial, basically—and Boxill boarded the plane to Nashville to testify in person. When she walked through the tunnel and into the Tennessee airport she laid eyes on the woman who had been, in a way, the source of all her grief.

There stood Debby Crowder.[76]

Even after she left the university, Crowder had closely followed the affairs of the department. She later said that her colleagues called her about seven times a day in the months that followed.[1] She frequently emailed her friends Gore and McMillan, and as the first NCAA investigation raged in 2010, she mused to Gore that it was "an interesting mess."[2] When the *Charlotte Observer* wrote an article about Wiley, the rogue tutor, Crowder emailed the link to Gore.[3] Having spent thirty years in a department, she no doubt found it difficult to turn away completely.

When her name started showing up in the news, she turned down media requests. When the university first launched reviews, she declined their requests to participate. But when the district attorney, Woodall, launched a criminal investigation, she was willing to talk.[4] And in the spring of 2014, when he dropped the investigation into Crowder and Nyang'oro on the condition that both cooperate, Crowder readied herself. She later recalled spending "untold hours" with Wainstein trying "in good faith to explain the situation." But when the report came out, she said, "I was crushed, because I did not think that it was an accurate representation of my personal interview."[5]

So when the NCAA mentioned Crowder in its first Notice of Allegations in the academic fraud case, she stayed silent. She didn't want to talk to anyone else. But when the association amended its notice for the last time, with the help of her new local attorney, Elliot Abrams,

Crowder filed an affidavit. She started by correcting what she saw as the Wainstein report's inaccuracies. The classes had been available to any student, not just the athletes. She hadn't masterminded these courses, nor had she put herself in the position of professor. Nyang'oro had just become "increasingly unavailable" as the years went on. Finally, she concluded with a philosophical statement, one that carried the weight of her experience as a student in the '70s. The university has a duty to educate its students, she said, but "institutional bureaucracy" represented a constant threat to that mission. So when it reared its head, "I believed we had a duty to protect the students and their futures—not by giving away grades, but by providing customized educational opportunities."

Two months later, she agreed to an interview with NCAA investigators. In a hotel conference room across the street from the center named after Friday, she told the room full of lawyers about the philosophy she'd laid out in the affidavit. Admitting a student to a university was like adopting a child. You had the duty to ferry them responsibly to adulthood. When Crowder met students one on one, she'd ask them about their goals, and sometimes that would lead them to discuss their problems. Such problems were legion in a huge bureaucracy like UNC, where it was easy to get lost in a crowd. And with mention of a problem, Crowder would spring into action: what could she do to help?[6]

An NCAA investigator named Kathy Sulentic broke in. In the real world outside of the university, there's no Debby Crowder to bail these students out. Don't they learn a lesson by making things work on their own? "Perhaps," Crowder answered. But if a student had come to her office "crying hysterically, threatening suicide," and she could help them by putting them in a class, she would put them in a class. "I would do that today after all of this."[7]

Wainstein had painted her as a mastermind, but she told the room that everything had developed gradually. She'd gotten the call from Taylor, learned that she could set up an impromptu class, supervised by Nyang'oro, to satisfy a perspective requirement. Every semester after that, the academic advising office would call over with a request.[8] That became another tool in the toolbox to help a struggling student. She hadn't "designed" any system, as Wainstein had said. It wouldn't have existed without her, but Nyang'oro by and large wrote the paper prompts and supervised many of the students—"whether he says he did or not," she said.[9] She graded papers, yes, but she hadn't wanted to. It was only when Nyang'oro was unavailable that she did so, when he asked her to do it. If she graded easily, that's because he told her to. "You have to work to get a C," he told her, she said, meaning your paper has to be especially bad to warrant a C.[10]

Crowder talked so much in that conference room that her voice became strained.[11] She wove a narrative that was both sympathetic and believable. What she said would have stayed under lock and key had an unlikely actor not deemed it incredibly useful information. That actor was the institution that had vilified Crowder for half a decade, and that was now looking for a way to escape penalties and preserve its athletic dominance.

The NCAA had begun its second investigation at a time of uncertainty for the university. UNC was still reeling from allegations from Willingham, who had just filed a lawsuit, and it was in the midst of the Wainstein investigation. When the results of the Wainstein probe were released, their severity signaled to observers that the university was almost certain to be hit with huge penalties, much worse, potentially, than it had faced after the NCAA investigation that Thorp had endured. In the days following the release of the report, the association's president, Mark Emmert, seemed to presage his organization's interest in intervention, calling the findings "absolutely disturbing."[12]

The NCAA's case against UNC had three major prongs.[13] First, it alleged that the university had provided impermissible benefits to athletes in the form of the paper classes. Second, it contended that Boxill had given improper academic assistance to athletes. Third, and most seriously, it alleged that the university had failed to monitor the administration of the paper classes, that the academic support office had manipulated these classes, and that Boxill's help for her athletes was over the line. The NCAA issued three notices of allegations against the university, with the case altered a little bit each time. By the third, it was clear that the association would not soft-pedal its allegations; that notice accused the university of using the paper classes not just as impermissible benefits for athletes, but as part of a broad-based and pernicious scheme manipulated by the athletic department. It also said that such a scheme violated NCAA rules governing sportsmanship and unethical conduct. It mentioned specifically the university's football and men's basketball teams, which had been absent from previous notices.[14] The NCAA might be looking to vacate championships and hand down postseason bans.

For the seven years that the NCAA had been poking around Chapel Hill, this had been fans' worst fear. James Moeser, the UNC chancellor who preceded Thorp and who hired both Butch Davis and Roy Williams, remarked in 2013 that the "real goal" of media outlets digging into the scandal was to "remove banners from the Smith Center," referencing the championship banners that hang in the rafters.[15]

That outcome now seemed more likely. As in 2010, the university had hired Rick Evrard from the firm Bond, Schoeneck & King to represent it before the NCAA. But unlike in its first go-round with the association, the university had an ingenious legal strategy up its sleeve that it hoped would spare it the severest penalties.

The NCAA had thrown the book at UNC. The university took the book and threw it right back, starting with Crowder's core contention: the classes she ran were available to both athletes and nonathletes on an equal basis. As such, they couldn't be called an impermissible benefit. Aimed at preserving amateurism, the rule seeks to ensure that athletes didn't get over-the-top benefits from their special status on campus. If the classes were open to and taken by everyone, how could they be called an impermissible benefit?[16]

The argument isn't exactly airtight. Nonathlete students don't have access to a separate team of advisers specifically charged with keeping them academically and athletically eligible. And indeed, the NCAA placed the academic-support program front and center in its allegations. "The institution and its athletics department," the NCAA wrote, "leveraged the relationship with Crowder and Nyang'oro to obtain and/or provide special arrangements to student-athletes."[17] But the academic-support program, the university argued, couldn't be lumped in with the athletic department, never mind that advisers had told Wainstein they felt beholden to coaches, and that their office was funded by the athletic department.[18] The reporting line was to the College of Arts and Sciences.[19] And how could the association seek to penalize a university for its academic advisers steering athletes to classes available to every student?[20] It was the NCAA, in fact, that mandated that each of its member institutions offer such a service. To punish UNC for that would be to do an about-face on its own rules.[21]

For the NCAA to hand down a punishment, the university argued, it would have to reach inside the classroom and rule on the content of a course. If it tried to do that, again, it would be going against its own rules and public statements. At its core, the NCAA existed to regulate and enforce the rules surrounding athletic competition.

UNC aimed to take full advantage of this limitation. After the release of the Wainstein report, two former UNC athletes had sued both the university and the NCAA over the fake classes, alleging they'd been denied a real education. In a filing to dismiss that lawsuit, the NCAA's lawyers had written that the association "did not assume a duty to ensure the quality of the education student-athletes received at member institutions or to protect student-athletes from the independent, voluntary acts of those institutions or their employees."[22] In other words, the NCAA could not be held responsible for curriculum-based complaints, for things that went wrong in the classroom. A federal judge went on to dismiss that lawsuit, a fact that the university's lawyers reminded the association of in response to its final notice.[23] Emmert himself had underlined the idea in 2015. "It's ultimately up to universities to determine whether or not the courses for which they're giving credit, the degrees for which they're passing out diplomas, live up to the academic standards of higher education," he said.[24]

The last piece of the university's hypocrisy argument was perhaps the most damning. The university had notified the NCAA of what it had first found in the department—the fishy courses run by Crowder and Nyang'oro—in 2011. The NCAA had responded, to Thorp's shock, by declaring to the university that those problems were not relevant to its then-ongoing investigation. And as part of that first investigation, the NCAA didn't mention those irregularities in its finding against UNC. The NCAA's own rules say a finding by the Committee on Infractions is "final, binding, and conclusive." If the NCAA wanted to punish UNC for course content, it would have to disavow or go against its previous ruling.[25]

The university's lawyers had constructed a minefield for the NCAA to walk, with the implied risk being legal action. For an example of how that might go, the NCAA needed only to look back a few years to the case of Penn State. The Jerry Sandusky child-abuse scandal had been a multiyear source of shame for the university, resulting in multiple criminal charges for university officials. The NCAA, too, felt called to issue punishment, so in 2012 it handed down decades of vacated wins, stringent scholarship caps, a four-year postseason ban, and a $60-million fine.[26] While the university didn't take the NCAA to court, others did. The state of Pennsylvania sued the NCAA over the penalties, saying it had overreached.[27] A state senator also sued. Within two years, the association had backed off the penalties almost entirely, lifting the postseason ban and saying it would let state lawmakers funnel the fine into programs within Pennsylvania, among other things.[28] Was it a recognition that the association had overreached? "I don't know how it could be perceived differently," one expert told *The New York Times*.[29]

The lawsuit filed by the state senator, Jake Corman, revealed evidence to that point. Internal NCAA emails made public through the discovery portion of the lawsuit showed an organization uncertain of its jurisdiction in handing down such large penalties. "I know we are banking on the fact the school is so embarrassed they will do anything," wrote the association's then-vice president of academic and membership affairs, "but I am not sure about that, and no confidence conference or other members will agree to that. This will force the jurisdictional issue that we really don't have a great answer to that one. . . ." Penn State called the emails "deeply disturbing," and referred to what the NCAA did as "bluffing" the university "to accept sanctions outside of their normal investigative and enforcement process."[30]

While the NCAA was running its standard enforcement process in the UNC case, officials would have had good reason to be sensitive about an overreach. The university's legal team had adopted a scorched-earth defense. They probably wouldn't take a conviction on what they saw as faulty charges lying down.

There's evidence that the Penn State case was on UNC's mind as it fought the NCAA. In a call with reporters after the NCAA released its final notice of allegations, Bubba Cunningham, the university's athletic director, surmised that the NCAA was relying on a lower standard of evidence than it had before. The conclusions of the notice that Cunningham cited were bolstered principally by the Wainstein report. In his remarks to reporters, Cunningham cited the Freeh report—the damning independent investigation of the Sandusky affair at Penn State, whose veracity was later questioned—as an example of a piece of evidence that could not qualify as an "appropriate level of documentation" in an NCAA investigation.[31]

UNC's lawyers took that skepticism and weaponized it in its final response to the NCAA, coming to a remarkable conclusion: the Wainstein report, which the university had commissioned, used as the basis to fire employees such as Boxill, and hailed as a final step in the healing process for a years-long scandal, was profoundly flawed.

Wainstein and his team, the university argued, had overcounted the number of athletes who took the paper classes—counting anyone who was ever an athlete during their time at UNC, as opposed to students who were athletes when they took a class.[32] The university also argued that Wainstein's statement that the grading standards of the paper classes were "lax" was an "interpretation" of Wainstein's, not a factual statement and certainly not one that could be treated as evidence in an NCAA proceeding.[33] And the report's determination that grades in the paper classes were "artificially high" was "flawed in several respects."[34] It made the same determination about the finding that athletes had "disproportionately" enrolled in the classes.[35] The university also cast doubt on the report's use of three experts to determine if papers in Crowder's classes had been plagiarized, saying it suffered "profound shortcomings."[36] The lawyers also said the Wainstein report's determination that 169 athletes had used the classes to stay academically eligible had "several flaws."[37]

It also poked holes in the case against Boxill. The alleged academic assistance was outside the NCAA's statute of limitations, the university argued, and each instance of the eighteen examples the association cited was "relatively modest."[38] Boxill was an "unconventional" member of the academic support staff, the university said, calling her a "a respected, full-time faculty member," "an expert in the field of sports ethics," and "exactly the kind of person universities routinely trust to educate their students."[39] Though the university conceded Boxill had shown "poor judgment,"[40] its defense of her was remarkable. The most notable human casualty of the Wainstein report, it appeared, was perhaps not as guilty as she seemed—in her former employer's eyes, at least.

The university's repudiation of certain aspects of the report, the lawyers wrote, was "not meant to criticize the [Wainstein] Report, but rather to show the danger of trying to use portions of it for purposes that [Wainstein] did not intend," adding that his team "quite simply was not tasked with determining whether student-athletes received a benefit not available to other students, which is the issue that is relevant here."[41]

In any case, such an about-face was striking. The university's legal strategy was so aggressive that it appeared to tear down the very report that had brought its furious self-examination to a conclusion. In critiquing the report's findings, it was disputing Wainstein's grand narrative. Crowder hadn't masterminded a scheme to keep athletes eligible, she'd just improvised unorthodox classes with her boss's approval and participation. The advisers in the academic-support office hadn't used the classes as part of a shadow curriculum, they were just doing their jobs. Boxill was a respected expert, not complicit. What UNC now backed away from was the very position it had welcomed and used as the basis to fire, force out, and demote several employees. It had gone even further than that. In a 2015 report to the university's accrediting agency, the university had affirmed the Wainstein report's finding that "the academic fraud was long-standing and not limited to the misconduct of just Nyang'oro and Crowder." That determination, UNC had said, is what led it to immediately fire or review several employees named in the report.[42]

But now the university did not seem so sure. A cynic could look at the university's response and see opportunism aimed at warding off the NCAA, with little observance of truth or principle. Cunningham boiled down the argument as a meaningful technicality: "Is this academic fraud? Yes, it is by a normal person's standard. But by the NCAA definition (it is not) . . . I'm telling you what happened was bad, but it's not against the rules."[43]

Crowder had not planned on going to Nashville to the Committee on Infractions' hearing. She'd planned to testify there via video conference, but Abrams, her attorney, got a message from the association that if she wanted to speak, she had to do it in person. Crowder was resistant. I can't get on an airplane for these people, she told Abrams. She feared she would just be signing up to get mistreated. The Friday before the Tuesday hearing she told Abrams she wasn't going. Her dogs were sick. It wasn't happening.

But on Monday, Crowder called Abrams again. If you drive me to the airport, she told him, I'll go. So he picked her up before daybreak and they got on the plane. Crowder, a dog lover, sat in a middle seat and played with another passenger's dog for the whole flight. They hadn't known it, but Boxill was on the same plane. The two former colleagues, now disgraced, saw each other when they exited the gate.

They hugged. But they weren't sure what they could say, given the NCAA's rules, so they took off individually for the hotel.

When they got there, they paused before the ballroom. An employee strapped a wristband on Crowder's arm, and she and Abrams walked in. To their left was stadium seating for everyone from the university: Roy Williams, the basketball coach; Larry Fedora, the football coach; Sylvia Hatchell, the women's basketball coach; Folt, the chancellor; and, finally, UNC's formidable legal team. To their right was a table of the NCAA's enforcement staff, the officials bringing the case against the university. Dead ahead was the Committee on Infractions, which would be judging the case. And right in the center of the room was a seat for a court reporter, fully equipped with a desk that could spin around at 360 degrees, to take accurate notes on all the action. Near her, Abrams recalled, were two small tables: one for Boxill and her attorney, and one for Crowder and Abrams.[44] The setup was symbolic. Two powerful institutions in a firefight, and two ordinary people caught in the middle.

The infractions committee was the critical body, a six-member group led by the commissioner of the Southeastern Conference and featuring a law professor, a former football coach, a former university president, an attorney, and Alberto Gonzales, the former U.S. attorney general. Boxill introduced herself to each member, and told Gonzales she'd used some of his writings in her classes.[45]

Abrams, as an observer, recognized that this was a credibility test. After Folt answered questions on behalf of the university, Crowder did the same. Then Boxill followed.[46] Both prepared to give versions of the defenses they'd already offered in writing—two people with good intentions and once-great reputations as bedrocks of a university that at its worst was an impersonal bureaucracy.

Boxill hadn't known if she would have a chance to present her case, and she was terrified. But, after asking a series of questions, someone from the NCAA asked her if she wanted to make a statement. She started talking. Unlike before, she didn't break down. She was firm, connecting the dots of the allegations and making her defense, telling the truth as she saw it. She spoke from the heart for twenty-five straight minutes, she remembered.[47] You could hear a pin drop as she spoke.

Sylvia Hatchell, the women's basketball coach who had worked with Boxill for decades, sat in awe.[48] When Boxill finally got the chance to tell her story in full, Hatchell said, it was captivating. "She was amazing," Hatchell said. The coach was so moved by Boxill's testimony that she nudged her attorney, who was sitting next to her, and said she wanted to stand up and speak in support of the professor. She's doing great, he replied. She doesn't need your help.[49]

Abrams, too, noticed some of the skepticism he'd sensed in the room begin to dissolve. Abrams, a UNC alumnus who had had Boxill as a professor in one of his classes, said she passed the credibility test with flying colors. "When you're sitting there listening to her you know she's telling the truth," he said. The same applied to Crowder. At the end of the hearing, one of the committee members gave her a hug and thanked her.

As Crowder left, she confessed to Abrams that she hadn't been sure about her decision to come. But now she knew that if she hadn't, she would have regretted it. She was satisfied. This process she had dreaded so much had gone just fine.[50]

Debby Crowder was an unlikely hero, and an even unlikelier villain. In the course of the years-long scandal, her reputation had traveled full circle. She was first an unassuming doer who sympathized with those who struggled, and was earning a salary of just over $36,000 when she retired.[51] Then she became the perpetrator of academic fraud, on whose doorstep an entire scandal was laid. Now the university had attempted to restore her to her former light, a sympathetic witness who just might—again—keep its athletic enterprise intact.

Several people who knew her expressed surprise that someone as modest and kindhearted as Crowder could end up at the center of the controversy. "The whole thing seems incredibly weird to me," a high school classmate of Crowder's told Kane.[52] Harris, the former department chair, told Smith, the faculty critic, in an email, "I have fond memories of Debby Crowder and am so saddened that she got caught up in all this madness."[53]

Hildebrand, who emerged with sharp criticism of the way his

department was treated, seemed to consider Crowder a tragic figure with pure intentions. "There are more than a few self-serving, pious hypocrites involved in this mess," he wrote during the scandal, "but she is not one of them."[54] Years later, he observed:

> Debby Crowder, her problem was that she, I think, identified a real problem, that there is a cost by trying to pretend that a professional minor league team is actually an extracurricular activity. Something has to give. And she saw that what was giving was that students were put in an untenable position. But it wasn't just athletes. She saw that with a whole range of students who didn't quite fit in and didn't know who to go to for help. They came to her. And she, using the power that she had—and then, ultimately, using more power than she had—tried to fix it for everybody and got into trouble. . . . She just got in over her head trying to do something based from her own experience, being lost in this big bureaucracy with all these students who felt very comfortable being here. . . . She wanted to throw herself in on the side of those others. Once that falls into a cauldron of race, and athletics, and politics, we're off to the races. Sanity goes out the window, and we'll never get it back.[55]

Crowder declined to be interviewed for this book. Abrams, her attorney, wrote in a message that she has been pained by the continued impression that she masterminded a scheme to help athletes cheat. He wrote in part:

> She gave her entire working life to the students of the University of North Carolina, and the psychological and reputational damage inflicted by the inaccurate portrayal of her conduct and motivations in the Wainstein Report are such that she has given up hope of repairing them through telling the truth. A case in point is that she told the truth and subjected herself to cross-examination in the NCAA infractions matter; the NCAA infractions judges found her entirely credible. . . . She is still regularly regarded as the mastermind of an effort to assist sports at the expense of student's education. She has resigned herself to the idea that this false narrative will persist regardless of her efforts to correct the record, and to attempt to do so again would merely expose her to worsening wounds that have not yet healed.[56]

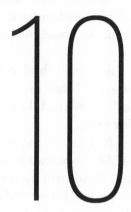

10

Early on Friday, October 13, 2017—three years, nearly to the day, after Boxill was handed a dismissal letter—her lawyer forwarded her a letter from the NCAA.

What she saw left her ecstatic. The NCAA's infractions committee had ruled that it could not conclude she had broken any rules. In doing so, it stated what Boxill already knew: ever since she had arrived at UNC in the late '80s, her role there had been complicated. She was a teacher and a counselor, a fan and a leader, a public-address announcer and a researcher. There were conflicts of interest. Lines got blurred. But after she was publicly derided and forced from the role to which she'd ascended, Boxill remained convinced that she—the ethicist—had never acted unethically. Now the NCAA was offering something of an affirmation, though centered on its own limitations:

> Considering the record and the instructor/counselor's credible statements at the hearing, the panel cannot conclude that she committed unethical conduct. Similarly, because she thoroughly explained her approach to all students and student-athletes she encountered, which is not refuted by the record material, the panel cannot conclude that she provided women's basketball student athletes with extra benefits. It is not clear on the face of the record that the conduct supported impermissible academic assistance. The dual role as instructor and academic counselor is a significant issue, one that member institutions

must approach with caution. Proper policies and procedures regarding appropriate behaviors are essential to ensure individuals have a clear understanding of what is appropriate and what is not.[1]

Boxill was thrilled. She jogged upstairs to tell her husband the good news, and then took out her phone and called her attorney.[2] Was this real? Later she told an *N&O* reporter of her relief.[3] It had been a hard few years.

And yet in the months after, Boxill found that—even with the NCAA's exoneration—the pain of those years still lingered. She was still humiliated by the reputation she carried. She was still tainted. People still believed what was in the newspapers. She was still angry at the university for how swiftly it had cast her aside after nearly thirty years of service. Though the institution had backed her up, to a degree, before the NCAA, it had done nothing to admit it had been wrong. She ran into the chancellor at a friend's retirement party and Folt gave her a hug. Boxill thought it was strange. Fire me, and then hug me?[4] (Folt wrote in an email that she did not recall this interaction and could not comment on employment-related decisions. But she said she considered Boxill "a kind person who cared deeply about her students and her work.")[5] To this day, Boxill believes the university owes her an apology.

Ever since she was a child she'd been busy. On the farm it was the relentless chores, done in the shadow of tragedy. Then it was the military, then it was school and sports. Then it was committees, speeches, presentations, books, games, tournaments, Olympic games. With all that gone in an instant, the void was vast. Among the only solaces she still had were her grandchildren. She shot hoops with them and told her grandson not to look at her Wikipedia page. She loved seeing her former players and students when they came back to town.

She'd been to South Campus a few times since she'd left, but never to North Campus, the heart of UNC where her office had been and where she spent most of her time. But in 2019 the Parr Center, which she used to lead, hosted an old friend of hers for a talk. She couldn't not go. She drove across town to campus, parked on the street, and walked the university grounds for the first time since she'd been forced to leave.

It was hard to be there, and she was worried. She arrived a little early for the event, so she picked up an issue of the *Daily Tar Heel* and read it at an outdoor table behind the dining hall, just a stone's throw from where Graham had pleaded with his faculty eighty years before. Students milled about in the beautiful mid-September weather. Sports, music, and teaching had always allowed her to feel at ease. But this university, which had been her home for thirty years, where she'd reveled in the energy and activity, had been another home. "I belong here," she thought to herself. "This is where I belong."

And yet she knew, after she left that day, that she would probably never come back.[6]

The same day Boxill got the good news, students and fans wearing Carolina blue stumbled down the hill toward the Dean E. Smith Center, a boxy shrine to the coach who'd lent his university the prestige of the Carolina Way. They chatted excitedly as the sunlight died in the autumn air. The campus was coming together for one of the most hotly anticipated nights of the year: the start of the basketball season. Every fall, the university puts on Late Night with Roy, a celebratory mix of skit, scrimmage, and ceremony built to excite the fans as well as the sought-after recruits in attendance. The basketball team had that spring won the NCAA national championship, one year after it lost at the last second in the championship game.[7] It was sweet redemption for Tar Heel fans. Tonight they'd have the perfect chance to celebrate.

But they were cheering more than a national championship. Incredibly, the university's legal strategy had worked like a charm. The NCAA had not handed down a single sanction.[8]

Crowder had credibly testified that the classes she'd arranged were available to all students, a claim supported even by the Wainstein report. That, the Committee on Infractions found, was ample evidence to prevent the NCAA from finding that the "benefit" of the classes was impermissible. And given that so many nonathletes found their way to Crowder's office to plead for a class, it didn't appear that the academic-support office's use of the classes could be considered a special benefit.[9]

And yet the NCAA had entertained a last-ditch option of finding UNC responsible: academic fraud. UNC had disavowed the paper classes and installed rules and reforms to keep them from happening again. Clearly, the university didn't believe they were above-board, and didn't believe the academic credit they conferred on students and athletes was altogether legitimate. This was possible groundwork for a determination of academic fraud, which was punishable under NCAA bylaws, separate from impermissible benefits.

But UNC was ready for this argument. At the hearing, the university defended the legitimacy of the classes. They didn't break any rules that were in place at the time. And the university continued to honor the grades earned in them.[10] This was the final step in an impressive contortion. University leadership had not only amplified the voice of the person it had long blamed for its most embarrassing scandal ever, it had defended her classes as being, at the time they were in place, completely legitimate.

The NCAA was stymied. It relies on member institutions to determine when fraud takes place, as it had said before—both publicly and in court. If a university insisted, as UNC did now, that no fraud occurred, the NCAA had to accept it. Even as it said it believed the classes had been fraudulent based on the common understanding of what constitutes fraud, that didn't matter. "What ultimately matters," the committee wrote, "is what UNC says about the courses."[11] And UNC said they were, at the time, just fine.

Not that the association's infractions committee was happy with the outcome. It made plain its displeasure with UNC's argument. It said it was "troubled" by the university's "shifting positions, including its positions related to the [Wainstein] report, depending on the audience."[12] How could it deny that academic fraud occurred when it had made public statements saying it had? Indeed, just two years earlier the university had told its accreditor that it considered the paper classes to be academic fraud. The university's leadership hadn't changed at all in the intervening years. The same chancellor, Folt, who oversaw the university's determination then was arguing before the NCAA that no fraud had occurred.

The NCAA asked: What accounted for the discrepancy? That statement to its accreditor, the university answered, was just a typo.[13]

Observers nationwide expressed outrage and disappointment at the decision. "The No Courage Athletic Association would be more fitting today," wrote Dan Wolken in *USA Today*.[14] Calling the NCAA's decision "arguably its most anticipated ruling ever," Pat Forde wrote in Yahoo Sports that by letting the university off the hook, the association "completed its descent from flawed to failed."[15]

The university welcomed the decision. "We believe this is the correct—and fair—outcome," Folt said in a statement. She continued: "We are as resolute as we have ever been to our commitment to excellence, guided by our historic mission to serve the people in our state and beyond."[16] Few had dared predict such a favorable outcome for Chapel Hill.

The university had argued to the NCAA that its accrediting agency was the proper arbiter of what was permitted in the classroom.[17] So the question came naturally: did it have anything to say about the way UNC had defended itself? In the days after the NCAA decision, the president of the Southern Association of Colleges and Schools Commission on Colleges, Belle Wheelan, commented to the *N&O*'s Kane that a few things the university had told the NCAA didn't "pass the smell test."[18] Days later, though, Wheelan wrote a letter to UNC apologizing and saying she hadn't found any problems in the NCAA report.[19] (The *N&O* published the recording of the conversation as Wheelan insisted the story lacked key context.)[20]

The collateral damage, too, didn't stop. Smith, the history professor and vocal critic, saw administrative blowback regarding a class he planned to teach on the history of college sports, which touched on the UNC scandal. In 2017, his department chair was approached by administrators who had concerns about the course, prompting the chair to cancel the course. Faculty came to Smith's defense, and the course was put back on the schedule. A faculty grievance committee investigated the administration's actions and determined that they had overstepped and violated Smith's academic freedom. Folt rejected that finding, and her determination was upheld by the governing board.[21]

The scandal's shock waves prompted national concern and talk of action. The month before the association's verdict, federal prosecutors announced the results of an investigation into a bribery scheme involving an Adidas executive and several college basketball coaches.[22] Though the prosecutors' case ultimately failed to deliver any earth-shattering findings of corruption, its genesis shook the college sports world, and the NCAA announced a commission to consider possible reforms. Among those it recommended: closing the loophole that allowed UNC to walk free. "Member institutions cannot be permitted to defend a fraud or misconduct case on the ground that all students, not just athletes, were permitted to 'benefit' from that fraud or misconduct," read the commission's report.[23] A working group within the NCAA recommended that the association add a bylaw that could be used to punish "egregious academic misconduct," a direct callback to the organization's failure to punish UNC.[24]

But when a bylaw was proposed precisely to that effect, the association's member institutions—led by their presidents—rejected it, citing "some but not significant support" among members.[25] And subsequent reporting by Kane revealed that a compromise plan—a one-time committee of college presidents to judge egregious examples of academic fraud—was also dropped.[26] Among colleges and universities like UNC, there was simply not an appetite to expose themselves to NCAA penalties for something that happens inside the classroom. As of 2021 the UNC loophole was still on the books.

That failed bylaw represented, in effect, the end of the scandal. The epic story had begun with the birth and growth of the Carolina Way, authored by Bill Friday and Dean Smith, cheered on by Debby Crowder, and embodied by Jan Boxill. Its middle act was the myth's swift unraveling, witnessed by Thorp and hastened by Willingham. The third act was perhaps the most surprising of all: despite all the evidence that the amateur ideal was at the root of the scandal, the university worked to resist any efforts at grappling with that fact. Instead, it endeavored to spare itself any penalties that might hamper its athletic dominance. The NCAA's acquittal completed the story: UNC was back in the game, its Carolina blue sheen more brilliant than ever.

Yet it would be a mistake to conclude that UNC hadn't paid a price for the scandal. It paid dearly. There was the financial toll. The university ultimately paid at least $21 million for legal representation and public-relations and investigative work related to the scandal.[27] That's not including the reputational hit exacted by seven years of bad headlines in a range of publications—from *Bloomberg Businessweek* to *Inside Higher Ed.* But such damage probably didn't make a dent in UNC's bottom line. Research has shown that some sports scandals seem to coincide with dips in student applications; that didn't happen in Chapel Hill.[28] Between 2010, when news of the scandal first broke, and 2016, when it was close to finished, undergraduate applications increased by a whopping 50 percent.[29]

Then there were the more intangible losses. On campus, the Carolina Way—as Thorp had accurately predicted—went more or less dormant. Faculty members spoke of a loss of pride, a profound sense of disappointment at what happened.[30] Professors in the African and Afro-American Studies department, now renamed the Department of African, African American, and Diaspora Studies, remained scarred by the scandal. Those fired or disciplined by the university grappled with upended lives.

The university's response to that cost was to shore up its defenses by implementing dozens of changes. No more confusion about who governs the Academic Support Program for Student Athletes; now it's firmly on the academic side of the house. The admissions office now uses a formula to predict athletes' GPA that it says does a better job of projecting academic fit. All grade-change forms must be signed by a dean. Any class with a 20 percent enrollment of athletes is flagged for follow-up by an administrator.[31] At one point administrators physically checked on classes to make sure they were really meeting.[32] And the university published more than a million documents related to the scandal online for the world to see, a trove of material on which much of this book is based. It's safe to say the paper-classes scandal that brought UNC to its knees would be impossible now.

And yet it's one thing to add many safeguards, and quite another to address the cause. In responding to the scandal, the university concentrated on the former, not the latter. The root cause was the athletics enterprise—specifically, its amateur myth. Graham had predicted that subsidizing one class of students by different standards than all others would create "campus problems undreamed of in our philosophy." That's exactly what happened. But rather than dust off his de-emphasis crusade, the university has made its patches and moved on.

In an email, Folt rejected this argument, saying that the "major root" of the scandal was "that there were weaknesses in some UNC academic processes"—weaknesses that have since been strengthened through the aforementioned safeguards. "I don't think any story about this matter would be complete," she wrote, in part, "without emphasizing all of the positive changes that occurred as a result of what happened, and recognizing the years of debate and reflection (beginning well before I arrived) that the community undertook openly and frankly."[33]

Such a defense is akin to blaming a dam break on hairline cracks.

Unmentioned is the role of the torrent of water bearing down on the dam at all hours, seeking any crevice to exploit. In the UNC scandal, the athletic imperative was that force. As one trustee remarked to an alumnus by email after the Wainstein report's release: "Of course, the ultimate root cause is big time college athletics. It is easy to say we should immediately terminate athletic scholarships and withdraw from intercollegiate sports, but it's just not that simple."[34]

College sports scandals come in many shapes and sizes.

Some are scandals of toxicity protected by privilege. In 2015 reports of sexual assault by Baylor University football players trickled into the public eye, forcing a damning internal report that cited "a cultural perception that football was above the rules," resulting in the ousters of the president, the athletic director, and the football coach.[35] Sometimes such cultures transcend campus boundaries. A 2014 investigation by the *New York Times* found that the Tallahassee Police Department had "on numerous occasions . . . soft-pedaled allegations of wrongdoing by Seminoles football players."[36]

Others tell of conflict between the academic and athletic spheres. In 2015, an investigative report revealed that the Rutgers University football coach had personally intervened with an instructor to try to raise the grade of one of his players, and even went as far as editing a thank-you letter the player wrote to the instructor. The coach, Kyle J. Flood, was suspended for three games and fined $50,000.[37] In May 2018, a University of Maryland at College Park offensive lineman named Jordan McNair collapsed at a team practice and was hospitalized. He died about two weeks later, and the resulting furor exposed allegations of toxicity inside the football program and athletic department. The saga climaxed when, as ESPN and other outlets reported, the university system's board told the College Park president, Wallace Loh, that he would be fired if he didn't reinstate the football coach, who had been placed on administrative leave. Loh subsequently announced plans to resign, and public outrage prompted him to fire the coach.[38]

To venture even further back into the annals of college sports history is to be confronted by scandals of eerie familiarity. A secretary who wrote papers for athletes at the University of Minnesota in the late 1990s.[39] Classes that didn't require athletes' attendance at the University of Southern California in the 1970s.[40] Slush funds throughout

West Coast universities in the 1950s.[41] Reading the 1929 Carnegie report that inspired a century of would-be reformers brings about a sense of déjà vu. That it is still so relevant speaks volumes about the failures to eliminate college sports scandals through reform. As historian John Thelin has observed, many of the practices decried back then were not outlawed in the ensuring years, but just cloaked in legitimacy. "The paradox of college sports reform" in the sixty years after the Carnegie report, Thelin writes, "has not been the corruption but, rather, what colleges and universities and the American public have come to accept as approved practices." He continues:

> The initial impulse in each era was to deplore the illegal and unethical activities in college sports, then to proceed to make them legal. If there is an epitaph for the demise of educationally sound athletic programs on the American campus, it will read, "The rules were unenforceable."[42]

The constant presence of scandal is perhaps the strongest piece of proof that intercollegiate athletics as a nationwide enterprise is remarkably buggy, when measured against higher education's highest aspirations of ethical stewardship and truth-telling. The two have never been squared; they have only coexisted, with colleges' academic sphere—as Thelin observed—in constant retreat. In analyzing how colleges responded to athletics scandals in the decade after 2010, the historian noticed a pattern: presidents and boards would express remorse and announce swift action as some on the campus clamored for a culture change. And yet in the face of that protest, leaders did little more than "rely on public relations as a source of 'crisis management' and 'damage control.'" The final phase of the process was the emergence of a collective determination that "the university must and would regain its athletic greatness."[43]

Such a pattern was remarkably costly in the UNC case, as the collapse of the Carolina Way mythology tarnished careers and lives. Take every sports scandal in higher education's history, add up the Boxills, the Thorps, the Willinghams, and there is a significant human toll. Add the cumulative reputational costs and embarrassment and one is stuck with quite a bill.

So why does higher education put up with it? Surely there must be some incredible benefit to balance the scales.

The knee-jerk answer—money—doesn't quite satisfy. No university has gold-plated coffers because of its winning teams. Typically, athletic departments spend what they bring in; ticket sales rarely subsidize decrepit libraries. Application bumps from championship seasons are only temporary. The utility of the president's box in fundraising is disputed. There's something deeper at work.

David Labaree, a Stanford University professor and author of a popular history of higher education, has argued that sports, particularly college football, has been American higher education's secret sauce. "Nobel prizes are great," he proclaimed in a 2017 article, "but college football is why American universities dominate the globe." Unlike the European schools that were their inspiration, the American university has never had a reliable source of funding; it has had to fight for every scrap, voraciously searching out any way to ensure its survival. Football did the trick, helping endear universities to their prospective students, who later attended and then became alumni with disposable income to give back. Sports also help soften the university's elitist edges, making it more palatable to state legislatures that are perpetually susceptible to America's populist streak.[44] When measured against this benefit, scandal is a cheap bill to pay, and one that colleges have paid again and again.

In doing so, colleges have allowed—or encouraged—athletics to become cemented among the core functions of state universities, Thelin argues. Recall the creation of the nation's land-grant institutions, an innovation that helped create public higher education—and, as a side effect, laid the groundwork for college football's ubiquity. Without the Ohio States, Texas A&Ms, and Auburns of the world—all land-grants—college sports would be a weaker force. Thelin has argued that in the early part of the twenty-first century the "A&M" tag that characterizes public higher education was rechristened in practice from the dated "Agricultural and Mechanical" to "Athletics and Medicine." These were "the front doors and neon signs that showcased an enterprising, dynamic state university," Thelin writes, that also allowed public universities a chance to be honest about these dual priorities, whose privileged status had become apparent with every new medical complex and football-stadium renovation. Among the costs of this ascendance, Thelin argues, was that "the historic academic core of the multipurpose state university became literally a step-child."[45]

It sounds like an astonishing case of mission creep. The proliferation of public higher education was about teaching technical skills to a relatively new nation; college football was a side effect of these new campuses' influence. Now big-time sports, Thelin argues, has finally supplanted public higher education's teaching mission as its primary calling card. But the historian points out that sports do fit within the spirit of the "A&M" brand of public service. Whereas teaching crop rotation was a critical service for the public of a developing nation, sports may also be a less critical but still significant service to the citizens of a developed one. "Who in the modern era," Thelin writes, "could not agree that a state university team in the BCS championship or in the NCAA basketball Final Four had not reached out to the entire state's population?"[46]

In the era of streaming television, they can reach a lot further than that. There can be no doubt that college athletics provides pleasure to millions upon millions of people, many of whom who have no other connection to a university. While it brings entertainment to the masses, it also brings intense pleasure to diehard fans. It is not uncommon for such fans to mention their favorite college teams in their obituaries—the ultimate marker of a fulfilling influence.[47] Contributing to a system that produces mass pleasure, even if it does not always produce something of value to the university, may be an end all its own.

When Folt stood before that skeptical student in the aftermath of the Wainstein report, she was challenged to defend the university's athletics enterprise. She did so by invoking the label of the "university of the people," the term Chapel Hill has for decades used to sum up its public mission as a resource to the state. Though Folt was referring specifically to the diversity athletes bring to campus, her remark may have reflected an awareness of UNC's duty to the public. In an era of global influence, athletics may be the most efficient means through which a university like UNC can offer national and global service.

Whether athletics is a silver bullet used to pacify the American public, or a freestanding service to that public, you would think universities would at least acknowledge it. But institutions like UNC are conspicuously bashful about their allegiance to athletics. In his study of college athletics, Clotfelter examined the mission statements of fifty-two colleges that offer big-time sports, and found that fewer than a tenth of them mentioned athletics. Nursing schools, pharmacy schools, and veterinary schools were all mentioned with greater frequency than sports, despite the irrefutable evidence that athletics touches far more lives than the future pharmacists who walk across the stage at commencement.[48]

What accounts for the silence? Sports isn't the only unique characteristic universities carry in the crowd of American organizations. They also pledge themselves to nobler aspirations. As one longtime university president described higher education's better angels,

> Universities must tell the truth. Other institutions are not tied as closely to transparency and veracity, because it's not their tradition, legacy, or expectation. To hold on to the trust of the public, and sometimes to even earn it or reclaim it, universities have to be associated with this kind of disclosure. When they fail to do that, they become just another corrupt institution that should be challenged in every dimension of its enterprise.[49]

Suppose truth telling and moral authority are as important to maintaining public trust as running minor-league sports programs. A catch-22 emerges, because universities must violate the first principle to satisfy the second. To participate in big-time sports, they must utter a transparent falsehood in violation of their higher calling—that their athletes are students first—and accept the ugly scandals that accompany that lie. Perhaps colleges' silence about athletics' primacy is a symptom of this contradiction, the uncomfortable dissonance that prevails when a university declares its adherence to truth while also telling an obvious lie.

This dissonance is far from academic. It requires bridges to be constructed, people to be enlisted to paper over the great divide. In a university profile of Betsy Taylor, the advising employee who Crowder claimed unwittingly provided the inspiration for the paper classes, a faculty member was quoted as saying, "She is one of the reasons that an institution as large as this one wears a human face."[50] The same could be said, to varying degrees, of each of the main characters in this story. Crowder was a consummate helper, seeking to ease the burdens of everyone she came across. "You could go home at night and feel like you had made a difference," she said of the work she did.[51] Boxill worked tirelessly to educate athletes and many other students, hoping some combination of sports and education would do for them what they'd done for her. Willingham worked one-on-one with struggling athletes, doing all she could to help them in the classrooms of this unfamiliar place. And Thorp, too, served as the face of UNC, and attempted shore up its moral authority when he fired Butch Davis, a signal that Carolina valued academics first.

And yet each of these people, whether they knew it or not, worked in their own ways to make the amateur lie seem true. Crowder may not have had preference for athletes, but many players were kept eligible because of her efforts. Boxill may not have known about the more unsavory parts of the paper classes, but she worked as one part of a system that offered only a partial university education to some of its athletes. Willingham, too, was complicit in this system for a time, and faced the wrath of its supporters when she stepped outside of it. Thorp, as an agent of the status quo, did not seek to make bold change while he held power. Enlisted in bridging the contradictions of the amateur myth, each person was eventually punished when things went south: Crowder was branded a mastermind, Boxill a cheat, Willingham was run out of a company town, and Thorp was left without a dream job— chancellor of his forefathers' university. There are no villains in this story, only well-intentioned people who suffered sobering fates.

Those fates should give the university pause. If these were good people, as many of their respective defenders have claimed, how bad must the conditions have been to produce their downfalls? The university presides over those conditions, which have now been altered by degrees ranging from the superficial to the substantive. The ultimate, indisputable condition that produced this outcome, though, was the amateur myth. For as long as it is maintained, it will produce pressures that look a lot like what sent UNC down the road toward scandal, and careers and livelihoods toward ruin.

Some partial reckoning for amateurism may be on the horizon. In 2019, California passed a law barring the state's universities from prohibiting their students from earning money off their own names, images, or likenesses. It was a direct affront to the NCAA, which after some saber rattling conceded that athletes should be allowed to earn some money from their likenesses—as long as such benefits fall squarely within the association's "collegiate model."[52] That phrase is a term of art that the NCAA leadership came up with years ago to describe a system in which the enterprise is commercial but the participants are amateurs.[53] Congressional lawmakers in late 2019 also demonstrated an interest in passing some regulation on compensation for players. College athletes might soon be allowed to seek some compensation; the requirement that they be students too has shown few signs of weakening.

As long as the amateur myth remains in place, the pressures that it exacts will carry a debt to reality. That debt might be deferred by a vigilant compliance staff at every turn. It might be paid by the role engulfment of the athletes who perform the labor. Or it might strike at the very heart of what a campus claims to be, revealing the ugly battle between the forces that tug at its heart. "My fundamental argument in all this business about intercollegiate sports has been the integrity of the university itself," Bill Friday said in 2010. "Are we what we say we are?"[54]

As the scandal at Chapel Hill so vividly demonstrates, the stakes are far from theoretical. Careers, reputations, and lives hang in the balance.

The Smith Center hardwood was lit gold that night as the 2017 season began.

This was a collective celebration, not of a single moment in time, but of a sterling history. Championship banners—1924, 1957, 1982, 1993, 2005, 2009—hung in silent witness of the joyous proceedings. The players took to the court triumphant amid cascading blue strobes, and danced in capes to the song "Holding Out for a Hero."[55] They reenacted the play that led to Michael Jordan's famous jump shot to win the 1982 national championship. Minutes later, they choreographed the game-winning jump shot that had secured the Tar Heels a place in the Final Four that very year. Swish. Cherished memories came to life, materializing in new and exciting forms. The cheering fans got goosebumps.[56]

With a proud history honored and affirmed, the moment came for the new addition. The beaming players and coaches gathered at center court, standing on the sky-blue likeness of the state of North Carolina, and craned their heads toward the rafters. The crowd stood, spontaneously, it seemed, in a show of reverence for what they were about to behold. Highlights from the previous season played on the big screen as a tear-jerking piano anthem blared. The crowd looked to the sky as one when, finally, the new banner was unfurled, white with a powder-blue border—"The University of North Carolina" emblazoned on it. It was one final assertion of the storied program's staying power.

After years of anxiety about a banner coming down, Chapel Hill fans had instead gained one. The thousands roared in deafening jubilation.[57]

"It was perhaps a trick," observed a *New York Times* reporter in attendance, "a hallucination produced by the outpouring of meaning from 21,000 fans invested in the moment, that it immediately felt as if the new flag had always been there, and that it would never go away." Absent some problem undreamed of, this banner was something no one could ever steal from the loyal and faithful masses. For them it meant bragging rights. It meant pride. It meant happiness.

In the crowd that night was a young man who had driven from across the state just hours after completing his application for admission. He hailed from a rural town roughly equidistant from the city where Thorp grew up and from another town simply named "Tar Heel." Amid the celebration, the NCAA verdict hung in the air, a welcome sign that the sorry tale had finally reached its coda. The new banner was just the cherry on top. "We're happy it's over," the young man told the *Times* reporter, channeling the sweet relief of the Tar Heel faithful.

"And even more happy nothing bad happened."[58]

As the winter of 2020 turned to spring, the college-sports world was preparing for its annual bonanza: the NCAA men's basketball championship. But the week before the announcement of the annual bracket, it became clear that COVID-19, the deadly disease caused by a new coronavirus, had arrived on American shores and was spreading beyond control.

Colleges abruptly closed their campuses, moving classes online and sending their students home.[1] Yet for about a week, colleges held out hope that the tournament—the NCAA's major source of revenue— could be played. The optics were bad: How could a college that had deemed campus life too dangerous for its students argue that basketball players should stick around? How could an institution that already suspended nonessential travel send teams on the road? The scenario further stretched the amateur ideal. Colleges were preparing to ask their athletes to do things they would ask of no other student.

On March 12, the NCAA canceled the tournament, and the spring sports season was suddenly over.[2] But the reluctance with which colleges conceded the season's end foreshadowed what would emerge as a striking, yet entirely predictable, theme of the pandemic. In order to preserve the normalcy that the sports calendar guarantees — regular football and basketball games, broadcast to the masses, and the revenue that flows from them—the big-time sports enterprise would have to all but admit that the assertion at the core of amateurism was false.

Even as much of American society shut down, the college-football season was treated in some athletic circles as a fait accompli. "I have zero doubt that we're going to be playing and the stands are going to be packed," said Dabo Swinney, Clemson University's football coach, on

April 3.[3] Those publicly advocating for a season made plain the role of the financial stakes in the decision. "In my opinion, we need to bring our players back," said Mike Gundy, football coach at Oklahoma State University. "They are 18, 19, 20, 21, and 22 years old and they are healthy and they have the ability to fight this virus off. If that is true, then we sequester them, and continue because we need to run money through the state of Oklahoma."[4]

By the early summer, universities in the Power Five conferences had welcomed their players back for workouts. At one point, roughly one-third of Clemson's football team tested positive for the coronavirus, and several other teams were forced to suspend workouts and practices due to outbreaks.[5] As the summer wore on—and coronavirus surged in response to reopening efforts nationwide—every league and conference except for the Power Five began canceling fall sports, saying the health risks were just too great. In August, two members of the Power Five, the Pac-12 and the Big Ten, postponed fall football, citing risks to athletes' health.[6] Several players who had tested positive for COVID-19 had also been diagnosed with a condition called myocarditis, an inflammation of the heart muscle, which might be especially dangerous for athletes.[7] Both conferences reversed course after facing pushback from players, coaches, and fans — and after securing enough tests to administer them to all athletes daily.[8]

Many of the same institutions that rushed to stage a football season decided it wasn't safe to allow students to live on campus. In early August, UNC's in-person fall plan quickly came unraveled just days into the new semester, with hundreds of students testing positive for COVID-19.[9] The university responded by effectively evacuating residence halls and moving all classes online.[10] But athletes were not included in the move. "So what's the difference in student athletes and regular students?" tweeted Garrison Brooks, a UNC basketball player, the same day the university moved classes online. "Are we immune to this virus because we play a sport?"[11] Months later, the University of Pittsburgh men's basketball coach weighed in on one consequence of college sports plowing ahead while much of the rest of society was locked down: "I don't think anyone can say anymore that these young men are amateurs," he said. "That's out the window. They're not. They absolutely aren't."[12]

This clarity translated, momentarily, into increased athlete activ-

ism. Pac-12 players sparked a movement that demanded health pro-
tections and greater revenue-sharing with players—demands that
were incorporated, in part, by the #WeWantToPlay campaign, which
also called for a players association for college athletes.[13] While such
an association is unlikely to come to fruition in the near term, its invo-
cation came amid favorable winds for the economic rights of athletes.
As of spring 2021, when this book went to press, Congress seemed
likely to weaken the NCAA's prohibition on athletes earning money
from their name, image, or likeness.[14] Universities' behavior during the
pandemic seemed to give athletes' advocates more ammunition. In a
filing to the Supreme Court, the plaintiffs in an antitrust suit against
the NCAA cited these "non-amateur realities," observing that programs had athletes "put their health at risk to continue generating
huge revenues for their schools during a pandemic, while other students are told to attend school remotely and stay in their dorms."[15]

That such realizations may be used most prominently in service
of athletes' economic rights, rather than as evidence of the need for
broader reform within universities, is characteristic of the state of
the anti-NCAA movement. As one publication put it, in an article
about how concerns over economic exploitation took over the college-
sports reform movement: "Seldom does the current discussion turn
on whether sports elbows out the needs of non-athlete students, or
corrupts the curriculum, or squanders the energies of university presidents and regents -- or whether it belongs anywhere near what are
supposed to be institutions of higher learning."[16]

A future of greater economic latitude for athletes looks assured. If
reform is limited to that sphere, it will do little to correct the contradictions that fueled the UNC scandal. For as long as colleges pretend
their entertainment arms are wholly united with their academic cores
— and that athletes are amateurs because they are students — they
will court scandal. Like Frank Porter Graham, we must gaze into the
decades ahead and confess a failure of imagination at the "undreamed
of" problems that colleges and their commercialized athletics will continue to produce.

ACKNOWLEDGMENTS

This book would not have been possible without the love and support of my wife, Colleen Murphy. She talked me through rough spots, endured my manic writing and reporting schedule, and was this manuscript's first reader. I am forever thankful to her.

I am grateful to my editor at the University of Michigan Press, Elizabeth Demers, who took a chance on a first-time author's proposal and provided deft editing and insight. Marcia LaBrenz, Daniel Otis, Jack Bernard, Theresa Schmid, Haley Winkle, and Mary Hashman were instrumental in the production and promotion process.

I am indebted to Scott Smallwood, who provided invaluable mentorship and feedback on this book at every stage in the process. This project would not have been possible without the work of Dan Kane, the *News & Observer* investigative reporter who brought much of the information shared in this book into the light of day.

My employer, the *Chronicle of Higher Education*, generously granted me time off to finish this manuscript. Conversations with my colleagues Brock Read, Lindsay Ellis, Emma Pettit, Dan Berrett, Jack Stripling, Eric Hoover, Dan Bauman, and others sharpened this work. Powell Latimer, Mark Simpson-Vos, Sarah Frier, Steve Kolowich, and Goldie Blumenstyk provided key direction in this book's earliest stages. I also appreciate my reviewers, whose suggestions made this work much stronger.

I appreciate the diligence of the staff at UNC's Wilson Special Collections Library, who lifted heavy box after heavy box for my benefit. I also extend my thanks to the staff of the North Carolina Digital Heritage Center, whose digitized newspapers were an invaluable resource.

I'm grateful to subscribers to my Writing a Book newsletter on Substack, where I chronicled this book's creation every step of the way. Their interest and encouragement kept me going. Thank you to the staff of Philz Coffee in Adams Morgan, where much of this book was written.

And I send special thanks to my friends Whitaker Brown and Joe Alter, who housed me during my reporting trips to the Triangle.

NOTES

CHAPTER 1

1. Holden Thorp, interview by author, Washington, D.C., December 16, 2019.

2. Thorp interview.

3. UNC-Chapel Hill, "Chancellor Thorp's Installation Speech," YouTube video, 30:46, October 14, 2008, https://www.youtube.com/watch?v=rmduXUrIchs

4. Thorp interview.

5. WRAL, "UNC Holds Press Conference on NCAA Investigation," WRALSportsFan.com, 22:32, August 26, 2010, https://www.wralsportsfan.com/rs/video/8197533/

6. Thorp interview.

7. The NCAA's highest tier, Division I, includes about 350 member colleges. "NCAA Division I," NCAA.org, National Collegiate Athletic Association, accessed November 7, 2019, http://www.ncaa.org/about?division=d1

8. The NCAA's principle of amateurism is defined in Article 2 of its constitution. NCAA Academic and Membership Affairs Staff, "2018-2019 NCAA Division I Manual," National Collegiate Athletic Association, August 1, 2018, ncaapublications.com/productdownloads/D119.pdf

9. See Chapter 5 for an expanded discussion of this issue.

10. Article 12 of the NCAA's bylaws prohibits athletes at member institutions from earning money through "his or her athletics skill." "2018-2019 NCAA Division I Manual."

11. Reginald Hildebrand, "Anatomy of a Scandal," accessed November 12, 2019, http://media2.newsobserver.com/content/media/2017/1/18/anatomy.pdf

CHAPTER 2

1. Graham appeared before the meeting of the faculty on January 13, 1938. "Athletic Policy Changes Will Be Discussed Today," *Daily Tar Heel*, Jan. 13, 1938, p. 1, http://newspapers.digitalnc.org/lccn/sn92073228/1938-01-13/ed-1/seq-1/. The high temperature observed in Chapel Hill on January 13 was 49 degrees, and the low was 33 degrees. "Record of Climatological Observations," National Oceanic and Atmospheric Administration, accessed November 7, 2019, https://web.archive.org/web/20191107211148/https://www.ncei.noaa.gov/orders/cdo/1936608.pdf

2. Allen Sack and Ellen Staurowsky, *College Athletes for Hire: The Evolution and Legacy of the NCAA's Amateur Myth* (Westport: Praeger Publishers, 1998), 11, 18-19.

3. Sack and Staurowsky 19.

4. John Thelin, *Games Colleges Play: Scandal and Reform in Intercollegiate Athletics* (Baltimore: Johns Hopkins University Press, 1994), Kindle edition, loc. 1021 of 3408.

5. William Snider, *Light on the Hill: A History of the University of North Carolina at Chapel Hill* (Chapel Hill: University of North Carolina Press, 1992), 106.

6. "The Sweetest Story Ever Told; N.C., 6-Va., 0," *Tar Heel*, Dec. 6, 1919, p. 1, http://newspapers.digitalnc.org/lccn/sn92073227/1919-12-06/ed-1/seq-1/

7. "Gift of $275,000 for Stadium Made by William R. Kenan," *Tar Heel*, Nov. 16, 1926, p. 1, http://newspapers.digitalnc.org/lccn/sn92073227/1926-11-16/ed-1/seq-1/

8. "Gifts to the University," *Tar Heel*, Nov. 16, 1926, p. 2, http://newspapers.digitalnc.org/lccn/sn92073227/1926-11-16/ed-1/seq-2/

9. "Athletics at the University," *Tar Heel*, Mar. 30, 1893, p. 1, http://newspapers.digitalnc.org/lccn/sn92073227/1893-03-30/ed-1/seq-1/

10. Sack and Staurowsky 24.

11. Howard Savage, *American College Athletics* (New York: Carnegie Foundation for the Advancement of Teaching, 1929), viii, http://archive.carnegiefoundation.org/pdfs/elibrary/American_College_Athletics.pdf

12. Savage 265.

13. "U.N.C. Tramples Terps, 33-0," *Daily Tar Heel*, Oct. 13, 1935, p. 1, http://newspapers.digitalnc.org/lccn/sn92073228/1935-10-13/ed-1/seq-1/

14. "Honor Violation Charges Brought Against Sniscak," *Daily Tar Heel*, Oct. 13, 1935, pp. 1, 4, http://newspapers.digitalnc.org/lccn/sn92073228/1935-10-13/ed-1/seq-1/

15. "Sniscak Charges Maryland Stars to Be Ineligible," *Daily Tar Heel*, Oct. 15, 1935, p. 1, http://newspapers.digitalnc.org/lccn/sn92073228/1935-10-15/ed-1/seq-1/

16. The following day's front page made it clear that Graham, not a faculty committee, had acted to dismiss Sniscak. "Faculty Dismisses Sniscak," *Daily Tar Heel*, Oct. 18, 1935, p. 1, http://newspapers.digitalnc.org/lccn/sn92073228/1935-10-18/ed-1/seq-1/

17. Andy Thomason, "One Man Had a Plan to Keep Money Out of College Sports. Here's What Happened," *Chronicle of Higher Education*, Aug. 12, 2014, https://www.chronicle.com/article/One-Man-Had-a-Plan-to-Keep/148359

18. "Rule 13 Now Stricken From Graham Plan," *Daily Tar Heel*, Dec. 12, 1937, p. 1, http://newspapers.digitalnc.org/lccn/sn92073228/1937-12-12/ed-1/seq-1/

19. "Text Of Graham's Speech On Athletics," *Daily Tar Heel*, Jan. 19, 1938, p. 1-2, 4, http://newspapers.digitalnc.org/lccn/sn92073228/1938-01-19/ed-1/seq-1/

20. Thomason.

21. Sack and Staurowsky 43–44.

22. Sack and Staurowsky 45.

23. Thelin 1430.

24. Walter Byers, *Unsportsmanlike Conduct: Exploiting College Athletes* (Ann Arbor: University of Michigan Press, 1995), Kindle edition, 73.

25. Sack and Staurowsky 47.

26. Sack and Staurowsky 68.

27. Taylor Branch, "The Shame of College Sports," *The Atlantic,* October 2011, https://www.theatlantic.com/magazine/archive/2011/10/the-shame-of-college-sports/308643/

28. Thelin 904.

29. Snider 264.

30. Biff Roberts, "We Cage A Cager," *Daily Tar Heel,* Sept. 24, 1952, p. 4, http://newspapers.digitalnc.org/lccn/sn92073228/1952-09-24/ed-1/seq-4/

31. Snider 264, 256.

32. William Link, *William Friday: Power, Purpose, and American Higher Education,* 2nd ed. (Chapel Hill: University of North Carolina Press, 1995), 105, https://books.google.com/books?id=hSlHAQAAQBAJ&printsec=frontcover#v=onepage&q&f=false

33. Link 106.

34. Dean Smith and Gerald Bell, *The Carolina Way: Leadership Lessons from a Life in Coaching* (New York: Penguin, 2004), 248.

35. Mark Asher and Paul Ensslin, "North Carolina Coach Dean Smith to Retire Today," *Washington Post,* Oct. 9, 1997, https://www.washington-post.com/archive/sports/1997/10/09/north-carolina-coach-dean-smith-to-retire-today/30e1563a-4c8b-4356-9529-64b37b22931e/

36. Brendan Marks, "With Four Corners Offense, Dean Smith Changed Basketball," *Daily Tar Heel,* Feb. 9, 2015, https://www.dailytarheel.com/article/2015/02/with-four-corners-offense-dean-smith-changed-basketball

37. Gary Smith, "The Relentless Scrimmage In Dean Smith," *Inside Sports,* Mar. 1982, https://thestacks.deadspin.com/the-relentless-scrimmage-in-dean-smith-1684918367

38. Cindy Boren, "Michael Jordan on Dean Smith: 'My Mentor, My Teacher, Second Father' (Updated)," *Washington Post,* Feb. 8, 2015, https://www.washingtonpost.com/news/early-lead/wp/2015/02/08/michael-jordan-on-dean-smith-my-mentor-my-teacher-my-second-father/

39. Gene Upchurch, "A Successful Basketball Coach Discusses the Value of College Education," *Daily Tar Heel,* Oct. 10, 1977, p. 6, http://newspapers.digitalnc.org/lccn/sn92073228/1977-10-10/ed-1/seq-6/

40. Dean Smith 218.

41. Gary Moss, "Dean Smith's Courage," *University Gazette,* Nov. 2013, https://www.unc.edu/posts/2013/11/20/dean-smiths-courage/

42. Kevin Blackistone, "Impact of Quiet Revolutionary Dean Smith Only Began on Basketball Court," *The Guardian,* Feb. 8, 2015, https://www.

theguardian.com/sport/2015/feb/08/impact-of-quiet-revolutionary-dean-smith-only-began-on-basketball-court

43. Bradley Saacks, "Dean Smith Was an Outspoken Democrat in North Carolina," *Daily Tar Heel*, Feb. 9, 2015, https://www.dailytarheel.com/article/2015/02/dean-smith-was-an-outspoken-democrat-in-north-carolina

44. Bill Fields, "Dean Smith: Becoming a Classic Over Time," *Daily Tar Heel*, Dec. 4, 1980, p. 11, http://newspapers.digitalnc.org/lccn/sn92073228/1980-12-04/ed-1/seq-18/

45. Dean Smith 256.

46. Madeline Levine, telephone interview by author, October 18, 2018.

47. Dean Smith 251.

48. S. L. Price, "Is Dean Smith Really God?," *Daily Tar Heel*, Mar. 31, 1982, p. 12, http://newspapers.digitalnc.org/lccn/sn92073228/1982-03-31/ed-1/seq-12/

49. Thelin 2326.

50. Sack 97.

51. Sack 98.

52. Thelin 2399.

53. Thelin 2423.

54. Charles Clotfelter, *Big-Time Sports in American Universities*, 2nd ed. (New York: Cambridge University Press, 2019), 66-70.

55. Thelin 2416-23.

56. Dean Smith, "Smith: More Emphasis On Academics," *Charlotte Observer*, Oct. 7, 1983, p. 1B.

57. "Bravo, Father LoSchiavo," *Charlotte Observer*, Aug. 8, 1982, p. 1B.

58. Dean Smith, *Carolina Way*, 250.

59. Associated Press, "Smith, Cosell Testify Before Subcommittee," *Charlotte Observer*, June 27, 1984, p. 1E.

60. Dean Smith, *Carolina Way*, 255.

61. "Space Jam—The Opening Scene [HD]," YouTube video, 2:27, posted by "DrSalvadoctopus," Aug. 7, 2013, https://www.youtube.com/watch?v=3axk73ToiFQ

62. Jim Naughton, "U. of North Carolina Is Proud of Its Balance of Big-Time Athletics and Quality Academics," *Chronicle of Higher Education*, Dec. 5, 1997, https://www.chronicle.com/article/U-of-North-Carolina-Is-Proud/99564

63. "Dean Smith UNC Chapel Hill Basketball Coach 1994," North Carolina People With William Friday, UNC-TV, 1994, 26:45, https://www.unctv.org/watch/unctv-originals/nc-people/

CHAPTER 3

1. Dan Kane, "Deborah Crowder's Story Could Bring NCAA Investigators to UNC," *News & Observer*, Apr. 15, 2014, https://www.newsobserver.com/news/local/education/unc-scandal/article10322303.html

2. "Deborah Crowder 5/10/17 Transcript," Bond, Schoeneck & King, May 10, 2017, p. 15, in "Exhibits Cited in Response to Second ANOA," University of North Carolina at Chapel Hill, May 25, 2017, https://carolinacommitment. unc.edu/files/2017/05/Exhibits-Table-of-Contents-Exhibit-1-1.pdf

3. Joe Sanders, "BSM Asks Removal Of Cathey, Henry," *Daily Tar Heel*, Dec. 12, 1968, p. 1, http://newspapers.digitalnc.org/lccn/sn920732 28/1968-12-12/ed-1/seq-1/

4. "'Cannot Provide Unique Treatment For Any Race,'" *Daily Tar Heel*, Feb. 4, 1969, p. 3, http://newspapers.digitalnc.org/lccn/sn92073228/1969-02-04/ ed-1/seq-3/

5. Charla Haber, "Dawson Appoints Members To Afro-American Body," *Daily Tar Heel*, Feb. 8, 1969, p. 6, http://newspapers.digitalnc.org/lccn/ sn92073228/1969-02-08/ed-1/seq-6/

6. Steve Plaisance, "Afro-American Degree Part Of '69 Curriculum," *Daily Tar Heel*, Apr. 19, 1969, p. 1, http://newspapers.digitalnc.org/lccn/ sn92073228/1969-04-19/ed-1/seq-1/

7. Fabio Rojas, *From Black Power to Black Studies: How a Radical Social Movement Became an Academic Discipline* (Baltimore: Johns Hopkins University Press, 2007), Kindle edition, 68-93.

8. "Bicentennial Fact Book 1993," University of North Carolina at Chapel Hill, 18, https://oira.unc.edu/files/2017/07/fb1994_bicent.pdf

9. John Thelin, *A History of American Higher Education*, 3rd ed. (Baltimore: Johns Hopkins University Press, 2019), 261.

10. Bicentennial 3.

11. Thelin, *A History* 260.

12. Norman Black, "Kepner Sees End to Overcrowding," *Daily Tar Heel*, Sept. 30, 1971, p. 1, http://newspapers.digitalnc.org/lccn/ sn92073228/1971-09-30/ed-1/seq-1/

13. Janet Langston, "Transfers Without Housing." *Daily Tar Heel*, Jul. 26, 1973, p. 1, http://newspapers.digitalnc.org/lccn/sn92073228/1973-07-26/ ed-1/seq-1/

14. Janet Langston, "Housing Shortage Hits Critical Stage," *Daily Tar Heel*, Aug. 28, 1973, p. 1, http://newspapers.digitalnc.org/lccn/ sn92073228/1973-08-28/ed-1/seq-1/

15. "Ah . . . Preregistration," *Daily Tar Heel*, Nov. 16, 1971, p. 1, http://news-papers.digitalnc.org/lccn/sn92073228/1971-11-16/ed-1/seq-1/

16. Jennifer Miller, "Drop-Add: From Gym to Tower," *Daily Tar Heel*, Aug. 29, 1974, p. 2A, http://newspapers.digitalnc.org/lccn/sn92073228/1974-08-29/ ed-1/seq-2/

17. Harry Smith, "Preregistration Begins Today," *Daily Tar Heel*, Nov. 15, 1971, p. 1, http://newspapers.digitalnc.org/lccn/sn92073228/1971-11-15/ ed-1/seq-1/

18. "Freshmen Offer First Week Impressions," *Daily Tar Heel*, Aug. 29, 1974, p. 5B, http://newspapers.digitalnc.org/lccn/sn92073228/1974-08-29/ ed-1/seq-13/

19. Kenneth Wainstein et al., *Investigation of Irregular Classes in the Department of African and Afro-American Studies at the University of North Carolina at Chapel Hill* (Cadwalader, Wickersham & Taft LLP), 1, Oct. 16, 2014, https://carolinacommitment.unc.edu/files/2014/10/UNC-FINAL-REPORT.pdf

20. Greg Turosak, "500 Students to Quit School," *Daily Tar Heel*, Nov. 23, 1971, p. 1, http://newspapers.digitalnc.org/lccn/sn92073228/1971-11-23/ed-1/seq-1/

21. Wainstein 1.

22. Roann Bishop, "BSM Protests UNC Insensitivity," *Daily Tar Heel*, Apr. 5, 1979, p. 1, http://newspapers.digitalnc.org/lccn/sn92073228/1979-04-05/ed-1/seq-1/

23. Michele Mecke, "Expansion of African Studies Cited," *Daily Tar Heel*, Feb. 21, 1978, p. 1, http://newspapers.digitalnc.org/lccn/sn92073228/1978-02-21/ed-1/seq-1/

24. Joy Thompson, "UNC Black Studies Takes Lead in Nation," *Daily Tar Heel*, Nov. 6, 1985, p. 2, http://newspapers.digitalnc.org/lccn/sn92073228/1985-11-06/ed-1/seq-2/

25. Liz Lucas, "Freshmen Must Adjust to Change in Curriculum," *Daily Tar Heel*, Aug. 30, 1982, p. 1, http://newspapers.digitalnc.org/lccn/sn92073228/1982-08-30/ed-1/seq-1/

26. Thompson 1.

27. Joy Thompson, "Hildebrand Leaves UNC," *Black Ink*, Sept. 17, 1985, p. 5, http://newspapers.digitalnc.org/lccn/2015236558/1985-09-17/ed-1/seq-5/

28. Newspaper clipping, Box 2:3, in Office of the Dean of the College of Arts and Sciences of the University of North Carolina at Chapel Hill Records #40076, University Archives, Wilson Library, University of North Carolina at Chapel Hill.

29. Letter to the *N&O* editor from Harris and Catharine Newbury, Box 2:3, in Office of the Dean of the College of Arts and Sciences of the University of North Carolina at Chapel Hill Records #40076, University Archives, Wilson Library, University of North Carolina at Chapel Hill.

30. Eric Bolash, "African Studies Seek Department Status," *Daily Tar Heel*, Mar. 28, 1991, p. 5, http://newspapers.digitalnc.org/lccn/sn92073228/1991-03-28/ed-1/seq-5/

31. Memo from Stephen Birdsall to Gillian T. Cell, Box 2:3, in Office of the Dean of the College of Arts and Sciences of the University of North Carolina at Chapel Hill Records #40076, University Archives, Wilson Library, University of North Carolina at Chapel Hill.

32. Wainstein 15.

33. Laura Ertel, "Supporting the Democratization of Africa," *Duke Law Magazine*, Spring 1997, p. 58-59, https://law.duke.edu/news/pdf/lawmag spring97.pdf

34. Wainstein 15.

35. Nicole Comparato, "Swept Up in Scandal," *Daily Tar Heel*, Aug. 21, 2012, https://www.dailytarheel.com/article/2012/08/swept_up_in_scandal

36. Sarah Suiter, "Teaching Award Winners Announced," *Daily Tar Heel*, Apr. 10, 1991, p. 1, http://newspapers.digitalnc.org/lccn/sn92073228/1991-04-10/ed-1/seq-1/

37. Reginald F. Hildebrand, interview by Charlotte Fryar, March 27, 2017, interview L-0460, transcript and recording, Southern Oral History Program Collection (#4007) at the Southern Historical Collection, Louis Round Wilson Special Collections Library, UNC-Chapel Hill, https://dc.lib.unc.edu/cdm/compoundobject/collection/sohp/id/27514/rec/1, 38-39.

38. Wainstein 17.

39. Memo from Nyang'oro to Curriculum faculty dated June 29, 1992, Box 2:3, in Office of the Dean of the College of Arts and Sciences of the University of North Carolina at Chapel Hill Records #40076, University Archives, Wilson Library, University of North Carolina at Chapel Hill.

40. Memo from Nyang'oro to Stephen Birdsall dated June 29, 1993, Box 2:3, in Office of the Dean of the College of Arts and Sciences of the University of North Carolina at Chapel Hill Records #40076, University Archives, Wilson Library, University of North Carolina at Chapel Hill.

41. "Deborah Crowder 5/10/17" 18.

42. "Deborah Crowder 5/10/17" 24.

43. Julius E. Nyang'oro, Acknowledgments of *The State and Capitalist Development in Africa: Declining Political Economies* (New York: Praeger Publishers, 1989).

44. Email from Julius Nyang'oro to Deborah Crowder, WRAL.com, Feb. 2, 2007, https://www.wral.com/search-thousands-of-unc-scandal-records/15030171/#174294. "Search thousands of UNC scandal records."

45. Letter from James W. Dean Jr. and Felicia A. Washington to S. Alphonse Mutima, University of North Carolina at Chapel Hill, Nov. 12, 2015, https://carolinacommitment.unc.edu/files/2015/11/MUTIMA-11.12.15.pdf

46. Tim McMillan, interview by Charlotte Fryar, November 29, 2017, interview L-0462, transcript and recording, Southern Oral History Program Collection (#4007) at the Southern Historical Collection, Louis Round Wilson Special Collections Library, UNC-Chapel Hill, https://dc.lib.unc.edu/cdm/compoundobject/collection/sohp/id/27535/rec/1, 74.

47. Michael Lambert, telephone interview by author, December 18, 2019.

48. Hildebrand interview 50-51.

49. *Request for Authorization to Attain Departmental Status for the Curriculum in African and Afro-American Studies at the University of North Carolina at Chapel Hill*, Feb. 26, 1996, Box 2:3 in Office of the Dean of the College of Arts and Sciences of the University of North Carolina at Chapel Hill Records #40076, University Archives, Wilson Library, University of North Carolina at Chapel Hill.

50. *African and Afro-American Studies 1997-98 Annual Report*, p. 1, Box 2:3, in Office of the Dean of the College of Arts and Sciences of the University of

North Carolina at Chapel Hill Records #40076, University Archives, Wilson Library, University of North Carolina at Chapel Hill.

51. Betsy Taylor, telephone interview by author, November 13, 2018.

52. Joseph Lowman, telephone interview by author, October 2, 2018.

53. Taylor.

54. "Deborah Crowder 5/10/17" 51.

55. "Deborah Crowder 5/10/17" 53.

56. Wainstein 17-18.

57. Wainstein 1.

58. "Deborah Crowder 5/10/17" 57.

59. "Deborah Crowder 5/10/17" 66-67.

60. Wainstein 42.

61. Email from Chris Faison to Deborah Crowder, WRAL.com, May 15, 2009, https://www.wral.com/search-thousands-of-unc-scandal-records/15030171/#1404164, "Search thousands of UNC scandal records."

62. Email from unnamed student to Deborah Crowder, WRAL.com, https://www.wral.com/search-thousands-of-unc-scandal-records/15030171/#1362495, "Search thousands of UNC scandal records."

63. *2014 Independent Inquiry Redacted Supplementary Documents*, University of North Carolina at Chapel Hill, 2014, p. 114, https://carolinacommitment.unc.edu/files/2014/10/UNC-FINAL-REPORT-EXHIBITS.pdf

CHAPTER 4

1. Jan Boxill, interview by author, Chapel Hill, N.C., February 13, 2019.

2. Brian Davis, telephone interview by author, December 17, 2018.

3. Lorenzo Middleton, "NCAA Toughens Rules, Says Athletes Must Complete 12 Credits Each Term," *Chronicle of Higher Education*, Jan. 19, 1981.

4. John A. Crowl, "NCAA Votes Stiffer Academic Requirements for Participants in Intercollegiate Sports," *Chronicle of Higher Education*, Jan. 19, 1983.

5. Davis.

6. John Blanchard, interview by author, Chapel Hill, N.C., November 14, 2018.

7. Beth Williams, "Sidewalk Restoration to End Project," *Daily Tar Heel*, Aug. 29, 1986, p. 3, http://newspapers.digitalnc.org/lccn/sn92073228/1986-08-29/ed-1/seq-3/

8. Phyllis A. Fair, "Field House Center to Aid Athletes," *Daily Tar Heel*, Apr. 7, 1986, p. 4, http://newspapers.digitalnc.org/lccn/sn92073228/1986-04-07/ed-1/seq-4/

9. Jan Boxill, telephone interview by author, December 17, 2019.

10. Tanya Lamb, telephone interview by author, July 3, 2019.

11. Kit Wellman, telephone interview by author, July 1, 2019.

12. Boxill, February 13.

13. Boxill, February 13.

14. Wainstein 14.

15. "Deborah Crowder 5/10/17" 34.
16. "Deborah Crowder 5/10/17" 40.
17. Lambert.
18. Handwritten note from Julius Nyang'oro to Steve Birdsall, Nov. 9, 1993, Box 2:3, in Office of the Dean of the College of Arts and Sciences of the University of North Carolina at Chapel Hill Records #40076, University Archives, Wilson Library, University of North Carolina at Chapel Hill.
19. Jay Smith and Mary Willingham, *Cheated: The UNC Scandal, the Education of Athletes, and the Future of Big-Time College Sports* (Lincoln, NE: Potomac Books, 2015), Kindle edition, loc. 437 of 6866.
20. Comparato.
21. Wainstein 16.
22. Lambert.
23. Timothy Shaw, telephone interview by author, June 22, 2019.
24. *2014 Independent* 90-92.
25. Wainstein 2.
26. Boxill, February 13.
27. Laura Stoehr, "UNC Honors Excellence in Teaching," *Daily Tar Heel*, Feb. 20, 1998, p. 3, http://newspapers.digitalnc.org/lccn/sn92068245/1998-02-20/ed-1/seq-3/
28. Dean Smith, foreword to *Sports Ethics: An Anthology*, edited by Jan Boxill (Malden, MA: Blackwell Publishing, 2003).
29. Boxill, February 13.
30. Caitlin McCabe, "Jan Boxill Elected to Lead the UNC Faculty Council," *Daily Tar Heel*, Apr. 26, 2011, https://www.dailytarheel.com/article/2011/04/jan_boxill_elected_to_lead_the_unc_faculty_council

CHAPTER 5

1. Mary Willingham, telephone conversation with author, December 11, 2019.
2. Felicia Paik, "Private Properties," *Wall Street Journal*, Oct. 15, 1999, https://www.wsj.com/articles/SB939937985918003898
3. Willingham.
4. Willingham.
5. Boxill, December 17.
6. Willingham.
7. "Common Data Set 2018-2019," University of North Carolina at Chapel Hill, 11, https://oira.unc.edu/files/2019/02/CDS_2018-2019_20190213.pdf
8. "Common Data Set 2018-2019," University of Louisville, 10, https://louisville.edu/oapa/institutional-research-and-planning/docs/copy_of_20182019CommonDataSet.pdf
9. "Intercollegiate Athletic Report 2004-2005," University of North Carolina Board of Governors, 3, https://devwww2.northcarolina.edu/sites/default/files/documents/intercollegiate_athletics_report_2004-2005.pdf

10. Blanchard.

11. Stanley Black, telephone conversation with author, March 11, 2019.

12. Email from Peter Coclanis to John Blanchard, WRAL.com, https://www.wral.com/search-thousands-of-unc-scandal-records/15030171/#161012, "Search thousands of UNC scandal records."

13. Email from Beverly Smith to Barbara Polk, WRAL.com, https://www.wral.com/search-thousands-of-unc-scandal-records/15030171/#161011, "Search thousands of UNC scandal records."

14. Email from Trudier Harris, Dec. 4, 2019.

15. "Faculty Committee on Athletic Admissions," WRAL.com,https://www.wral.com/search-thousands-of-unc-scandal-records/15030171/#315675, "Search thousands of UNC scandal records."

16. Blanchard.

17. Data sent from Stephen M. Farmer to Vince Ille, Aug. 3, 2012, WRAL.com, https://www.wral.com/search-thousands-of-unc-scandal-re-cords/15030171/#998192, https://www.wral.com/search-thousands-of-unc-scandal-records/15030171/#998197, https://www.wral.com/search-thousands-of-unc-scandal-records/15030171/#998198, and https://www.wral.com/search-thousands-of-unc-scandal-records/15030171/#998199, "Search thousands of UNC scandal records."

The SAT's shortcomings as a measure of academic preparedness or intelligence are well documented; it is an imperfect measure, but one that is widely used in college admissions.

18. *Annual Report: Academic Support Program for Student-Athletes*, 1996-1997, 3, Box 1:1, in Office of the Dean of the College of Arts and Sciences of the University of North Carolina at Chapel Hill Records #40076, University Archives, Wilson Library, University of North Carolina at Chapel Hill.

19. Willingham.

20. Bradley Bethel, telephone conversation with author, October 21, 2019.

21. Patricia Adler and Peter Adler, *Backboards & Blackboards: College Athletes and Role Engulfment* (New York: Columbia University Press, 1991), 167.

22. Steve Delsohn, "UNC's McCants: 'Just Show up, Play,'" *ABC News*, June 6, 2014, https://abcnews.go.com/Sports/uncs-mccants-show-play/story?id=24023238

23. Chrystal Baptist, telephone conversation with author, January 17, 2019.

24. *Annual Report*.

25. Blanchard.

26. Willingham.

27. Wainstein 94.

28. Blanchard.

29. Tom Friend, "Peppers Turns to Former Advisor for Help," *ESPN The Magazine*, Feb. 19, 2003, http://a.espncdn.com/nfl/columns/misc/1511385.html

30. Dan Kane, "Sports Agent Taught Class at UNC-CH," *News & Observer*, Aug. 27 2011, https://www.newsobserver.com/news/local/education/unc-scandal /article15573086.html

31. "Summaries of Rules Changes Approved by Delegates At Last Week's NCAA Convention," *Chronicle of Higher Education*, Jan. 16, 1991, https://www. chronicle.com/article/Summaries-of-Rules-Changes/86906

32. Douglas Lederman, "NCAA Raises Academic Standards for College Athletes," *Chronicle of Higher Education*, Jan. 15, 1992, https://www.chronicle. com/article/NCAA-Raises-Academic-Standards/81762

33. Welch Suggs, "NCAA Approves New Academic Standards for Athletes," *Chronicle of Higher Education*, Nov. 1, 2002, https://www.chronicle.com/ article/NCAA-Approves-New-Academic/115093

34. Sara Lipka, "NCAA Officials Establish New Penalties for Teams With Consistently Poor Academic Performance," *Chronicle of Higher Education*, Aug. 4, 2006, https://www.chronicle.com/article/NCAA-Officials -Establish-New/118843

35. Jaimie Lee, interview by author, Chapel Hill, N.C., August 23, 2019.

36. Baptist.

37. Associated Press, "North Carolina Names Butch Davis New Head Coach," Nov. 13, 2006, https://www.espn.com/college-football/news/sto ry?id=2659982

38. Willingham interview.

39. Blanchard.

40. *Intercollegiate Athletics Report*, University of North Carolina Board of Governors, August 2010, https://www.northcarolina.edu/sites/default/files/ documents/intercollegiate_athletics_report_2007-2008_and_2008-2009. pdf, 6.

41. Data from Farmer, https://www.wral.com/search-thousands-of-unc -scandal-records/15030171/#998198

42. *Intercollegiate Athletics Report*, University of North Carolina General Administration, April 2013, https://www.northcarolina.edu/sites/default/ files/documents/intercollegiate_athletics_report_2010-2011_and_2011- 2012.pdf, 4.

43. Data from Farmer.

44. Willingham interview.

45. "Deborah Crowder 5/10/17" 45.

46. Email from Deborah Crowder to Wayne Walden, WRAL.com, https://www. wral.com/search-thousands-of-unc-scandal-records/15030171/#488385, "Search thousands of UNC scandal records."

47. Email from Deborah Crowder to Jaimie Lee, WRAL.com, https://www. wral.com/search-thousands-of-unc-scandal-records/15030171/#503945, "Search thousands of UNC scandal records."

48. Email from Deborah Crowder to Brent Blanton, WRAL.com, https://www. wral.com/search-thousands-of-unc-scandal-records/15030171/#611088, "Search thousands of UNC scandal records."

49. Smith and Willingham 3862-73.

50. Smith and Willingham 3902-13.

51. Smith and Willingham 3791.

52. Willingham interview.

53. Mary Willingham, "Academics & Athletics—A Clash of Cultures: Division I Football Programs," master's thesis, University of North Carolina at Greensboro, 2009, http://citeseerx.ist.psu.edu/viewdoc/download?doi=10.1.1.469.5236&rep=rep1&type=pdf

54. Willingham interview.

55. Wainstein 42.

56. "Deborah Crowder 5/10/17" 19.

57. Email from Cynthia Reynolds to Deborah Crowder, WRAL.com, https://www.wral.com/search-thousands-of-unc-scandal-records/15030171/#580411, "Search thousands of UNC scandal records."

58. Email from Wayne Walden to Deborah Crowder, WRAL.com, Nov. 11, 2008, https://www.wral.com/search-thousands-of-unc-scandal-records/15030171/#618633, "Search thousands of UNC scandal records."

59. Email from Brent Blanton to Deborah Crowder, WRAL.com, May 28 2009, https://www.wral.com/search-thousands-of-unc-scandal-records/15030171/#606003, "Search thousands of UNC scandal records."

60. Email exchange between Robert Mercer and Harold Woodard, WRAL.com, Oct. 16, 2009, https://www.wral.com/search-thousands-of-unc-scandal-records/15030171/#631748, "Search thousands of UNC scandal records."

61. "Morrisville, NC Weather History," Weather Underground, Nov. 3, 2009, https://www.wunderground.com/history/daily/KRDU/date/2009-11-3

62. Wainstein 66.

63. Blanchard.

64. Wainstein 85.

65. Wainstein 103-4.

66. Wainstein 22-23.

67. Lambert.

CHAPTER 6

1. "Morrisville, NC Weather History," Weather Underground, Oct. 12, 2008, https://www.wunderground.com/history/daily/KRDU/date/2008-10-12

2. "Chancellor Thorp's Installation Speech," YouTube video, 30:46, posted by "UNC-Chapel Hill," Oct. 14, 2008, https://www.youtube.com/watch?v=rmduXUrIchs

3. Snider 256.

4. David E. Brown, "Holden Thorp '86 Named 10th Chancellor," *Carolina Alumni Review*, May 8, 2008, https://alumni.unc.edu/news/holden-thorp-86-named-10th-chancellor/

5. Bruce Egan, "The Art of the Possible," *Carolina Alumni Review*, January/February 2002, http://www.carolinaalumnireview.com/carolinaalumnireview/20020102/MobilePagedReplica.action?pm=2&folio=20#pg22

6. Thorp interview.

7. Brown.

8. Brown.

9. *Fact Book 2008-2009*, Office of Institutional Research and Assessment, University of North Carolina at Chapel Hill, p. 48, https://oira.unc.edu/files/2017/07/fb2008_2009.pdf

10. Allie Grasgreen, "An Academic Slam Dunk," *Inside Higher Ed*, March 18, 2013, https://www.insidehighered.com/news/2013/03/18/academic-performance-tournament-bracket-march-madness-higher-ed-crowd

11. Thorp interview.

12. Michael Workman, "Smith, UNC Ink $4.7 Million Deal With Nike," *Daily Tar Heel*, Oct. 4, 1993, p. 1, http://newspapers.digitalnc.org/lccn/sn92068245/1993-10-04/ed-1/seq-1/

13. Joe Giglio, "UNC and Nike Headed for Another Contract But Don't Expect Ohio State or Texas-Type Money," *News & Observer*, Jan. 22, 2018, https://www.newsobserver.com/sports/college/acc/unc/article195996949.html

14. Email from Holden Thorp to Bernadette Gray-Little, Elmira Mangum, and Bruce Carney, Box 14, in the Office of Chancellor of the University of North Carolina at Chapel Hill: H. Holden Thorp Records #40321, University Archives, Wilson Library, University of North Carolina at Chapel Hill.

15. Seth Wright, "Kenan Readies for Expansion," *Daily Tar Heel*, April 8, 2008, p. 8, http://newspapers.digitalnc.org/lccn/sn92068245/2008-04-08/ed-1/seq-8/

16. Thorp interview.

17. Email from Holden Thorp to Caroline Johnson, dated Nov. 16, 2009, Box 14, in the Office of Chancellor of the University of North Carolina at Chapel Hill: H. Holden Thorp Records #40321, University Archives, Wilson Library, University of North Carolina at Chapel Hill.

18. Handwritten card from Holden Thorp, dated Nov. 11, 2009, Box 14, in the Office of Chancellor of the University of North Carolina at Chapel Hill: H. Holden Thorp Records #40321, University Archives, Wilson Library, University of North Carolina at Chapel Hill.

19. Handwritten card from Holden Thorp, dated Nov. 30, 2010, Box 14, in the Office of Chancellor of the University of North Carolina at Chapel Hill: H. Holden Thorp Records #40321, University Archives, Wilson Library, University of North Carolina at Chapel Hill.

20. Thorp interview.

21. Roger Perry, telephone interview by author, November 13, 2019.

22. *Keeping Faith With the Student-Athlete: A New Model for Intercollegiate Athletics*, Knight Commission on Intercollegiate Athletics, Mar. 1991, https://

www.knightcommission.org/wp-content/uploads/2008/10/1991-93_kcia_report.pdf

23. "The N.C.A.A. Gets It Right," *New York Times*, Jan. 23, 1996, https://www.nytimes.com/1996/01/23/opinion/the-ncaa-gets-it-right.html

24. Art & Science Group, LLC, *Quantitative and Qualitative Research with Football Bowl Subdivision University Presidents on the Costs and Financing of Intercollegiate Athletics: Report of Findings and Implications*, Knight Commission on Intercollegiate Athletics, Oct. 2009, p. 2, https://www.knightcommission.org/wp-content/uploads/2017/09/kcia-president_survey_2009.pdf

25. Art & Science 18.

26. Art & Science 16.

27. Art & Science 44.

28. Art & Science 43.

29. Art & Science 42.

30. Art & Science 31.

31. Art & Science 31-32.

32. Art & Science 30.

33. Art & Science 16.

34. Art & Science 15.

35. Thorp interview.

36. Jason Kirk, "UNC's 7-Year-Long NCAA Scandal Started When a Player Tweeted a Rick Ross Lyric at 6 a.m. in 2010," *SB Nation*, Oct. 13, 2017, https://www.sbnation.com/2017/10/13/16468658/north-carolina-ncaa-sanctions-scandal-investigation

37. J. P. Giglio, "Austin: 'I Messed Up' at UNC," *News & Observer*, Jan. 22, 2011, https://web.archive.org/web/20110808035234/http://www.newsobserver.com:80/2011/01/22/936299/austin-i-messed-up.html

38. Art & Science 20.

39. Committee on Infractions, *University of North Carolina, Chapel Hill Public Infractions Report*, National Collegiate Athletic Association, Mar. 12 2012, p. 11, https://apsa.unc.edu/files/2019/06/NCAA-Public-Infractions-Report-Appendix-2-March-2012.pdf

40. *Request for Reinstatement and/or Self Report of NCAA Secondary Violation (Level I)*, WRAL.com, Sept. 2010, p. 6, https://wwwcache.wralsportsfan.com/asset/colleges/unc/2012/10/26/11706694/Documents_for_Production_10-26-12.pdf

41. *Request* 17.

42. Thorp interview.

43. WRAL, "UNC Holds."

44. "Marvin Austin Suspended Indefinitely," *ESPN.com*, Sept. 1, 2010, https://www.espn.com/college-football/news/story?id=5520574

45. Heather Dinich, "Thirteen Tar Heels Ruled Out for Opener," *ESPN.com*, Sept. 3, 2010, https://www.espn.com/college-football/news/story?id=5527407

46. Thorp interview.

47. Ray Glier, "Short-Handed Tar Heels Rally But Fall Short," *New York*

Times, Sept. 5, 2010, https://www.nytimes.com/2010/09/05/sports/ncaa-football/05unc.html

48. Charles Robinson, "Money Trail Ties Agent, Ex-UNC Coach," *Yahoo! Sports*, Sept. 29, 2010, https://sports.yahoo.com/news/money-trail-ties-agent-ex-235700914-ncaaf.html

49. "2010 North Carolina Tar Heels Schedule and Results," Sports Reference, https://www.sports-reference.com/cfb/schools/north-carolina/2010-schedule.html

50. Associated Press, "UNC Clips Tennessee in 2OT After Controversial Final Drive in 4th," *ESPN.com*, Dec. 31, 2010, https://www.espn.com/college-football/recap?gameId=303642633

51. "Timeline of UNC Investigation," *News & Observer*, Jul. 28, 2011, p. 3C.

52. Thorp interview.

53. Bob Winston, telephone interview by author, December 19, 2019.

54. *Notice of Allegations to University of North Carolina, Chapel Hill*, National Collegiate Athletic Association, 21 June 2011, p. 7, https://assets.sbnation.com/assets/642328/NCAA_NOA_062111.pdf?_ga=2.87599313.89265454.1575894095-1015018707.1573675031

55. *Notice of Allegations* 1-7.

56. *Notice of Allegations* 17-21.

57. Christina Gough, "NCAA March Madness Basketball Tournament Average TV Viewership From 2013 to 2019 (in Million Viewers)," *Statista*, April 2019, https://www.statista.com/statistics/251560/ncaa-basketball-march-madness-average-tv-viewership-per-game/

58. Derek Volner, "CFP National Championship—Alabama vs. Clemson: 25.3 Million Fans Watched, Up from the Same Matchup Two Seasons Ago," *ESPN*, Jan. 8, 2019, https://espnpressroom.com/us/press-releases/2019/01/cfp-national-championship-audience-is-reported-at-25-2-million-and-will-continue-to-grow-more-fans-watched-alabama-clemson-this-season-than-same-matchup-two-seasons-ago/

59. Clotfelter 68-69.

60. Clotfelter 242-46.

61. Clotfelter 249.

62. Natalie A. Brown and Andrew C. Billings, "Sports Fans as Crisis Communicators on Social Media Websites," *Public Relations Review*, Mar. 2013, https://www.sciencedirect.com/science/article/abs/pii/S036381111200183X?via%3Dihub, and Natalie A. Brown et al., "'May No Act of Ours Bring Shame': Fan-Enacted Crisis Communication Surrounding the Penn State Sex Abuse Scandal," *Communication & Sport*, Dec. 2013, https://journals.sagepub.com/doi/abs/10.1177/2167479513514387?journalCode=coma

63. Alex Scarborough, "Welcome to College Football's Never-Ending Online Tailgate," *ESPN.com*, Jul. 12, 2018, https://www.espn.com/college-football/story/_/id/24011044/message-boards-texags-tigerdroppings-keep-college-football-weird

64. *Michael McAdoo vs. University of North Carolina at Chapel Hill et al.*, Durham County Superior Court, Jul. 1, 2011, https://web.archive.org/web/20110725183849/http://www.ncicl.org/assets/uploads/article/McAdoo%20Verified%20Complaint%20Final.pdf

65. Appendix to *Michael McAdoo vs. University of North Carolina at Chapel Hill et al.* Durham County Superior Court, Jul. 1, 2011, p. 127, https://web.archive.org/web/20121208071634/http://media2.newsobserver.com/smedia/2011/07/05/22/21/NQ5tK.So.156.PDF

66. Adam Hochberg, "NC State Fan Site Investigates UNC Football Player, Media Follow," *Poynter*, Jul. 21, 2011, https://www.poynter.org/reporting-editing/2011/nc-state-fan-site-investigates-unc-football-player-media-follow/

67. Jonathan Jones and Kelly Parsons, "Paper in McAdoo Lawsuit Shows Evidence of Plagiarism," *Daily Tar Heel*, Jul. 8, 2011, https://www.dailytarheel.com/article/2011/07/paper_in_mcadoo_lawsuit_shows_evidence_of_plagiarism

68. Hochberg.

69. "Harsh Spotlight—Plagiarism, a Lawsuit and Hesitant Leadership Demand a Sharp Focus on UNC-Chapel Hill's Problems," *News & Observer*, Jul. 19, 2011, p. 8A.

70. Perry.

71. Thorp interview.

72. Calendar entry for July 26, 2011, in Calendar, 2011, Box 1, in the Office of Chancellor of the University of North Carolina at Chapel Hill: H. Holden Thorp Records #40321, University Archives, Wilson Library, University of North Carolina at Chapel Hill.

73. Bruce Feldman, "Despite Being Cleared in Scandal at UNC, Davis Still Waiting for a Gig," *CBSSports.com*, Dec. 11, 2013, https://www.cbssports.com/college-football/news/despite-being-cleared-in-scandal-at-unc-davis-still-waiting-for-a-gig/

74. Pat Forde, "Bad Timing on Butch Davis' Dismissal," *ESPN.com*, Jul. 28, 2011, https://www.espn.com/college-football/story/_/id/6810094/north-carolina-tar-heels-football-coach-butch-davis-dismissed

75. Jonathan Outlaw, "Carolina Makes Football Coaching Change," *UNC News*, Jul. 27, 2011, https://uncnewsarchive.unc.edu/2011/07/27/carolina-makes-football-coaching-change-2/

76. Thorp interview.

77. "Thorp's Trial—The UNC-Chapel Hill Chancellor Takes Undeserved Heat for Making a Good Call on His Football Coach," *News & Observer*, Aug. 7, 2011, p. 16A.

78. Anne Blythe, "News Spreads; Talk Is Why Now," *News & Observer*, Jul. 28, 2011, p. 1A.

79. Willingham interview.

80. Dan Kane, "Austin's UNC Transcript Raises Questions," *News & Observer*, Aug. 21, 2011, https://www.newsobserver.com/news/local/education/unc-scandal/article10349711.html

81. Thorp interview.

82. Thorp interview.

83. ABC7, "UNC Professor Resigns Amid Football Investigation," ABC7. com, Sept. 2, 2011, https://abc7.com/archive/8338877/

84. "NCAA Tells Carolina It Has No AFAM Issues," *Carolina Alumni Review*, Aug. 31, 2012, https://alumni.unc.edu/news/ncaa-tells-carolina -it-has-no-afam-issues/

85. Thorp interview.

86. Boxill, December 17.

87. Thorp interview.

88. "NCAA Tells Carolina."

89. "UNC Proposes Self-Imposed Sanctions for Football," *Carolina Alumni Review*, Sept. 19, 2011, https://alumni.unc.edu/news/unc-proposes-self-impo sed-sanctions-for-football/

90. "UNC Banned from 2012 Postseason," *ESPN.com*, Mar. 12, 2012, https://www.espn.com/college-football/story/_/id/7677271/north-carolina -tar-heels-handed-postseason-ban-2012-ncaa

91. Thorp interview.

92. Jonathan Hartlyn and William L. Andrews, *Review of Courses in the Department of African and Afro-American Studies, College of Arts and Sciences*, UNC-Chapel Hill, https://carolinacommitment.unc.edu/files/2012/05/Hart- lynAndrews-report.pdf

93. "Criminal Charge Against Nyang'oro Dropped," *Carolina Alumni Review*, Jul. 3, 2014, https://alumni.unc.edu/news/criminal-charge-against -nyangoro-dropped/

94. Dan Kane, "UNC Players Made Up 39 Percent of Suspect Classes," *News & Observer*, May 8, 2012, https://web.archive.org/web/20120511115129/ http://www.newsobserver.com/2012/05/07/2050241/unc-football-basket- ball-players.html

95. "SBI Probing Fraud Report in African, Afro-American Studies," *Carolina Alumni Review*, May 14, 2012, https://alumni.unc.edu/news/ sbi-probing-fraud-report-in-african-afro-american-studies/

96. Maxine Swann, "The Professor, the Bikini Model and the Suitcase Full of Trouble," *New York Times Magazine*, Mar. 8, 2013, https://www.nytimes. com/2013/03/10/magazine/the-professor-the-bikini-model-and-the-suit case-full-of-trouble.html

97. Claire McNeill, "UNC Professor Paul Frampton Still in Argen- tine Prison," *Daily Tar Heel*, Mar. 25, 2012, https://www.dailytarheel.com/ article/2012/03/drugs_prof

98. Jessica New, "Frampton Supporters Ramp Up Efforts," *Daily Tar Heel*, Aug. 28, 2012, https://www.dailytarheel.com/article/2012/08/ frampton-supporters-ramp-up-efforts

99. Letter from Reginald Hildebrand to Holden Thorp dated Aug. 29, 2012, Box 2, in the Office of Chancellor of the University of North Carolina at Chapel Hill: H. Holden Thorp Records #40321, University Archives, Wilson Library, University of North Carolina at Chapel Hill.

100. Hildebrand, Oral History 57.

101. Jack Jakucyk, "Jack Jakucyk: Programs Are Sops," *News & Observer*, May 18, 2012, in Box 2, in the Office of Chancellor of the University of North Carolina at Chapel Hill: H. Holden Thorp Records #40321, University Archives, Wilson Library, University of North Carolina at Chapel Hill.

102. Andrew Levine, "Academic Fraud Scandal Requires Drastic Fix," *Daily Tar Heel*, Aug. 20, 2012, https://www.dailytarheel.com/article/2012/08/academic-fraud-scandal-requires-drastic-fix

103. Jane Stancill, Twitter post, February 7, 2013, 12:13 p.m., https://twitter.com/janestancill/status/299566513239752704

104. Letter from Hildebrand.

105. *Request for Authorization.*

106. Hildebrand, *Anatomy* 6.

107. Hildebrand, *Anatomy* 7.

108. Email from Perry A. Hall to faculty—athletics-forum@listserv.unc.edu, WRAL.com, Jul. 27, 2012, https://www.wral.com/search-thousands-of-unc-scandal-records/15030171/#246437, "Search thousands of UNC scandal records."

109. *Resolution 2012-9. On Affirming the Academic Integrity of African and Afro-American Studies,* Faculty Council, UNC-Chapel Hill, Sept. 7, 2012, http://faccoun.unc.edu/files/2011/03/Res2012-9OnAfAmStudies.pdf

110. *Journal of Proceedings of the General Faculty and Faculty Council: September 7, 2012,* Faculty Council, UNC-Chapel Hill, Sept. 7, 2012, https://facultygov.unc.edu/faculty-council/meeting-materials-past-years/meeting-materials-2012-13/september-7-2012/

111. Hildebrand, *Anatomy* 7.

112. Hildebrand, Oral History 60.

113. Hildebrand, Oral History 59.

114. Hildebrand, Oral History 40-2.

115. Hildebrand, Oral History 40.

116. Branch.

117. Jane Stancill, "UNC to Change Which Kenan Is Honored on Kenan Stadium," *News & Observer*, Oct. 3, 2018, https://www.newsobserver.com/news/local/article219461160.html

118. Craig Calcaterra, "UNC Stadium Honoree Was Captain In Wilmington Massacre," *WBUR*, Nov. 9, 2018, https://www.wbur.org/onlyagame/2018/11/09/unc-kenan-stadium-massacre

119. Hildebrand, Oral History 65.

120. Hildebrand, Oral History 53-54.

121. Hildebrand, Oral History 56.

122. Reginald F. Hildebrand, interview by Rob Stephens, April 21, 2010, interview FON_0127, transcript and recording, Marian Cheek Jackson Center, https://archives.jacksoncenter.info/items/show/469, 4.

123. Hildebrand, Oral History 56.

124. Thorp interview.

125. Dan Kane, "Peppers' Transcript Might Point to Broader Academic Issues at UNC," *News & Observer*, Aug. 13, 2012, https://www.newsobserver.com/news/local/education/unc-scandal/article15573542.html

126. "What Gives?" *News & Observer*, May 14, 2012, in Box 2, in the Office of Chancellor of the University of North Carolina at Chapel Hill: H. Holden Thorp Records #40321, University Archives, Wilson Library, University of North Carolina at Chapel Hill.

127. Email from Craig Fox to Holden Thorp, dated May 4, 2012, in the Office of Chancellor of the University of North Carolina at Chapel Hill: H. Holden Thorp Records #40321, University Archives, Wilson Library, University of North Carolina at Chapel Hill.

128. Email from Morgan Dickerman to Holden Thorp, dated May 4, 2012, in Box 2, in the Office of Chancellor of the University of North Carolina at Chapel Hill: H. Holden Thorp Records #40321, University Archives, Wilson Library, University of North Carolina at Chapel Hill.

129. Email from David Speer to Holden Thorp et al., dated May 4, 2012, in Box 2, in the Office of Chancellor of the University of North Carolina at Chapel Hill: H. Holden Thorp Records #40321, University Archives, Wilson Library, University of North Carolina at Chapel Hill.

130. Email chain from Tom Ross to Holden Thorp, dated May 9, 2012, in Box 2, in the Office of Chancellor of the University of North Carolina at Chapel Hill: H. Holden Thorp Records #40321, University Archives, Wilson Library, University of North Carolina at Chapel Hill.

131. Thorp interview.

132. Holden Thorp, "Steps Taken to Address Problems at UNC-CH," *News & Observer*, Aug. 22, 2012, in Box 2, in the Office of Chancellor of the University of North Carolina at Chapel Hill: H. Holden Thorp Records #40321, University Archives, Wilson Library, University of North Carolina at Chapel Hill.

133. Email from Burley Mitchell to Holden Thorp, dated Aug. 17, 2012, in Box 2, in the Office of Chancellor of the University of North Carolina at Chapel Hill: H. Holden Thorp Records #40321, University Archives, Wilson Library, University of North Carolina at Chapel Hill.

134. In the spring semester of 2012, I had Smith as a professor in a class on the French Revolution. I earned a B+.

135. Email from Jay Smith to Holden Thorp, dated Aug. 16, 2012, in Box 2, in the Office of Chancellor of the University of North Carolina at Chapel Hill: H. Holden Thorp Records #40321, University Archives, Wilson Library, University of North Carolina at Chapel Hill.

136. J. Andrew Curliss, "Chancellor Thorp Flew With Former UNC Fundraisers," *News & Observer*, Sept. 18, 2012, https://www.newsobserver.com/news/local/education/unc-scandal/article15573620.html

137. Nicole Comparato, "Chancellor Holden Thorp to Step Down in June," *Daily Tar Heel*, Sept. 17, 2012, https://www.dailytarheel.com/article/2012/09/chancellor-holden-thorp-to-step-down-in-june

138. Thorp interview.

139. Hannah Lang, "On the Steps of South Building: The Decade According to UNC's Chancellors," *Daily Tar Heel*, Dec. 4, 2019, https://www.dailytarheel.com/article/2019/12/chancellor-decade

140. Thorp interview.

141. Kevin Kiley, "The Virginia Effect," *Inside Higher Ed*, Sept. 25, 2012, https://www.insidehighered.com/news/2012/09/25/reaction-unc-chancellor-resignation-shows-influence-virginia-controversy

142. J.AndrewCurliss, "Thorp: UNC's Standards for Athletes Will Rise," *News & Observer*, Sept. 26, 2012, https://web.archive.org/web/20121106025022/http://www.newsobserver.com/2012/09/26/2371972/thorp-uncs-standards-for-athletes.html

143. Email from Wade Hargrove to John Ellison, dated Sept. 27, 2012, in Box 2, in the Office of Chancellor of the University of North Carolina at Chapel Hill: H. Holden Thorp Records #40321, University Archives, Wilson Library, University of North Carolina at Chapel Hill.

144. Email from Jeff Thornton to Wade Hargrove et al., dated Sept. 29, 2012, in Box 2, in the Office of Chancellor of the University of North Carolina at Chapel Hill: H. Holden Thorp Records #40321, University Archives, Wilson Library, University of North Carolina at Chapel Hill.

145. Email from Walter Lowry Caudill to Alston Gardner, dated Oct. 4, 2012, *News & Observer*, http://media2.newsobserver.com/static/content/multimedia/interactive/uncblindspot/pdf/day02-caudill.pdf

146. Brian Barbour, "About Those New Academic Standards Holden Thorp Proposed," *Tar Heel Blog*, Oct. 17, 2012, https://www.tarheelblog.com/2012/10/17/3519284/about-those-new-academic-standard-holden-thorp-proposed

147. Thorp interview.

148. "Can Strong Academics and Winning Athletics Coexist At Carolina?," YouTube video, 1:16:43, posted by "UNC GAA," May 30, 2013, https://www.youtube.com/watch?v=_P8Qt7O-hOs&t=520s

149. Barry Jacobs, "Jacobs: Athletics a Pressure Point for University Leaders," *News & Observer*, Feb. 1, 2015, https://www.newsobserver.com/sports/college/acc/unc/article10243649.html

150. Vinayak Balasubramanian, "Former UNC-System President Bill Friday Dies at 92," *Daily Tar Heel*, Oct. 12, 2012, https://www.dailytarheel.com/article/2012/10/bill-friday-dies

151. Thorp interview.

152. "Memorial Service for William C. Friday," *UNC-TV* video, 1:36:12, October 16, 2012, https://video.unctv.org/video/nc-people-memorial-service-william-c-friday/

153. Perry.

154. Winston.

155. John Drescher, "Drescher: Thorp Shared Traits With UNC

Hero Graham," *News & Observer*, Sept. 21, 2012, https://web. archive.org/web/20130130113627/http://www.newsobserver. com/2012/09/21/2359099/drescher-thorp-was-an-able-chancellor.html

CHAPTER 7

1. Willingham interview.

2. Dan Kane, "UNC Tolerated Cheating, Says Insider Mary Willingham," *News & Observer*, Nov. 17, 2012, https://www.newsobserver.com/news/local/education/unc-scandal/article15573761.html

3. Dan Kane, "A Prosecutor's Choice Leads to Origins of UNC's Bogus Classes," *News & Observer*, Sept. 21, 2016, https://www.newsobserver.com/news/special-reports/carolinas-blind-side/article102701612.html

4. "The Read on UNC-CH," *News & Observer*, Nov. 19, 2012, https://web.archive.org/web/20121121192024/http://www.newsobserver.com/2012/11/19/2495456/the-read-on-unc-ch.html

5. Recording of interview of Mary Willingham by James G. Martin, provided to the author by Willingham.

6. Jay Smith, telephone conversation with author, November 22, 2019.

7. "Martin Says Fraud Isolated to African Studies Department," *Carolina Alumni Review*, Feb. 1, 2013, https://alumni.unc.edu/news/martin-says-fraud-isolated-to-african-studies-department/

8. James G. Martin, *The University of North Carolina at Chapel Hill Academic Anomalies Review Report of Findings*, University of North Carolina at Chapel Hill, Dec. 19, 2012, pp. 8-9, https://carolinacommitment.unc.edu/files/2013/01/UNC-Governor-Martin-Final-Report-and-Addendum-1.pdf

9. Dan Kane et al., "Martin Report: Suspect UNC Classes Stretched Back to 1997," *News & Observer*, Dec. 21, 2012, https://www.newsobserver.com/news/local/education/unc-scandal/article15573890.html

10. Mary Willingham, "The Martin Report," *Athletics vs Academics* (blog), December 20, 2012, https://web.archive.org/web/20130114013611/http://athleticsvsacademics.com/the-martin-report/#comment-87

11. Kane, "Martin Report."

12. Dan Kane, "Martin Says He Misspoke About UNC Scandal," *News & Observer*, Jul. 25, 2015, https://www.charlotteobserver.com/news/local/education/article28709758.html

13. Dan Kane, "As Revelations Mounted On UNC's Bogus Classes, Leaders' Tension Grew," *News & Observer*, Sept. 20, 2016, https://www.newsobserver.com/news/special-reports/carolinas-blind-side/article102613232.html

14. Thorp interview.

15. "Drake Group Honors UNC Administrator for Defending Academic Integrity," The Drake Group, March 14, 2013, https://www.thedrakegroup.org/wp-content/uploads/2019/03/rmh2013.pdf

16. Willingham interview.

17. Mary Willingham's speech in acceptance of the Drake Group's Robert Maynard Hutchins Award, Apr. 18, 2013, https://web.archive.org/web/20140805183736/http://drakegroupblog.files.wordpress.com/2013/04/rmh-2013-willingham-speech.pdf

18. Willingham interview.

19. Bradley Bethel, telephone interview by author, October 21, 2019.

20. Dan Kane, "Psychologist Who Collaborated With Mary Willingham at UNC-Chapel Hill Has Contract Canceled," *News & Observer*, Apr. 11, 2014, https://www.newsobserver.com/news/local/education/unc-scandal/article10321373.html

21. Email from Lyn Johnson to Jan Boxill, WRAL.com, Jul. 8, 2013, https://www.wral.com/search-thousands-of-unc-scandal-records/15030171/#1389417, "Search thousands of UNC scandal records."

22. Document entitled "History of Screening/Testing Scholarship Student-Athletes," WRAL.com, https://www.wral.com/search-thousands-of-unc-scandal-records/15030171/#1327852, "Search thousands of UNC scandal records."

23. Bethel.

24. Evaluation of Mary Willingham by Harold Woodard, dated June 27, 2012, Information regarding grievance filed by Mary Willingham, November 1, 2013-August 11, 2014, Box: 1, Folder: 7. Mary Willingham archive, SCU-RBSC-2017-8. Irvin Department of Rare Books and Special Collections, http://archives.library.sc.edu:8081//repositories/5/archival_objects/250586

25. Willingham interview.

26. Evaluation of Mary Willingham by Harold Woodard, dated June 20, 2013, Information regarding grievance filed by Mary Willingham, November 1, 2013-August 11, 2014, Box: 1, Folder: 7. Mary Willingham archive, SCU-RBSC-2017-8. Irvin Department of Rare Books and Special Collections, http://archives.library.sc.edu:8081//repositories/5/archival_objects/250586

27. Willingham interview.

28. Email from Mary Willingham to James Dean, WRAL.com, Jul. 18, 2013, https://www.wral.com/search-thousands-of-unc-scandal-records/15030171/#483458, "Search thousands of UNC scandal records."

29. "The University of North Carolina at Chapel Hill—Faculty Athletics Committee—Minutes of Meeting: December 10, 2013," http://faccoun.unc.edu/files/2010/10/20131210FACMinutes.pdf

30. Sara Ganim, "CNN Analysis: Some College Athletes Play Like Adults, Read Like 5th-Graders," *CNN.com*, Jan. 8, 2014, https://www.cnn.com/2014/01/07/us/ncaa-athletes-reading-scores/index.html

31. Sara Ganim, "CNN Analysis: Some College Athletes Play Like Adults, Read Like 5th-Graders," *CNN.com*, Jan. 8, 2014, https://www.cnn.com/interactive/2014/01/us/college-scores/index.html

32. Transcript of interview with Mary Willingham, *CNN.com*, Jan. 9, 2014, http://transcripts.cnn.com/TRANSCRIPTS/1401/09/sn.01.html

33. Paul M. Barrett, "In Fake Classes Scandal, UNC Fails Its Athletes—and Whistle-Blower," *Bloomberg Businessweek*, Feb. 27, 2014, https://www.bloomberg.com/news/articles/2014-02-27/in-fake-classes-scandal-unc-fails-its-athletes-whistle-blower

34. Sara Ganim, "Death Threats and Denial for Woman Who Showed College Athletes Struggle to Read," *CNN.com*, Jan. 14, 2014, https://www.cnn.com/2014/01/09/us/ncaa-athletes-unc-response/index.html

35. Willingham interview.

36. "UNC Statement on Student-Athlete Reading Ability," University of North Carolina at Chapel Hill, Jan. 16, 2014, https://carolinacommitment.unc.edu/unc-statement-on-student-athlete-reading-ability/

37. Recording of conversation between Mary Willingham, Jay Smith, and Jim Dean, provided to the author by Willingham.

38. Bradley Saacks, "Willingham's Research Applications Raise Questions," *Daily Tar Heel*, May 15, 2014, https://www.dailytarheel.com/article/2014/05/mary-willingham-application-0515

39. Letter from Jeanne Lovmo to Mary Willingham, Jan. 16, 2014, https://www-cache.wral.com/asset/news/education/2014/05/16/13651472/2014.01.21_Dukes_Response_5.15.2014.pdf, p. 46.

40. Barrett.

41. Dan Kane, "2005 UNC Champs Relied on Suspect Classes, Records Show," *News and Observer*, June 6, 2014, https://www.newsobserver.com/news/local/education/unc-scandal/article10332632.html

42. Doc Kennedy, "Willingham Leaks AFAM Grades of 2005 Title Team," *Tar Heel Blog*, June 7, 2014, https://www.tarheelblog.com/2014/6/7/5788400/willingham-leaks-afam-grades-of-2005-title-team

43. Kane, "2005 UNC."

44. "Executive Summary of External Independent Review," University of North Carolina at Chapel Hill, Apr. 11, 2014, https://carolinacommitment.unc.edu/files/2014/04/Executive-Summary-of-External-Independent-Review.pdf

45. Mary Willingham, "Response to UNC's Independent Evaluation of Research," *Paper Class Inc.* (blog), Apr. 15, 2014, https://web.archive.org/web/20140623164300/http://paperclassinc.com/response-uncs-independent-evaluation-research/

46. Willingham interview.

47. Blanchard.

48. Recording of conversation between Mary Willingham and Carol Folt, provided to the author by Willingham.

49. Willingham interview.

50. Dan Kane, "UNC Whistle-Blower Resigns After Meeting With Chancellor" *News & Observer*, Apr. 21, 2014, https://www.newsobserver.com/news/local/education/unc-scandal/article10323344.html; Sara Ganim, "Whistle-Blower in University of North Carolina Paper Class Case Files Lawsuit," *CNN*.

com, Jul. 1, 2014, https://www.cnn.com/2014/07/01/us/university-north-carolina-paper-class-lawsuit/index.html

51. Sara Ganim, "UNC 'Fake Classes' Whistleblower to Get $335K in Settlement," *CNN.com*, Mar. 17, 2015, https://www.cnn.com/2015/03/17/us/north-carolina-willingham-unc-settlement/index.html

52. The panel was chaired by Jefferson Brown, who is, coincidentally, the father of a childhood friend of mine.

"Decision of the Board of Trustees in the EPA Non-Faculty Grievance of Mary Willingham," dated Aug. 11, 2014, Information regarding grievance filed by Mary Willingham, November 1, 2013-August 11, 2014, Box: 1, Folder: 7. Mary Willingham archive, SCU-RBSC-2017-8. Irvin Department of Rare Books and Special Collections, http://archives.library.sc.edu:8081//repositories/5/archival_objects/250586

53. Dan Kane, "UNC Critic Mary Willingham Accused of Plagiarism in Thesis," *News & Observer*, Aug. 4, 2014, https://www.newsobserver.com/news/local/education/unc-scandal/article10030394.html

54. Willingham interview.

55. Email from Christine Kelly-Kleese, Aug. 31, 2020.

56. Willingham interview.

57. Marc Tracy, "N.C.A.A. Is Reopening Inquiry Into Academic Violations at North Carolina," *New York Times*, June 30, 2014, https://www.nytimes.com/2014/07/01/sports/ncaa-is-reopening-university-of-north-carolina-inquiry.html

58. Willingham, "Response."

59. Carol Folt, "A Message from Chancellor Carol L. Folt," University of North Carolina at Chapel Hill, Feb. 21, 2014, https://uncnewsarchive.unc.edu/2014/02/21/message-chancellor-carol-l-folt/

60. Kane, "A Prosecutor's Choice."

CHAPTER 8

1. Dan Kane, "UNC Faculty Leader Pushed Rewrite of Key Report to Keep NCAA Away," *News & Observer*, Jul. 20, 2013, https://www.newsobserver.com/sports/college/acc/unc/article21678294.html

2. Boxill, February 13.

3. Kane, "UNC Faculty Leader."

4. Jane Stancill, "UNC Professors Declare Support for Faculty Leader Jan Boxill," *News & Observer*, Jul. 30, 2013, http://blog.ecu.edu/sites/dailyclips/blog/2013/07/30/chapel-hill-unc-professors-declare-support-for-faculty-leader-jan-boxill-education-newsobserver-com/

5. Ran Northam, "Boxill: N&O Took 'Booster' Email Out Of Context," *Chapelboro.com*, Aug. 29, 2013, https://chapelboro.com/news/unc/boxill-no-took-booster-email-out-of-context

6. Boxill, December 17.

7. Blanchard.

8. Boxill, April 11.

9. Thorp interview.

10. Boxill, December 17.

11. Randall M. Roden, "Jan Boxill: Response to Amended Notice of Allegations," Tharrington Smith, L.L.P., Aug. 1, 2016, https://drive.google.com/file/d/0B9MDZdoTx7ZWcjcxTkZnUUN2clk/view, 43-46.

12. Boxill, December 17.

13. Wainstein.

14. "Full Video of UNC Report on Academic Fraud," YouTube video, 1:43:58, posted by "The News & Observer," October 22, 2014, https://www.youtube.com/watch?v=XPg4pGGu1e4

15. Transcript of the press conference concerning the Wainstein report's release, University of North Carolina at Chapel Hill, Oct. 22, 2014, https://carolinacommitment.unc.edu/files/2015/01/UNC-Oct-22-Press-Conference-Transcript.pdf, p. 33.

16. "UNC-Chapel Hill Leaders Discuss Wainstein Report With Campus Community," YouTube video, 1:14:45, posted by "UNC-Chapel Hill," October 28, 2014, https://www.youtube.com/watch?v=heWiXWEJ6f8&t=2452s

17. Journal of Proceedings of the General Faculty and Faculty Council: October 31, 2014, Faculty Council, UNC-Chapel Hill, Oct. 31, 2014, https://facultygov.unc.edu/faculty-council/meeting-materials-past-years/meeting-materials-2014-2015/october-31-2014/

18. Front page of the *New York Times*, October 23, 2014, http://www.nytimes.com/images/2014/10/23/nytfrontpage/scan.pdf

19. Wainstein 19.

20. Wainstein 42.

21. Wainstein 60.

22. Brad Wolverton, "The Ethicist Who Crossed the Line," *Chronicle of Higher Education*, Oct. 24, 2014, https://www.chronicle.com/article/The-Ethicist-Who-Crossed-the/149619

23. Wainstein 40.

24. Sarah Lyall, "U.N.C. Investigation Reveals Athletes Took Fake Classes," *New York Times*, Oct. 22, 2014, https://www.nytimes.com/2014/10/23/sports/university-of-north-carolina-investigation-reveals-shadow-curriculum-to-help-athletes.html

25. Kevin Armstrong, "Probe Reveals Shocking Scope of Academic Fraud at University of North Carolina," *New York Daily News*, Oct. 22, 2014, https://www.nydailynews.com/sports/college/probe-reveals-shocking-scope-academic-fraud-north-carolina-article-1.1983362

26. Wolverton.

27. Wainstein 40.

28. Wainstein 56-57.

29. Wolverton.

30. Boxill, February 13.

31. "Deborah Crowder 5/10/17" 107.

32. James Duderstadt, *Intercollegiate Athletics and the American University: A University President's Perspective* (Ann Arbor: University of Michigan Press, 2000), 100.

33. Lambert.

34. Jan Boxill, interview by author, Chapel Hill, N.C., April 11, 2019.

35. Jean DeSaix, telephone conversation with author, December 20, 2019.

36. Mary Willingham, telephone conversation with author, January 26, 2019.

37. Jay Smith interview.

38. Boxill, April 11.

39. Wainstein 67.

40. Boxill, April 11.

41. Willingham, January 26.

42. Email from Carol Folt, Dec. 23, 2019.

43. Copied portions of an email from Carol Folt, Jan. 2, 2020.

44. Press conference transcript, p. 4.

45. Wainstein 22.

46. "Two More UNC Staff Fired Over Athletics-Academics Issues," *Carolina Alumni Review*, Nov. 13, 2015, https://alumni.unc.edu/news/two-more-unc-staff-fired-over-athletics-academics-issues/

47. Wainstein 21.

48. Wainstein 5.

49. "Two More."

50. Wainstein 93–94.

51. Wainstein 24.

52. Letter from James W. Dean Jr. and Felicia A. Washington to Samuel Travis Gore, dated November 12, 2015, University of North Carolina at Chapel Hill, https://carolinacommitment.unc.edu/files/2015/11/GORE-11-12-15.pdf

53. Jack Stripling, "Where the Buck Stopped in the UNC Fraud Scandal (Hint: Not at the Top)," *Chronicle of Higher Education*, Oct. 13, 2017, https://www.chronicle.com/interactives/unc-scandal

54. Lambert.

55. Hildebrand, Southern Oral History 62–65.

56. Boxill, December 17.

57. Jan Boxill, interview by author, Carrboro, N.C., October 30, 2019.

58. Randall Roden, interview by author, Chapel Hill, N.C., April 11, 2019.

59. Boxill, April 11.

60. Roden, April 11.

61. Boxill, April 11.

62. Boxill, December 17.

63. "University Statement Regarding Jan Boxill's Resignation," University

of North Carolina at Chapel Hill, Mar. 5, 2015, https://carolinacommitment. unc.edu/university-statement-regarding-jan-boxills-resignation/

64. Letter from James W. Dean Jr. and Felicia A. Washington to Jeanette M. Boxill, dated October 22, 2014, University of North Carolina at Chapel Hill, https://carolinacommitment.unc.edu/files/2015/03/Boxill-_-Notice-Letter. pdf

65. Amanda Albright, "More Evidence Emerges on Jan Boxill," *Daily Tar Heel*, Nov. 14, 2014, https://www.dailytarheel.com/article/2014/11/ more-evidence-emerges-on-jan-boxill

66. Amanda Albright and Sara Salinas, "Jan Boxill Says She Did Not Teach 160 Independent Study Courses at UNC," *Daily Tar Heel*, Apr. 27, 2015, https:// www.dailytarheel.com/article/2015/04/jan-boxill-independent-studies

67. "University Statement."

68. Jay Smith.

69. Boxill, December 17.

70. Lamb.

71. Boxill, October 30.

72. The first notice can be found at https://carolinacommitment.unc.edu/ files/2015/06/NCAA-NOA.pdf. The second notice can be found at https://car-olinacommitment.unc.edu/files/2016/04/NOA_Amended_042516_North-Carolina.pdf. The third notice can be found at https://carolinacommitment. unc.edu/files/2016/12/NCAA-third-notice-of-allegations.pdf

73. Roden, "Jan Boxill."

74. Lamb.

75. Boxill, October 30.

76. Boxill, December 17.

CHAPTER 9

1. "Deborah Crowder 5/10/17" 20.

2. Email from Deborah Crowder to Travis Gore, WRAL.com, Sept. 13, 2010, https://www.wral.com/search-thousands-of-unc-scandal-re-cords/15030171/#537192, "Search thousands of UNC scandal records."

3. Email from Deborah Crowder to Travis Gore, WRAL.com, Nov. 15, 2010, https://www.wral.com/search-thousands-of-unc-scandal-records/1503 0171/#190778, "Search thousands of UNC scandal records."

4. Kane, "A Prosecutor's."

5. "Deborah Crowder 5/10/17" 14.

6. "Deborah Crowder 5/10/17" 25.

7. "Deborah Crowder 5/10/17" 29.

8. "Deborah Crowder 5/10/17" 64.

9. "Deborah Crowder 5/10/17" 65.

10. "Deborah Crowder 5/10/17" 66-67.

11. "Deborah Crowder 5/10/17" 69.

12. Michael Marot, "NCAA's Emmert Calls N. Carolina Report Troubling," *Associated Press*, Oct. 27, 2014, https://web.archive.org/web/20160402040636/http://collegefootball.ap.org/article/ncaas-emmert-calls-n-carolina-report-troubling

13. This excludes two charges of noncooperation, one against Crowder and one against Nyang'oro.

14. "Second Amended Notice of Allegations to the Chancellor of the University of North Carolina, Chapel Hill," *National Collegiate Athletic Association*, Dec. 13, 2016, https://carolinacommitment.unc.edu/files/2016/12/NCAA-third-notice-of-allegations.pdf

15. McClatchy News Service, "Ex-Chancellor Moeser Criticizes Coverage of UNC Scandal," *Times-News*, May 21, 2013, https://www.thetimesnews.com/20130521/ex-chancellor-moeser-criticizes-coverage-of-unc-scandal/305219865

16. "Response to NCAA Second Amended Notice of Allegations," University of North Carolina at Chapel Hill, May 16, 2017, p. 1, https://carolinacommitment.unc.edu/files/2017/05/UNC-Response-to-2016-2nd-Amended-NOA-1.pdf

17. "Second Amended" 2.

18. Wainstein 94.

19. "Response" 13.

20. "Response" 8.

21. "Response" 42.

22. "Memorandum in Support Of Defendant the National Collegiate Athletic Association's Motion to Dismiss," United States District Court for the Middle District of North Carolina, Mar. 20, 2015, p. 15, in *Exhibits Cited in Response to Second ANOA*, the University of North Carolina at Chapel Hill, 25 May 2017, https://carolinacommitment.unc.edu/files/2017/05/Exhibits-Table-of-Contents-Exhibit-1-1.pdf

23. "Response" 12.

24. Luke DeCock, "NCAA Leaders Explain Response to UNC Lawsuit," *News & Observer*, Apr. 2, 2015, https://www.newsobserver.com/sports/spt-columns-blogs/luke-decock/article17234402.html

25. "Response" 15-16.

26. Pete Thamel, "Sanctions Decimate the Nittany Lions Now and for Years to Come," *New York Times*, July 23, 2012, https://www.nytimes.com/2012/07/24/sports/ncaafootball/penn-state-penalties-include-60-million-fine-and-bowl-ban.html

27. Steve Eder, "Governor Sues Over Penalties to Penn State," *New York Times*, Jan. 2, 2013, https://www.nytimes.com/2013/01/03/sports/ncaafootball/governor-announces-lawsuit-against-ncaa-over-penn-state-penalties.html

28. Jeré Longman, "A Boost From the State Capitol Helped Penn State Escape N.C.A.A. Penalties," *New York Times*, Feb. 4, 2015, https://www.

nytimes.com/2015/02/05/sports/ncaafootball/how-one-legislator-helped-penn-state-escape-ncaas-harsh-penalties.html

29. Steve Eder and Marc Tracy, "N.C.A.A. Decides to Roll Back Sanctions Against Penn State," *New York Times*, Sept. 8, 2014, https://www.nytimes.com/2014/09/09/sports/ncaafootball/penn-states-postseason-ban-is-lifted.html

30. Kevin Horne, "Internal Emails Show NCAA Questioned Authority to Sanction Penn State," *Onward State*, Nov. 5, 2014, https://onwardstate.com/2014/11/05/internal-emails-show-ncaa-questioned-jurisdiction-over-penn-state/

31. Andrew Carter, "UNC's Third Notice of Allegations: Questions and Answers," *News & Observer*, Dec. 24, 2016, https://www.newsobserver.com/sports/college/acc/unc/unc-now/article122813999.html

32. "Response" 6-7.

33. "Response" 32-33.

34. "Response" 35-36.

35. "Response" 38.

36. "Response" 34.

37. "Response" 40.

38. "Response" 80.

39. "Response" 79-80.

40. "Response" 51.

41. "Response" 36.

42. "Response to the Southern Association of Colleges and Schools Commission on Colleges (SACSCOC) Letter of November 13, 2014," *University of North Carolina at Chapel Hill*, Jan. 12, 2015, p. 29, https://oira.unc.edu/files/2017/07/UNC-Chapel-Hill-Report-to-SACSCOC-Redacted-for-Public-Release.pdf

43. Dan Kane, "NCAA Faces Criticism for UNC Decision," *News & Observer*, Oct. 13, 2017, https://www.newsobserver.com/sports/college/acc/unc/article178784981.html

44. Elliot Abrams, interview by author, Raleigh, N.C., February 12, 2019.

45. Boxill, December 17.

46. Abrams.

47. Boxill, December 17.

48. Hatchell resigned in 2019 after a university review found she had made racially insensitive comments to players.

49. Sylvia Hatchell, telephone interview by author, December 5, 2019.

50. Abrams.

51. Stripling.

52. Kane, "Deborah Crowder's Story."

53. Email from Trudier Harris to Jay Smith, WRAL.com, Aug. 22, 2013, https://www.wral.com/search-thousands-of-unc-scandal-records/15030171/#594938, "Search thousands of UNC scandal records."

54. Hildebrand, *Anatomy* 7.

55. Hildebrand, Southern Oral History 66-7.

56. Text message from Elliot Abrams, Dec. 11, 2019.

CHAPTER 10

1. NCAA Committee on Infractions Panel, "University of North Carolina at Chapel Hill Public Infractions Decision," *National Collegiate Athletic Association*, Oct. 13, 2017, p. 19, https://www.ncaa.org/sites/default/files/Oct2017_University-of-North-Carolina-at-Chapel-Hill_InfractionsDecision_20171013.pdf

2. Boxill, December 17.

3. Jane Stancill, "Jan Boxill, Former Professor, Counselor to UNC Women's Team, Relieved With NCAA Result," *News & Observer*, Oct. 13, 2017, https://www.newsobserver.com/sports/college/acc/unc/article178794761.html

4. Boxill, December 17.

5. Copied portions of an email from Carol Folt, Jan. 2, 2020.

6. Boxill, December 17.

7. "Redemption—UNC Captures 6th NCAA Title," *News & Observer*, Apr. 3, 2017, https://www.newsobserver.com/news/local/counties/durham-county/article142529099.html

8. It did find Crowder and Nyang'oro guilty of noncooperation (Crowder for the period before she agreed to participate in the infractions process), but because neither has gone on to work for an NCAA member institution, the findings carried little effect.

9. "Public Infractions Decision" 2.

10. "Public Infractions Decision" 16-18.

11. "Public Infractions Decision" 18.

12. "Public Infractions Decision" 17.

13. "Public Infractions Decision" 11.

14. Dan Wolken, "NCAA Has Never Seemed So Impotent After Decision on North Carolina Academic Scandal," *USA Today*, Oct. 13, 2017, https://www.usatoday.com/story/sports/college/columnist/dan-wolken/2017/10/13/ncaa-has-never-seemed-so-impotent-after-decision-north-carolina-academic-scandal/761563001/

15. Pat Forde, "North Carolina Ruling Proves NCAA Is Useless," *Yahoo! Sports*, Oct. 13, 2017, https://sports.yahoo.com/north-carolina-ruling-proves-ncaa-useless-162457632.html

16. "Message From Chancellor Carol L. Folt on NCAA Decision," *University of North Carolina at Chapel Hill*, Oct. 13, 2017, https://carolinacommitment.unc.edu/message-from-chancellor-carol-l-folt-on-ncaa-decision/

17. "Response" 11.

18. Dan Barkin, "UNC's Statements to the NCAA Didn't 'Pass the Smell

Test,' Accreditor Said," *News & Observer*, Nov. 22, 2017, https://www.newsob server.com/news/local/education/unc-scandal/article186019288.html

19. Letter from Belle S. Wheelan to Carol L. Folt, dated 13 Nov. 2017, *Southern Association of Colleges and Schools Commission on Colleges*, https://carolinacommitment.unc.edu/files/2017/11/Letter-from-Belle-Wheelan.pdf

20. Barkin.

21. Jane Stancill, "UNC Leaders Reject Finding That Administrators Meddled in Controversial Sports History Class," *News & Observer*, May 3, 2018, https://www.newsobserver.com/news/local/article210286749.html

22. "U.S. Attorney Announces The Arrest Of 10 Individuals, Including Four Division I Coaches, For College Basketball Fraud And Corruption Schemes," *U.S. Department of Justice*, Sept. 26, 2017, https://www.justice.gov/usao-sdny/pr/us-attorney-announces-arrest-10-individuals-including-four-division-i-coaches-college

23. Commission on College Basketball, "Report and Recommendations to Address the Issues Facing Collegiate Basketball," April 2018, p. 11, https://web.archive.org/web/20180429053027/https://www.ncaa.org/sites/default/files/2018CCBReportFinal_web.pdf

24. "Defining the NCAA's Role in Academic Matters: Final Report from the NCAA Division I Academic Misconduct Working Group to the NCAA Division I Presidential Forum," *National Collegiate Athletic Association*, January 2019, http://www.ncaa.org/sites/default/files/2019AMWG_Final_Report_20190130.pdf

25. Dan Kane, "NCAA Drops Proposed Academic Fraud Reform," *News & Observer*, Aug. 9, 2019, https://www.newsobserver.com/news/local/education/unc-scandal/article233693507.html

26. Dan Kane, "NCAA Rejected Recommendations to Halt Academic Fraud, Newly Released Documents Show," *News & Observer*, Oct. 6, 2019, https://www.newsobserver.com/sports/college/article235794402.html

27. Dan Kane, "New Legal Bills Push UNC's Tab for Academic Scandal to $21 Million," *News & Observer*, Aug. 10, 2018, https://www.newsobserver.com/latest-news/article216462745.html

28. Dina Gerdeman, "Prospective Students Steer Clear of Schools Rocked by Scandal," *Harvard Business School*, Aug. 10, 2016, https://hbswk.hbs.edu/item/prospective-students-stay-clear-of-schools-rocked-by-scandal

29. "Fact Book: Thirtieth Edition, 2016-2017," Office of Institutional Research and Assessment, University of North Carolina at Chapel Hill, November 2017, p. 19, https://oira.unc.edu/files/2018/06/Fact-Book-16-17_20180608.pdf

30. Joe Nocera, "Dean Smith's Shadow Looms Over U.N.C. as It Struggles With a Scandal's Fallout," *New York Times*, Feb. 12, 2016, https://www.nytimes.com/2016/02/13/sports/ncaabasketball/dean-smiths-shadow-looms-over-unc-as-it-struggles-with-a-scandals-fallout.html

31. "Actions & Initiatives," University of North Carolina at Chapel Hill, https://carolinacommitment.unc.edu/actions-and-initiatives/actions-and -initiatives/

32. Lindsay Ellis and Robin Wilson, "Professors in Class on Time? Check," *Chronicle of Higher Education*, Jan. 6, 2014, https://www.chronicle.com/article/ Professors-in-Classroom-on/143813

33. Copied portions of an email from Carol Folt, Jan. 2, 2020.

34. Kane, "A Prosecutor's Choice."

35. Marc Tracy, "Baylor Sexual Assault Report Produces Punishment, but No Paper Trail," *New York Times*, Jul. 15, 2016, https://www. nytimes.com/2016/07/16/sports/ncaafootball/baylor-sexual-assault-report-no-paper-trail.html; Suzanne Halliburton, "Baylor's Ken Starr Resigns as Chancellor in Wake of Rape Scandal," *Austin American-Statesman*, Sept. 3, 2016, https://www.statesman.com/news/20160903/ baylors-ken-starr-resigns-as-chancellor-in-wake-of-rape-scandal

36. Mike McIntire and Walt Bogdanich, "At Florida State, Football Clouds Justice," *New York Times*, Oct. 10, 2014, https://www.nytimes. com/2014/10/12/us/florida-state-football-casts-shadow-over-tallahassee-justice.html

37. Des Bieler, "Rutgers Football Coach Kyle Flood Suspended, Fined for Interventions With Academic Staff," *Washington Post*, Sept. 16, 2015, https:// www.washingtonpost.com/news/early-lead/wp/2015/09/16/rutgers-football-coach-kyle-flood-suspended-fined-for-interventions-with-academic-staff/

38. Adam Rittenberg and Tom VanHaaren, "Timeline: Everything That Led to DJ Durkin's Firing at Maryland," *ESPN.com*, Nov. 1, 2018, https://www.espn.com/college-football/story/_/id/24351869/maryland -terrapins-football-jordan-mcnair-death-dj-durkin-scandal-line

39. Sam Farmer, "A Losing Record for NCAA Whistle-Blower," *Los Angeles Times*, Mar. 30, 2001, https://www.latimes.com/archives/la-xpm-2001-mar-30-mn-44594-story.html

40. Thelin, *Games* 2399.

41. Thelin, *Games* 1848.

42. Thelin, *Games* 2689.

43. Thelin, *A History* 405.

44. David F. Labaree, "Nobel Prizes Are Great, But College Football Is Why American Universities Dominate the Globe," *Quartz*, Oct. 7, 2017, https:// qz.com/1095906/nobel-prizes-are-great-but-college-football-is-why-american-universities-dominate-the-globe/

45. Thelin, *A History* 381-85.

46. Thelin, *A History* 382.

47. Clotfelter 251.

48. Clotfelter 37-38.

49. Adam Harris, "Career Advice From a Groundbreaking President,"

Chronicle of Higher Education, Jan. 1, 2018, https://www.chronicle.com/article/Career-Advice-From-a/242131

50. "Elizabeth B. Taylor," C. Knox Massey Distinguished Service Awards, Oct. 6, 2004, https://masseyawards.unc.edu/elizabeth-b-taylor/

51. "Deborah Crowder 5/10/17" 65.

52. Dan Murphy, "NCAA Clears Way for Athletes to Profit From Names, Images and Likenesses," *ESPN.com,* Oct. 29, 2019, https://www.espn.com/college-sports/story/_/id/27957981/ncaa-clears-way-athletes-profit-names-images-likenesses

53. Richard M. Southall and Ellen J. Staurowsky, "Cheering on the Collegiate Model: Creating, Disseminating, and Imbedding the NCAA's Redefinition of Amateurism," *Journal of Sport and Social Issues,* 2013, https://journals.sagepub.com/doi/abs/10.1177/0193723513498606

54. Libby Sander, "'It Was Just Work, and Giving Back': William C. Friday Reflects," *Chronicle of Higher Education,* Oct. 12, 2012, https://www.chronicle.com/article/It-Was-Just-WorkGiving/135130

55. "unc late night with roy 2017 part 1," YouTube video, 14:16, posted by "ethan williams," October 15, 2017, https://www.youtube.com/watch?v=6KzuEZaylKA

56. "unc late night with roy 2017 part 2," YouTube video, 13:42, posted by "ethan williams," October 15, 2017, https://www.youtube.com/watch?v=2mRpLrJ5cOg

57. "UNC 2017 National Title Banner Unveiled," YouTube video, 5:24, posted by "Tar Heel Illustrated," October 13, 2017, https://www.youtube.com/watch?v=-yYLV-ftOH4

58. Marc Tracy, "At North Carolina, a Sigh of Relief and a New Championship Banner," *New York Times,* Oct. 14, 2017, https://www.nytimes.com/2017/10/14/sports/ncaabasketball/north-carolina-tar-heels-roy-williams.html

AFTERWORD

1. Emma Dill, Karin Fischer, Beth McMurtrie, and Beckie Supiano, "As Coronavirus Spreads, the Decision to Move Classes Online Is the First Step. What Comes Next?" *The Chronicle of Higher Education,* Mar. 6, 2020, https://www.chronicle.com/article/as-coronavirus-spreads-the-decision-to-move-classes-online-is-the-first-step-what-comes-next/

2. Steve Almasy, "The NCAA is canceling March Madness," *CNN,* Mar. 12, 2020, https://www.cnn.com/2020/03/12/us/march-madness-withdrawals-spt/index.html

3. Scott Gleeson, "Clemson's Dabo Swinney has 'zero doubt' NCAA football season will start on time with 'packed' stadiums," *USA Today,* Apr. 3, 2020, https://www.usatoday.com/story/sports/ncaaf/2020/04/03/clemsons-dabo-swinney-has-zero-doubt-football-season-starts-time/2942212001/

4. Robert Allen, "Mike Gundy Eager, Planning to Get Back to Work and Football," *Sports Illustrated*, Apr. 7, 2020, https://www.si.com/college/oklahomastate/football/mike-gundy-on-college-football-and-the-coronavirus

5. Joshua Needelman, "Nearly a third of Clemson's football roster tests positive for coronavirus," *Post and Courier*, Jun. 26, 2020, https://www.postandcourier.com/sports/clemson/nearly-a-third-of-clemsons-football-roster-tests-positive-for-coronavirus/article_7f74aff4-b7fa-11ea-97c2-db740a68c867.html; Elizabeth Redden, "College Football Hit by Coronavirus," *Inside Higher Ed*, Jun. 22, 2020, https://www.insidehighered.com/news/2020/06/22/college-football-programs-hit-covid-after-resumption-voluntary-workouts

6. Brakkton Booker, "The Big Ten, Pac-12 Postpone Football, Other Fall Sports Over Coronavirus Concerns," *NPR*, Aug. 11, 2020, https://www.npr.org/sections/coronavirus-live-updates/2020/08/11/901081822/the-big-ten-postpones-football-other-fall-sports-over-coronavirus-concerns

7. Paula Lavigne and Mark Schlabach, "Heart condition linked with COVID-19 fuels Power 5 concern about season's viability," *ESPN*, Aug. 10, 2020, https://www.espn.com/college-football/story/_/id/29633697/heart-condition-linked-covid-19-fuels-power-5-concern-season-viability

8. Associated Press, "Pac-12 to kick off seven-game football season in November," NBC Sports, Sep. 24, 2020, https://www.nbcsports.com/washington/ncaa/pac-12-reverses-decision-football-kick-seven-game-season-november

9. Kate Murphy, "More than 200 new COVID-19 cases among students reported at UNC Chapel Hill," *News & Observer*, Aug. 24, 2020, https://www.newsobserver.com/news/coronavirus/article245194165.html

10. Scott Carlson, "Anger, Confusion, and Resignation as Chapel Hill's Campus Rapidly Empties," *Chronicle of Higher Education*, Aug. 19, 2020, https://www.chronicle.com/article/anger-confusion-and-resignation-as-chapel-hills-campus-rapidly-empties

11. Garrison Brooks, Twitter post, August 17, 2020, 10:27 p.m., https://twitter.com/__garro/status/1295547824227192833

12. Craig Meyer, "'Something just doesn't feel right about it right now': Pitt's Jeff Capel conflicted about playing during pandemic," Pittsburgh Post-Gazette, Dec. 7, 2020, https://www.post-gazette.com/sports/Pitt/2020/12/07/pitt-panthers-jeff-capel-basketball-covid-19-pandemic-ncaa-christmas/stories/202012070102

13. Ben Kercheval and Barrett Sallee, "Trevor Lawrence sparks united #WeWantToPlay movement, players association goal as 2020 season hangs in balance," CBS Sports, Aug. 10, 2020, https://www.cbssports.com/college-football/news/breaking-down-the-11-real-college-football-playoff-title-contenders-for-the-2020-season/

14. Ross Dellenger, "As Congressional Power Shifts, NCAA Reform and Athletes' Rights Are Firmly in the Crosshairs," Sports Illustrated, Jan. 20, 2021, https://www.si.com/college/2021/01/20/ncaa-athlete-rights-compensation-congress-nil

15. https://www.supremecourt.gov/DocketPDF/20/20-512/170800/20210303124341538_FINAL%20-%20Brief%20For%20Respondents.pdf

16. Daniel Libit and Luke Cyphers, "Silencing the Spoilsports: How 'Pay the Players' Drowned Out College Sports' Fiercest Critics," Sportico, Dec. 17, 2020, https://www.sportico.com/leagues/college-sports/2020/ncaa-reform-pay-players-movement-critics-1234618397/

BIBLIOGRAPHY

Adler, Patricia, and Peter Adler. *Backboards & Blackboards: College Athletes and Role Engulfment.* New York: Columbia University Press, 1991.

Boxill, Jan, ed. *Sports Ethics: An Anthology.* Malden, MA: Blackwell Publishing, 2003.

Byers, Walter. *Unsportsmanlike Conduct: Exploiting College Athletes.* Ann Arbor: University of Michigan Press, 1995.

Clotfelter, Charles. *Big-Time Sports in American Universities,* 2nd ed. New York: Cambridge University Press, 2019.

Duderstadt, James. *Intercollegiate Athletics and the American University: A University President's Perspective.* Ann Arbor: University of Michigan Press, 2000.

Link, William. *William Friday: Power, Purpose, and American Higher Education,* 2nd ed. Chapel Hill: University of North Carolina Press, 1995.

Nyang'oro, Julius E. *The State and Capitalist Development in Africa: Declining Political Economies.* New York: Praeger Publishers, 1989.

Rojas, Fabio. *From Black Power to Black Studies: How a Radical Social Movement Became an Academic Discipline.* Baltimore: Johns Hopkins University Press, 2007.

Sack, Allen, and Ellen Staurowsky. *College Athletes for Hire: The Evolution and Legacy of the NCAA's Amateur Myth.* Westport: Praeger Publishers, 1998.

Smith, Dean, and Gerald Bell. *The Carolina Way: Leadership Lessons from a Life in Coaching.* New York: Penguin, 2004.

Smith, Jay, and Mary Willingham. *Cheated: The UNC Scandal, the Education of Athletes, and the Future of Big-Time College Sports.* Lincoln, NE: Potomac Books, 2015.

Snider, William. *Light on the Hill: A History of the University of North Carolina at Chapel Hill.* Chapel Hill: University of North Carolina Press, 1992.

Thelin, John. *Games Colleges Play: Scandal and Reform in Intercollegiate Athletics.* Baltimore: Johns Hopkins University Press, 1994.

Thelin, John. *A History of American Higher Education,* 3rd ed. Baltimore: Johns Hopkins University Press, 2019.